ANTHROPOLOGICAL PAPERS

MUSEUM OF ANTHROPOLOGY, UNIVERSITY OF MICHIGAN
NO. 71

PERSIAN DIARY

1939–1941

by
WALTER N. KOELZ

ANN ARBOR, MICHIGAN
1983

©1983 Regents of the University of Michigan
The Museum of Anthropology
All rights reserved

Printed in the
United States of America

ISBN 0-932206-93-X

To Eugene F. McDonald, Jr.,
in whose company my wanderings began

CONTENTS

Biographical Introduction,
    by Carolyn Copeland ix
Introduction to Iran in 1939–41,
    by Henry T. Wright. xi
Author's Preface xiii
Introduction. xv

    I.   The Medieval Sea Gate and the Coast. 1
    II.   Kirman and the Great Date Oases. 15
    III.   Isfahan Nim-Jahan. 43
    IV.   Shiraz, Jahrum, and Niriz. 55
    V.   Khuzistan. 73
    VI.   Dorud and Tī. 83
    VII.   The Capital 93
    VIII.   The Caspian Shore, from Below Sea Level to
            Above the Clouds 99
    IX.   The Borderland of the Soviets and Ghengiz's Hordes—
            the Turkomans. 105
    X.   Holy Meshed. 115
    XI.   Khorasan, Land of Lost Cities and Great Poets 121
    XII.   Again in the Great Forest 149
    XIII.   Again in the Capital 151
    XIV.   Azerbaijan and the Turks 163
    XV.   The Land of the Medes. 191
    XVI.   At the Gates of Mesopotamia 197
    XVII.   Where My Soul Has Longed to Go 209

LIST OF ILLUSTRATIONS

Walter N. Koelz viii
Regions of Iran x
Map of Iran, Showing Route of Travel xvi
Wangyel, the Thakur Rup Chand, and Rinchen Gialtsen 2
Paths in the Bedrock near Bandar Abbas 4
A Landscape in Southern Iran 5
The Camel is the Desert Truck 7
Digging the Shaft of a Qanat 9
A Kirman Oasis 17
Deh Shib in Kirman 18
A Fig Tree at Deh Bala, Kirman 20
Dugout Homes of the Desert Poor in Kirman 22
Rup Chand and a Golden Eagle near Kirman 27
The Shrine at Mahun 34
Mountain Forest near Deh Bakri in Kirman 35
Reed Houses in Tomogaon, Kirman 39
Storks, a Common Inhabitant of Many Towns in the Country 51
The Shaking Tower at Isfahan 51
The Blind Spinner at Eylit 58
Persepolis or Takht-i Jamshid 60
Persepolis 61
Persepolis 62
The Bagh Safa at Shiraz 63
An Old Tombstone Dating from the Last Period of the Moghuls 67
A Grave Marker in Jahrum, Fars 68
Wild Almonds at Dehrisk, Jiroft 69
Lifting Water from Well at Ahwaz by Cattle Team 74
Lifting Water from Well at Ahwaz 75
Another Method of Irrigating 77
A Roadside Cairn in the Bakhtiari Oak Forest 79
Market Day in Khuzistan 81
Trucking in Khuzistan 82
A Lur "Village" in Luristan 87
Tents of Tibetan Nomads 88
A Leaf of Wild Rhubarb Common in Iran and Afghan Mountains 90
The Peacock Throne 94
A Street Restaurant 96
A Muskmelon Collection 101
Tea on the Caspian Slope 103
A Mulberry Tree in the Himalayan State of Chamba 110
The Lovely Mosque of Hazrat Masumeh at Qom 118
A Goat Flock on the March Near the Afghan Border 124
The Bagh Gulshan at Tabas 128
Camp at Deh Bala near Yezd in a Field Beside a Mulberry Tree 130
"Sobhanah Rabii al'Alah va bahumdah!" 138
The Zurkhana 140
A Collection of Squash from Quetta 141
On the Road 145
Plowing at Shahrud 146

vi

Tinning Copper Dishes 147
Muhamed Reza Pahlevi, the Crown Prince at the Time of this Account 152
The Shah of Iran with the Crown Prince 153
A Water Seller in the Capital. 155
Threshing 160
The Tibetan Counterpart of the Mountaintop Cairn, a *Burje*, on Taklung Pass 165
Tree Growing in a Persian Garden 170
A Wild Peach Tree in the Himalayan State of Chamba 173
A Fleet of Camels. 175
A Collection of Water Mills in the Himalayas 177
An Extreme Development in the Fattailed Sheep 178
Kurdish Men 182
The Bazaar in a Kurdish Town. 184
At Work at Camp, Skinning a Collection of Flamingos. 187
A Gleaner 195
Threshing 205
On the Road 206
A Well-Tended Garden of Assorted Trees and Flower Beds 212
Kurd Nomad Women Milking the Sheep. 216
A Kurdish Dance 221
Piggie, the Pet Wild Boar 224

WALTER N. KOELZ. Photograph taken in Ann Arbor during the 1940s.

BIOGRAPHICAL SKETCH OF WALTER N. KOELZ
by
Carolyn A. Copeland
College of Literature, Science and the Arts, The University of Michigan

Walter Norman Koelz was born in Waterloo, Michigan, on September 11, 1895, and, after many years spent abroad, once again resides in the house where he was born. He attended Olivet College as an undergraduate and did his graduate work at the University of Michigan, receiving the degree of Doctor of Philosophy in June of 1920. His graduate studies of the Coregonid fishes of the Great Lakes brought him not only a government appointment with the U.S. Bureau of Fisheries, but also an appointment as a Curator of Fishes in the Museum of Zoology at the University of Michigan.

During the summer of 1925, Walter Koelz served as naturalist with the MacMillan Arctic Expedition. This was the first of many expeditions that would take Dr. Koelz to the far corners of the world. In the spring of 1930, he began a two year appointment as a biologist for the Himalayan Research Institute of the Roerich Museum in Kulu, India. In the autumn of 1932, he was appointed by the Regents of the University of Michigan as a Research Fellow on the Charles L. Freer fund, and he returned to India to collect Tibetan materials for the Museums of Anthropology and Natural History. He returned to Ann Arbor in the spring of 1934 and during 1934 worked on a government parks project, acquiring land for the Waterloo Recreation Area. As of January 1, 1936, he became a plant explorer for the U.S. Department of Agriculture, and he left for India once more. He returned to spend the winter of 1939 in Brunswick, Georgia, but was back in Bombay in July. December 14 of that year is the first entry in the *Diary* that follows. In January of 1946, Dr. Koelz left Persia for further explorations in India, Nepal, and Assam, which lasted until October of 1953. In 1956, he was awarded the Meyer Memorial Medal for outstanding contributions to world agriculture. Dr. Koelz continues to hold an appointment with the University of Michigan as an Adjunct Research Investigator with both the Museum of Zoology and the Botanical Gardens.

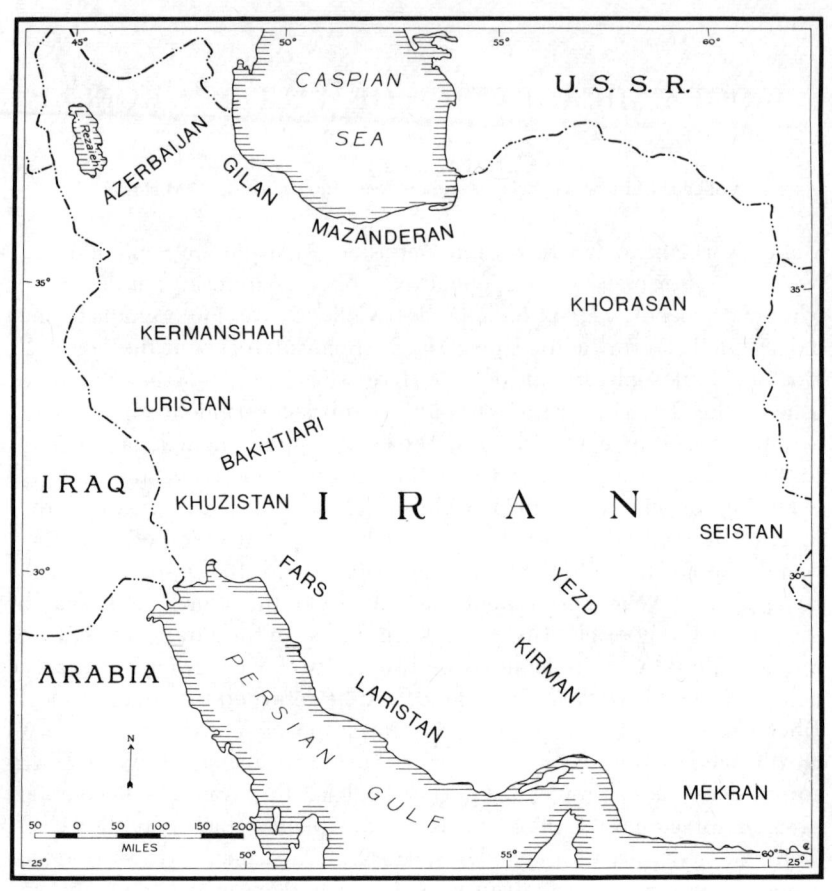

Regions of Iran Mentioned in the Diary.

INTRODUCTION
by
Henry T. Wright
University of Michigan Museum of Anthropology

When Walter Koelz and his assistants arrived in Bandar Abbas late in 1939, Iran was an island of relative tranquility in a world at war. Though rumors of war reached him during his naturalist's odyssey, he found Iran hovering at a structural moment, seemingly stable after more than a decade of firmly centralized rule of the Shah, Reza Pahlevi. There is no intimation of the rapid invasion which Britain and Russia would launch during 1941 in response to German advances toward Cairo and Baku, overthrowing Reza Shah and again bringing the threats of banditry, famine, and epidemics to the countryside. The reader is thus privileged to see, through the eyes of Koelz, the effects of Reza Shah's programs of reform and "modernization," and to assess the quality of Iranian life at a crucial step in recent history.

The perspective that one gains is different from that offered by other travelers, for Koelz tarried little in major cities or along main routes. He was seeking a diversity of agricultural patterns as well as the best-preserved remnants of Iran's pre-agricultural natural landscapes. Most of the description is therefore of small towns, villages, and mountain tracks. In his photographs we see wooded slopes today stripped bare and traditional houses and tents where today there are pre-fabricated government buildings. The document provides a baseline in words and pictures of a sort rarely available before the development of aerial photography and rural economic surveys.

It is, of course, a thoroughly human document. In many ways—in his view of human failings, his opinions of business and government, and his love of distant and rugged places—Koelz is quintessentially an American of his time. His comments on the people he met and the frequent delays he met in his work adequately convey this aspect of his person. In other ways—in his love of birds and flowers, in his moments of poetic response the countryside, and in his acute feeling for the hardships of the lives of ordinary nomads and farmers and the practicality of their responses to life—he is seen to be a true natural historian, a sort all too unusual in our own day of narrow scientific and scholarly specialities. Indeed, certain biological, ethnographic, and historical specialists will no doubt wish that these diaries were less human and more technical. To such people, we hasten to say that, as far as the editors can tell, these pages contain most of what was written down in the field. It is true that some of the hand-written volumes are unavailable but those that it has been possible to examine closely parallel the typescript Koelz himself edited in the early 1950s. We ourselves have, after a great deal of thought, made few changes in the typescript, and those we made were characteristically for reasons of clarity. We decided that if Koelz chose, while sitting in an Iranian village, to digress and write about an incident in India, he had good reason to do so. Similarly, if Koelz expresses a strong personal opinion, to retain it gives the reader an honest appreciation of his personal perspective at the time he was writing.

There do exist other documents relevant to Koelz's travels. In the first place, there is a parallel diary, kept in Urdu by another member of his team, of which an English translation is retained at the University of Michigan Herbarium. There are also his botanical field catalogues, one copy also at the Herbarium, another in Vienna, where many of Koelz's botanical specimens repose. No doubt there are other documents of which we are unaware, for example reports to the U.S. Department of Agriculture, which supported the trip. At first, much effort was expended trying to integrate some of this material into the following publication, but in the end it was felt that both editors lacked the specialized knowledge required in the preparation of a fully critical edition.

Our additions are therefore in the form of a few footnotes drawn, unless otherwise noted, from maps and from a volume entitled *Persia*,[1] one of the anonymous geographical handbooks prepared by the Naval Intelligence Division of the Royal Navy of Great Britain during the Second World War and available to the public since 1954. The information assembled in this handbook was current to 1941, and much of it complements the picture one can draw from the *Persian Diary*. It is methodical, focused on towns and main routes, and filled with second-hand background information. If some of its contents are dubious, it does provide the reader with an idea of what the scholarly and diplomatic world found useful to know about Iran at the beginning of the World War. We hope that the footnotes will be useful to those not familiar with Iran as it was four decades ago.

---

1. British Naval Intelligence Division, *Persia*, Geographical Handbook Series, B.R. 525. Produced and printed for official purposes during the war 1939/45. (Oxford: The University Press for H.M. Stationery Office, 1945).

AUTHOR'S PREFACE

This book is a selection of pages from my diary, written during travels in Iran on a project of plant exploration sponsored by the United States Department of Agriculture. Its period extends from late 1939 to the beginning of 1941. With me were three companions from the Tibetan province of Lahul who had accompanied me in several years of earlier explorations in India and Afghanistan. The Thakur Rup Chand, known to American newspaper readers by his Tibetan name of Surja Dawa, had also spent several years with me in the United States. Wangyel and Rinchen Gialtsen made their first sea voyage on this trip.

The government of Iran received us hospitably and did all possible to facilitate our travels, usually even sending a representative of its Department of Agriculture to smooth our way. These men mostly acquitted themselves of their unwonted and not-easy task in a manner that would reflect credit on the citizenry of any nation.

Some 3000 samples of seeds, 4000 collections of herbarium specimens, and a comprehensive collection of birdskins were gathered on the expedition. Many of the seeds are varieties of cultivated plants that have been a useful addition to our seed and fruit-tree catalogs. Others, of wild and cultivated stock, may be used for breeding experiments in producing disease-resistant, drought-tolerant, and other agriculturally important strains of cultivated plants. Among them also are representatives of the numerous species of wild flowers that glorify the Persian plain and mountain.

The days thus spent were happy days, and I am grateful to those who helped make them so. To my friend, B.Y. Morrison of the Office of Plant Introduction, is due the conception of the program, and to his skillful administration belongs the credit of its successful execution. My Tibetan companions would be puzzled at my thanks for their part; moreover, I can find no words to thank them for a relation that transcends friendship. To the gentle and friendly Persian people I have the pleasantest obligation, and perhaps my voluntary sojourn among them is its most convincing expression.

Walter N. Koelz
Waterloo, Michigan

INTRODUCTION

We are going to Persia, Persia the land of Zoroaster,—of a people who saw in fire a symbol of worship, not fire the consumer, but fire the cleanser, fire the emblem of purity and of light. And as the eternal fires lighted their ancient altars, for long centuries after, the fires of genius lighted the Persian soul and the glow of their sunset reflections still lingers. In the years of our wanderings in India our eyes were ever drawn to that western afterflow. For, Circus of Creation as it is, with its sideshows of marvels and horrors, India nevertheless does show the sublimest works of the hand of man and those miracles of man drew from the inspiration of Persia, ennobled, it may be, by the contemplation of the sublimest works of the hand of God, which stand before them, the Himalayas—the mystic "Abode of Snow" that in all ages was the cynosure of Indian philosophers, from which even the noonday sun of Realism has not dispersed its supernatural haze. We had seen the morning sun gild Everest and Nanga Parbat and felt the soul tug to be free in the rare air of the heights before these outposts of the Infinite. We had dreamed in the fabulous flowerstrewn uplands of Kashmir and languished in the oppression of scent and color of Ceylon. To senses steeped in this magic atmosphere the monuments of Persian thought, among which the revelation in white marble at Agra rises supreme, stand in transfiguring light and the comprehension quickens of the meaning of Beauty—that infinite formless Something that hovers above Creation and to which, the poets say, the artist gives a local habitation. And as mankind has ever been drawn by the mystery of Beginnings to worship the river's source or the rising sun or the birthplace of an embodied idea, we were drawn toward the source of inspiration of these things of supernal beauty and turned our steps toward Persia with a pilgrim's devotion.

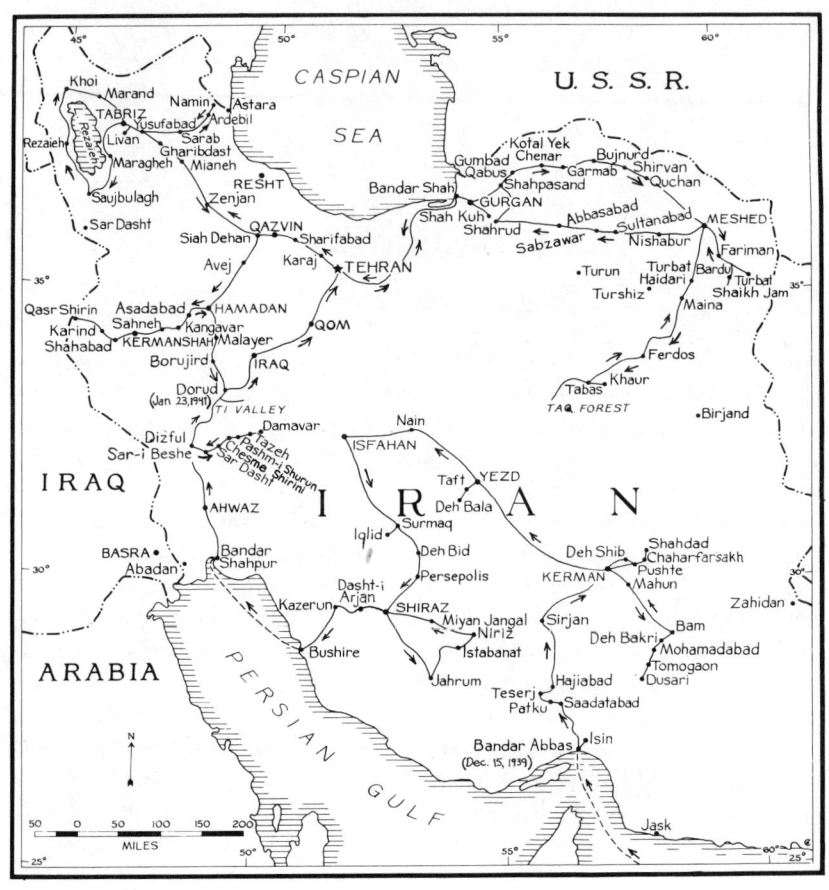

MAP OF IRAN, SHOWING THE ROUTE OF TRAVEL AND PLACES MENTIONED IN THE DIARY.

Chapter I

THE MEDIEVAL SEA GATE AND THE COAST

December 14. The boat that has brought us from Karachi is one of the line that runs regularly into the Persian Gulf and makes stops at all the ports. Our ship is not the gull-winged bark of poet's fancy that is fit to touch the romantic shores of the Medes and Persians, of Babylon and Nineveh and the Arabian Nights, but an old slow steamer as dreary as the barren shores it plods along and with British aloofness, never touches. The crew and cargo are also drab, products of India though they be, for even myrrh and sandalwood have nothing of romance about them done up in gunny sacks, nor natives, however shiny-limbed and limpid of eye, if they are dressed in dingy pants and shirt. When we stop and the little boats come from shore to take a box or a sack or two that the shallows don't allow us to deliver, for a few moments there is something to see: a strange rug woven in black and white in one of the boats; a bunch of dates as it was cut from the tree; queer fish that look like Japanese drawings, swimming in the clear water around the boat; but we are soon off again, and the cheerless atmosphere of a country church settles on us once more. It would have been pleasanter if I could have stayed on deck with my friends. They had taken food along for the journey and cooked on their charcoal fire and slept under the balmy sky of the subtropic winter. For me there is a Goese chef's interpretation of the bleak British cookbook, and I sleep in a tiny cabin, darkened from fear of submarines. A representative of the United States Department of Agriculture, the subject of diplomatic representations and official reception, must travel first class.

The servant of the British Consul at Bandar Abbas is returning with his master. He has been on a visit to his folks in Kashmir. He complains that vacations cost a lot and you're apt to find things at home changed and not for the better. His brother has died, now he has to support the widow and her children, and he got into a cudgel fight with his other brother. He brought a pot of honey from his village for his master. He got it with his own hands

WANGYEL, THE THAKUR RUP CHAND, AND RINCHEN GIALTSEN. These three Tibetans were my constant companions in my long exile in India, Afghanistan, and Iran. The Thakur Rup Chand has friends in Ann Arbor and is a staff member at the University Botanical Gardens.

because his master wanted it clean, and last night he spilled it on the deck and had a bad time scraping it up again. He warned my men not to tell me what had happened or I'd be sure to blab to the Consul. He knew what great folks talked about at the table. At Lucknow a domestic every morning poured water from one glass to another and from time to time plunged his finger in it. We found he had boiled the water and was cooling it. His master would brush his teeth only in sterilized water. Verily, what you don't know won't hurt you.

The sea has hardly been disturbed by a breeze in the four days since we left India, and Rinchen Gialtsen thinks sea travel is pleasant. Rup Chand knows the horrors of seasickness and told him how a rough sea can make you long for the calm of the grave, but Rinchen Gialtsen is of the opinion that he would find it exhilarating and hopes the wind will blow.

We anchored off Bandar Abbas[1] at nine. The ship's help had been trying

---

1. Bandar Abbas (27°11′N, 50°17′E, 20 feet). This undistinguished port had 15,000 people of

hard since supper to catch their two longhaired cats but couldn't. They said enterprising thieves picked up pets and sold them back to them on the return trip. The young Fourth Engineer said he was sorry I was leaving because the food is better when there is a first class passenger aboard. A group of pleasant Persian officials said they had had telegraphic instructions about us from the capitol. They asked about nothing but our guns and cartridges and made out a slip for each gun for me to sign. At midnight they loaded our luggage into a launch and in an hour we were ashore. They took us to a building fronting the sea and lodged us in two richly and heavily carpeted rooms with no wall ornaments but photographs of the king, a fine regal personage, and of the good-looking crown prince. A magnificent meteor shower in the northern sky and a hideous chorus of jackals in the street below us, both extraordinary performances of their kind, closed our day and ushered in our Persian adventures.

December 15. Everyone on the ship, even the Kashmiri, had told us what a dirty place the town was and we wondered what filth we should see if an Indian were shocked. The streets, however, look clean enough to us, and the sandy beach is clean, too. The people are plain featured, very swarthy, and well mannered. Somewhere in the environs they say are remains of the forts the Portuguese, Dutch, or British had held three centuries ago in the days of Shah Abbas, the last great administrator of the remnants of the Empire of the Medes and Persians. Along the beach are plenty of wintering birds, mostly curlews, plovers, gulls and the like, and also flocks of oyster catchers that I had never seen before in Asia. They say that there are plenty of fish at certain seasons and the best of them are the *qodr, zalaibi, shirmahi, ghobat, puru, habur, rashku,* and the like. Some Danes have a sardine factory here and put out a good but rather expensive product.

---

mixed Persian, Arab, and Baluchi background. Established perhaps as early as the twelfth century A.D. and known as "Gombrun" or "Comru" before and during the Portugese occupation of nearby Hormuz, it was refounded as "Bandar Abbas" by Shah Abbas after he drove out the Portuguese in 1622. It was Iran's major Indian ocean port until the mideighteenth century, when Bushire, farther up the Gulf and closer to Shiraz, became important. It remains the regional port for southwestern Iran and was occupied by the Omanis in the early nineteenth century and the British at the end of World War I. At the time of Koelz's visit the town's anchorage, protected by nearby Hormuz and Qishm Islands, was serviced by dhows using the beach and a single dock. Dates, nuts, cloth from a new mill, and fish from a new cannery were traded. The town itself was on the sandy coastal strip, marked by acacia and jujube shrubs and a few date orchards, all that could survive with only 5 inches of winter rain per year and intense summer heat. City water was provided by cisterns and wells, malaria was common and plague had been recorded as recently as 1924. A dirt road entered a pass to the north toward Kirman and beyond. In 1940 the town had several banks, a British consulate, a customs office, a hospital, an airstrip, and one garage.

PATHS IN THE BEDROCK NEAR BANDAR ABBAS. These grooves have been worn in the rock by the feet of travellers who have gone that way through the centuries. On the Pariz massif near Dorud in Luristan the ibex herds, forced to descend for water in summer, have carved on the cliff face a similar record. Their path is nearly sheer and the marble that records it has been polished to glisten.

Children along the shore are fishing with a basin over which they tied a cloth with a hole in the center. A crushed crab is the bait. When they pull the basin up, they often have a couple of fish, like perch.

December 16. Some beautiful brown donkeys with smooth silky coats came for us in the morning. We loaded three of them and started off at half past ten for Isin, toward Kuh-i Ganu,[1] a rather sizable peak that looks to be some 15 miles inland. The way soon runs over a limestone ridge through which a stream has dug a narrow gulch. In the broad bed of the stream are now pools of very salty water in which plenty of minnows are swimming. The path over the bare rock is deeply cut into narrow troughs, some of them to a foot in depth, often a dozen of them together, where the feet of the ages have worn away the stone. There is little vegetation, and what there is is mostly shrubby and grows best in the cracks of the rocky walls. There are few birds, but we found a little sparrow (*Emberiza striolata*) that we sometimes found in India only among the barren ruins of ancient buildings.

---

1. Kuh-i Ganu (27°26′N, 58°10′E, ca. 7700 feet).

A Landscape Like This Might Be Found Anywhere in Southern Iran near Mountains, Whence Water Could Be Brought to Irrigate the Dates. The donkey is the commonest and cheapest mode of transport in the area, and the little traffic the traveller meets in the great spaces of the desert is sustained by this admirable beast. In some places there are fine breeds and some people ride animals of which they are obviously proud, but too often it is otherwise. The normal load the donkey is expected to carry is about what a horse usually does, and it is no rare sight to see the owner riding on top of the load. The goods are carried in bags, woven, in pairs, of goat hair usually, and are thrown across the animal's back.

On the way is a large cistern closed in with a domed roof in which is collected the winter rain. Along the coast the wells are brackish and the water here, though fresh, is dark and stagnant. A sweet cold drink from a spring is a thing unknown in the desert. Long hewn bars of stone set in the wall provide the rungs of a ladder to descend to the scummy water level.

Isin is a bright spot of cultivation in the broad plain that slopes gently down from the mountain. There are large groves of date palms, with trees 20 to 40 feet apart, and tiny lawnlike fields of grain. The houses are humble shelters, often in walled-in gardens, where, crowded together for protection against the blasting desert wind, are found at least a few sorts of most of the subtropical fruits—papayas, sapistas, citrus, bananas, mangos, and even mulberries. There are at least five kinds of citrus, the commonest a lime, a fine fragrant thing that is dried and forms one of the indispensables of the Persian cuisine in all parts of the country. All gardens have at least a few vegetables too: melons are beginning to run; corn is earing; tomatoes and lettuce have been freshly transplanted; purple carrots are ready to pull. In the trees were flocks of large wood pigeons, and gray partridges (*Francolinus pondicerianus*) which they call *karmanzil* were feeding along the fields. A black and white woodpecker (*Dryobates assimilis*) makes a living on the palm trunks, which seem infested with borers. They say date palms are set out from root-shoots and come to bear in about seven years. The weather is springy like a fine late April day at home. Clouds floated high all day, and in the afternoon heavy storm clouds swept from behind the mountain and with thunder and lightning fled seaward, leaving the desert in a strip a mile wide covered with pools.

December 23. Wangyel guessed that the solstice is at hand from the position of Orion on the horizon. Tibetans call the constellation Golak. The nomad Tibetans have names for all the constellations and keep their calendar by their position in the sky. All the men here wear felt hats that sit on their mops of hair like birds' nests, often at a right angle with the ground. I hear the hats aren't of their own choice but an item of the king's reforms that are designed to modernize the country. The women no longer are veiled, and there is no seclusion of the women as one sees in Afghanistan and India. They say the women liked the veils (*chaddar*) because they could wear what they pleased under them, and for prostitutes the institution was a heaven-sent blessing since no one could recognize them. That it gets sweltering-hot under the airproof garment that constitutes the *chaddar* and that it seems impossible to keep clean doesn't detract from its popularity.

There was a shower yesterday, and they are planting grain. We left Sabi or Saadatabad (the reforms mentioned above have reached even the names of places and any number of towns; streets and even the country itself have changed names) for a trip among some of the date-growing villages, to rejoin the Bandar Abbas-Kirman road after four days of march. We sent what we didn't need on ahead by truck and set off across the plain to Patku. For a few miles the plain is strewn with tamarisk trees that harbor a little owl (*Athene brama*), last seen in India. The tamarisks here are scrubby but in other parts of the south they become well grown trees 2 or 3 feet in diameter. When the tamarisks petered out, the desert became soft and springy and the walking therefore a bit troublesome, but my Tibetan friends seemed to like it. Heavy alkali content often gives the desert this physical quality, and the vegetation then is of low and fleshy halophytes. Five bustards (Persians call them *ahubareh*; the scientific name is *Chlamydotis mcqueenii*) flew up almost at our feet, and we wondered how they managed to conceal themselves so well. These same birds usually are

THE CAMEL IS THE DESERT TRUCK, AS THE DONKEY IS THE DESERT FORD. Camels and goats are the only domestic animals that you seldom feel sorry for. Both beasts are able to wrest what they need from the parsimonious desert and bear well the demands of their host. The camel by its size and wit has established its position in the transport scheme as satisfactorily as the Brotherhood of Railway Engineers, and more permanently. It gets what is needs. It gets no abuse, because it tolerates none. This caravan is bringing forage. Loads are commonly prepared in two flaps that straddle the animal's back. It is convenient to load and unload such packages. The method of loading, however, varies from place to place, and all methods are not equally effective. The path has been marked by foot traffic but, if it were not, an experienced camel would find the way just the same.

unapproachable in the open. I have noticed birds that can hide well seem to know when they are hidden. Members of the chicken tribe are particularly clever at disappearing, large and bright-colored as they are, and I have several times seen them in the Himalayas freeze into inconspicuousness against a tuft of grass or in the open on the leaf-strewn ground. There were plenty of pig and gazelle tracks, and once we came near three gazelles (Persian *ahu*). Patku is a village of a few houses surrounded by date palms and a few huge wild jujube trees. As always, a pleasant clean place was ready for us in the second story of the best house. The owner had apparently gone somewhere else to make room for us but the goats didn't know it, and when they were brought home in the evening, in spite of all the shepherd boy could do to stop them, they got up the stairs to their usual quarters. We had some nice dates and good rice, said to be grown here. They say the rice has to be watered every evening, and one wonders how they can spare the water in such a desert.

December 25, Teserj. We went down to a huge spring that comes out at the foot of a low cliff. A strong stream, usually too deep to wade and 10 to 15 feet across, flows from it and, cloaked in cattails and bulrushes, runs out of sight among the bare rocky hills. There are plenty of fish in the stream, some probably 8 pounds in weight, and in the swampy border are numbers of wild pigs. No one seems to bother them, and I came upon several monsters at thrillingly close range. There are plenty of black partridges (*Francolinus francolinus*; Persian *toraj*) among the cultivation; we were surprised at finding such a hunter's paradise. It seems fish in most parts of Iran are not often eaten and pigs of course are forbidden by the Muslim religion, while the partridges are too difficult to shoot with the sort of guns the natives would have, if they should happen to be allowed any at all.

I was called to see a wounded man, bedridden with hideous gashes in the thighs. He said a boar had attacked him when he ran into him (the boar) asleep in a dry irrigation ditch. The wound was old but clean and was healing nicely. A boy had a lesser wound that he got yesterday when he surprised a sleeping pig among the rocks. It seems that people often are attacked when the animal is taken unawares and doesn't see a clear way to escape, but since then, I have seen an old boar leave a travelling herd on the open plain and take after a peasant he happened to catch sight of, with no provocation at all. The peasant ran for his life, and the pig chased him a few minutes but probably only because he ran. The wild boar we later kept as a pet in Persia delighted in chasing anyone who would run from him but would never hurt his victims even if they fell in their terror. He waited instead till they got up again and then started off after them anew. He especially liked to stampede donkeys, and I have seen other wild pigs attack them, too. Donkeys seem to have a natural fear of pigs, and Piggy was the cause of many a donkey-rider's being dumped in the dirt by his frightened mount.

The soldiers who are escorting us found no sugar here so we have to move on to the next village. (Persians must have sugar for their indispensable tea, and here the people use dates instead, but that savors of poverty.) News has come of brigands in the neighborhood and our guard has been increased to ten, a fearful visitation on a small population, and we feel we must hurry along. There is rich black soil in the valley and the date palms thrive.

December 28. The truck had stood all day without anyone thinking of making any repairs. Cars are often not disturbed, even to the extent of refueling, as long as they will run, and such treatment may make things unpleasant for travellers. Hardly out of the town our car balked, and for the

DIGGING THE SHAFT OF A QANAT. The underground irrigation canals that water many of the Persian settlements are dug by sinking shafts and burrowing in both directions from these shafts. The digger is in the hole and signals when he has a load of earth to be hauled up. The *qanats* run commonly for 8 or 10 miles, and the shafts, though ordinarily not more than 50 feet, may be much deeper. The strings of mounds that mark their course on the plain are a common feature of the Persian landscape.

first couple of hours we got as many miles. When at last stops were no longer necessary, we began, out of habit probably, to stop all along and for long periods at small adobe huts called "coffee houses." We had a place on the dates our truck was hauling and could stretch out and rest so the stops didn't matter. Our Persian friends preferred the seat with the driver and they always got out and went in for refreshment too. After these halts everyone came back happy and laughed at our snoring, and off we went again till we got to another of these entertainment places. In the morning we arrived at one of the villages of the Sirjan group and had breakfast. The Persians borrowed our .22 and shot some desert larks which they plucked and roasted. We offered them some partridges that we had killed but since we hadn't cut the throat as their religion requires, the flesh wasn't edible, wasn't what they call *halal*. The Mohamedan religion enjoins its followers to eat meat of no warm-blooded animal that hasn't died by having its throat cut "in the name of God." In the case of game—often dead when you get to it—many people are broadminded and perform a postmortem throat-cutting. The town superficially seemed to be a collection of ruined mud walls, and numbers of little desert owls were sunning themselves on them.

I wanted a few for my collection, but the first one fell into a bottomless well and the next stuck on top of a high frail wall and was as inaccessible as the first.

At ten we got to Sirjan[1] and were taken to a large public building in a huge garden apparently newly laid out. A nice-looking youth who is the agricultural agent here later invited us to his home to lunch. His room was hung with embroidered and woven shawls of the style sometimes seen in India and there recognized often as Persian-made. The material from which shawls were woven is "cashmere" (Persian *kurk*)—the soft underhair that some kinds of goats develop in winter. The Indians weave their shawls from such goat hair brought from Tibet, where it is called *lena* (Urdu *pasham*), and aside from the fact that the style of design of Indian shawls is different, they are usually softer in texture. The Persian *kurk* resembles very fine wool. They say shawls are still made in Kirman and Yezd, and one often sees furniture upholstered in a shawl-like material said to come from these places. The old shawls seem to be rarer here than in India, and those that show up are most often quilted squares said to have been used in the bath.

The youth apparently had expected us and had prepared a wonderfully varied and well cooked feast. Already on the table were the *ajeel*, a collection of hazelnuts, *pistas* (English pistachio) and watermelon and pumpkin seeds, all roasted and coated with salt and turmeric. *Ajeel* is very popular in the country and is an important social institution. The host puts his guests at ease by employing their hands and teeth, which is the best he can do without a radio. Tea was served with short cupcakes and a strangely scented marshmallow-like cake, with disks of a kind of butterscotch. Tea in Persia is served everywhere, even in public offices, and you can hardly make a call in one on any matter without being offered tea. Certainly you will have tea if you call at any house, however humble. It is served in small glasses, silver-based if possible, with cube sugar or loaf sugar on the side, which the Persian often puts in his mouth and dissolves with the tea. Porcelain teacups may be offered at important social gatherings and often with lemon slices as an accompaniment, but I don't recall ever having seen

---

1. Sirjan (29°27′N, 55°43′E, 5790 feet), renamed "Saidabad" in the time of Reza Shah, is a small crossroads town, reported to have a population of about 9000 sometime before Koelz's visit. It had been the political center of Kirman province until the tenth century A.D. but little remains to indicate its former status. The saline Sirjan Plain had about 60 villages, sustained by *qanats* and known for their cotton crops. Many small nomad groups spent some of their year here as well. Most groups, both sedentary and nomad, were Persian-speaking. Sirjan was on the main motor road from Bandar Abbas to Kirman but had a caravan link across the salt flats to Niriz and hence Shiraz.

milk. The custom of tea drinking is said to have been introduced from Russia about a century and a half ago.

Then followed several courses of meat (mutton, chicken, quails) with *pilo*—buttered boiled rice seasoned with saffron, almonds, *pistas*, and currants. *Pilo* (English pilau, supposed to have come in from Malay) is a staple Moslem dish and the decorative elements vary, but fat seems to be a weighty item. The Persian, like the Afghan, likes grease and also sugar, and it seems nothing can be too greasy or too sweet for his palate. I have been served fried eggplant drowned in melted butter and smothered in cream, and the dish was stone cold to boot. Jaundice conditions are common among them and the cause is ascribed to burnt food, which is of course accordingly avoided. I have never seen a Persian who wouldn't, I believe, sooner eat a spider than a piece of burnt bread. They also have a horror of dust, though heaven knows in this desert they see and breathe plenty of it, but especially they dread dust raised by the broom. Toward the end of the meal a pink quince preserve was brought in and vodka scented with lemon, and such fruits as still were in season: apples, pears, grapes, pomegranates, melons.

In the bazaar, I found my size in *giveh*, the comfortable native shoes so commonly worn. They are made ankle height, without laces, of white cotton thread crocheted onto a sole. The sole may be leather, or sometimes a piece of old auto tire, though rubber soles are believed to be bad for the eyes, and in some places a special sole is made of small strips of rags pounded down and strung on thongs. The quality of the *giveh* depends on the fineness of the thread and the sole. The nicest have a design crocheted on the toe and around the top. For ordinary wear they are durable and of course can readily be slipped off and on—an important consideration for people who don't like to carry the dirt of the street into their houses.

I went then with three of the young men of the company to look at the cultivation. The gardens were all walled-in with mud walls 10 feet and more high, but people were friendly and always let us in when we asked. Many had only bushtrees of *pista* 10 to 15 feet high; some had trees of apple and other deciduous fruits. The trees were widely spaced, and grain had been sown under them. By mistake I used a cartridge Rup Chand had loaded with lead slugs (in case he came upon a pig) to shoot at a little owl but missed ignominiously. All three boys volunteered to do the shooting henceforth, so I gave one the gun. He asked where to aim. I said at the head and with the first shot he got two crows. He gravely examined the corpses and seeing blood in the mouth said he had hit where I had told him. Persians seem to like guns, but no one we ever came across showed any skill in handling one. Just now their possession is much restricted in the country, and the contraband sort are apt to be of ancient models and not suited for displays of skill. We have, however, almost everywhere been told of remarkable feats that are commonly performed, such as shooting a dime in the air with a revolver, and very often someone has told us that when he owned a gun, in the days before the government disarmed everybody, he used to shoot game half a mile away and that we tried always to get too close.

The agriculture officer knows some French and calls me "*Musoo.*" Many people, even peasants, know as much French as that, and we are generally called that or something like it. French is the foreign language most commonly taught in schools, and many educated people know it. Numbers of Persians of both sexes have been schooled abroad, mostly in France. The little son of the caretaker of our building who has been watching our housekeeping, prodded by his father, greeted me with: "Bon soir, monsieur, comment allez-vous?" When I obviously understood him, the father nearly burst with pride. He knew one more French sentence that had, however, no conversational value.

The town is the usual uninteresting accumulation of mud-walled one-storied houses. It lies on a plain perhaps 50 miles across, with mountains all around; those toward Kirman and Shiraz are snow-capped.

December 29. A youth from the agricultural office came this morning to take us over to Ahmedabad, 9 miles off, where they said there was good hunting. We have had to emphasize the hunting or else our guide would hustle us across the landscape with the promise of having all the seeds we could want sent after us, and it works out all right because the best hunting is in the best-cultivated regions, since food for game is more abundant there. The plain is strewn with rows of mounds that mark the course of a *qanat* or *kariz*, the underground channel through which irrigation water is conducted, often for 10 or 15 miles, across the desert. The amount of labor in making such subterranean channels may be imagined. The excavated earth is brought to the surface in pails on a windlass through shafts, like wells, sunk at regular intervals, and the mounds are the sites of these shafts. Here the streams run about 50 feet underground, but I have been told many are much deeper, even (at Yezd) to 300 feet. The upkeep of a *qanat* is much less than of a surface ditch since these are always being clogged by plants and by the perpetually drifting dust of the Persian desert that has buried even great cities so that their sites are unknown. Then there is the colossal loss of water by evaporation under the thirsty air, pilfering by plant volunteers, and seepage through the walls of the ditch. The *qanat* channels appear to be well cemented with minerals precipitated out of the water they carry and probably lose little to the surrounding earth. *Qanats* are seen almost everywhere in desert Iran, and I had once seen very shallow ones too at Mukur in Afghanistan. One often sees numerous blind chains marking *qanats* abandoned and left to fill in, the people say, after the massacre of the population in the course of the savage wars that swept the country. In places these ruined systems are more numerous than those now in use, and from this it has been argued the ancient population of the country was greater than now. Certainly the population may be in proportion to the water available for irrigating the land, for the country is fertile in general, and the amount of land now under cultivation is proportionally as insignificant as the pupil is to the rest of the eye. The *qanat* wells or shafts are usually left open and, naturally, all kinds of hapless animals fall into them. Fish are usually to be seen at the mouths. Without the *qanat*, great stretches of Iran must remain desert waste.

Our companion often asked the peasants we met how much farther it was to Ahmedabad, and one boy showed on his finger the proportion between the distance we had come and that yet to go. Near the village there were nice fields of grain, some neatly planted in rows such as I never had seen anywhere but in Japan. Almost everywhere from India to here the seed is broadcast and then plowed under. Plenty of the fields had been planted to cotton, and the yard-high stalks were still standing. There were flocks of sand grouse in the stubble, some great blue herons on the dry plain, and flocks of green-winged teal in the green grain. We walked from eight to five. Our poor friend who wasn't used to such exertion nevertheless firmly refused to hire a donkey, though we said we'd ride too, and we got him home with no more visible effects of his excursion than a fiery face. He hadn't recognized the town from the distance and thought we ought to turn sharply to the right.

People here are very interested in our doings. A crowd of both sexes sits and watches our activities and from time to time makes comments on the plants or the birds. A soldier said it was a sin to shoot wagtails, and I can quite understand how he got the idea. They are pleasant to look at with their neat black and white bodies seemingly so delicately balanced on wiry little legs, and they are so cheerful and friendly in habit. They commonly come to open pools and streams, even in city patios. At Karaj they fed at our window box and nested somewhere on the roof. The doors in our room are of plane-tree wood (*chenar*) of beautiful grain but said to be frail. In the market there are handsome fragrant sweet quinces, 5 inches through, two kinds of good pomegranates, and nice large walnuts. We found no cucumber or cabbage seed in our search. Cabbage is a rare vegetable in all the countries of Asia I have visited, but cucumbers are usually found everywhere.

Chapter II

KIRMAN AND THE GREAT DATE OASES

January 3. We left Sirjan for Kirman[1] yesterday on a truckload of dried limes that is going to Tehran and had to change over to a truckload of stovewood at a town 5 *farsakhs*[2] from Kirman at half past two this morning. Distances in Iran are measured in *farsakhs* (about 3 miles) but most people know kilometer too, though no two people seem to have the same conception of either one, and my ideas on both are completely different from anyone else's. After an hour we started off, breezily and perilously perched on a top-heavy load of twisted limbs that writhed and slipped under every jolt of the road. Soon something fell off. The driver made an imprudent attempt to back up for it and sent one wheel off the shoulder. The load tottered for a horrible second and threatened to catapult us off into the dark and the desert. Unlocked by the sway, the sinuous limbs slid sharply and with a lurch shifted the balance of the load to the other side and we stayed

---

1. Kirman, or Kerman (30°17′N, 57°05′E, 5650 feet). This large and well-known city of 50,000 was founded perhaps in Classical, certainly by Sasanid, times. After the tenth century, it had become the capital of a series of local dynasties, a center of pilgrimage, and a commerical entrepôt. It was frequently pillaged in the eighteenth century, but recovered during the nineteenth. The town lies near the center of a mountain-enclosed basin, surrounded by walled gardens and villages, watered by *qanats* or underground tunnels carrying water from nearby foothills. Its mud-brick wall still existed at the time of Koelz's visit, but a broad avenue had been cut into the heart of the traditional city. The city is overwhelmingly Persian-speaking, and there were substantial communities of Zoroastrians and Bahais among the Moslem majority. Kirman has been world-famous for its carpet industry since the mid-nineteenth century, but other fabrics and metalwork were also important. Kirman was a hub in the road network, with dirt roads leading to Khorasan to the north, Seistan to the east, Fars to the west, and the Gulf ports to the south. There was at this time also a landing field. As at Bandar Abbas, there were banks, a British consulate, a hospital, and several garages.

2. Legally 6.34 kilometers, the *farsakh* proves to be a flexible unit of measure in rural Iran, not unlike the "country mile"; it can be shorter if the speaker wishes to encourage the trip but longer if he wishes to discourage travel.

upright. Someone walked back to get what had fallen off. Then the car broke down, and it was eight o'clock when we got to Kirman. In the dismal dark of early dawn we plowed through swarms of donkeys that were bringing loads of dry desert plants to town to sell for fuel. They would arrive before daylight. I could not see why one need thus take Time by the forelock, and the sight depressed lower still my weary spirits. I dislike to get up early myself and therefore feel sorry for anyone who does. Even when one surmounts the natural sloth that makes him loathe to leave his bed untimely, there still is the cold, the wet, the dark, and the loneliness, and the need must be great that can drive one over all of these.

Kirman lies at one end of a great plain walled in by chains of barren mountains. Here and there at the base of the enclosing wall where springs give up the mountains' hoard of winter water, small villages can be seen, and here and there too over the floor of the desert plain are scattered spots of cultivation where *qanats* have brought down from the mountain some hidden stream. With this you have the setting of most of the towns of Iran, and the only variant is the quantitative one: the spots of cultivation are fewer or smaller and the distances less. The urban beauty treatment that has come in vogue with the new "era of progress" has done little more to Kirman than eyebrow-plucking, and its pleasant Persian character has not been blotted from its weatherbeaten old face. Poor and humble it is, to be sure, but poor and humble it still would be even if the streets took on the metropolitan mainstreet width that, with the erection of a two-story government building or two, has face-lifted most Persian towns into staring frights. How much better warm water and a soapy rag would have been and afterwards maybe a little judicious rouge. The old roofed-in bazaar still stands—the word 'bazaar' is properly used only for this section of commercial life of a city that has the streets covered over and thus in summer is sheltered from the heat and in winter from the snow and mud and provides an advantage in the bitter struggle that poverty-stricken Asia wages without end against the elements. Whatever is on the market is to be had in the bazaar, and that isn't much besides the staple products of the country. Inexpensive articles of foreign manufacture that the simple housekeeping and husbandry require and a luxury or two in the way of some good foreign cloth or a fine assortment of common German drugs are found, but the bazaars of most towns of all the country couldn't compete in variety of stock in general with an average Woolworth store and would be sorely worsted in a competition of quality. Goods are offered for sale piled on shelves or on the floor, in small rooms or booths fully open to the street and often with a living room joined on behind, and it isn't necessary usually to go inside to shop. If the proprietor is out he generally indicates his absence by hanging a piece of cloth across the front of the booth. The cloth covers only the lower part of the opening and you can see that the shop is empty, but without the cloth you might think the owner was in the back room or at his neighbor's.

The buildings are of adobe, of one story, with domed roofs and arched

A Kirman Oasis. The settlements in all of Iran, except along the Caspian Sea, are like this, larger or smaller, as the supply of water is more or less. Here the magic fluid is brought from mountain springs by canals, their course marked by the pollarded willows. The bridge is of several centuries ago, probably from the reign of Shah Abbas, who left many architectural monuments throughout his realm. It is a winter landscape, else there would be no clouds.

doors and windows, yet the limitations of materials have not prevented the attainment of grace and dignity. Often the houses are set in walled-in gardens that have shrubs and trees: pines, cypresses, Judas trees, or a willow with fiery branches like a red osier, and their tended freshness bespeaks a love of home that in the East is not so often manifested in this way. We were shown into one of these gardens and lodged in two pleasant rooms that as usual were heavily carpeted. A friendly woman hastily made a blaze of straw in the stove, apparently as a symbol of warmth and welcome, and said her husband would be along in a minute to see what else we needed. Outside in the garden petunias and calendulas still defied the winter with a stray flower or two, while a Judas tree and some narcissus were already welcoming the spring with theirs.

My first business was at the bank, and Nikbur asked me as tactfully as his simple nature allowed him to wear the nice clothes I had on yesterday.

Clothes are as important in these parts as in others, and I often have to be reminded of it. In the Himalayas a Tibetan horseman once told my men to ask me to wear better clothes since my appearance touched on his honor, though nobody could see how, except that servants are proud of the figure their masters cut. Indian servants, for example, take great pride in the quantity of their master's luggage, though often it is only a headache for them. On that score at least no servant of ours ever had cause to complain, for however hard we tried to go light, carrying for subsistence and comfort only the minimum that seemed scant even to the Tibetan nomads, we inevitably accumulated great bundles, bags, and boxes of specimens so nondescript in appearance that we were sometimes taken for one of the numerous wandering groups of jugglers and dancers that roam from the Himalayas to Afghanistan. These wanderers travel with their miserable goods tied on donkeys and with a following of curs and children. Invariably there is in the caravan a corded wooden bedstead under which its donkey bearer is completely hidden so that it seems to be floating along by itself except that the several hens which always to be seen tied on top stagger and totter from the jolting of some unseen cause. Our resemblance to them wasn't quite complete, but the difference must have seemed small because

DEH SHIB IN KIRMAN. The houses in the Kirman settlements are often single, not clustered into the defense unit that constitutes the usual village of this part of the world. The walls are solid and built with care. The openings are arched in the typical manner of the country.

we were even asked now and then to give a performance of our skill. The bank manager spoke German well and gave me 17 *rials* for my dollar. In the produce market there are the usual winter vegetables and late season fruits, and also plenty of two kinds of wild partridges. There are good tangerines, a sort of Valencia orange, a fine orange-colored lemon that can be peeled and segmented like a navel orange, very good pomegranates, and a few watermelons, still edible. Pumpkins, of the sort we call Japanese, are common; cabbage is tender and mild; the carrots are a foot and more long, smooth, black, purple, or yellow. Potatoes seem to be rare and are, I understand, not much eaten, except by those who have nothing else. It may be that they don't know how to use them in their diet, for after all you can't do much with a potato without milk, fat, or gravy. Beets and turnips are a godsend to the poor and are sold steaming hot by street-vendors. Here the people usually raise their voices to make us understand better; at Balvard they often whispered.

January 7. The village of Deh Bala lies a few hours walk from Kirman, well hidden against the bare hills in an enlargement of the valley. The name means "The Upper Village," and there must be dozens of settlements of that name in the country. Hussainabad, Yusufabad, Aliabad, Mohamedabad, and the like are also much multiplied designations, perpetuating as they do the names of popular religious figures. Huge fig trees grow about 18 inches in diameter, often five or more in a clump, tall and vigorous as an old apple tree. I had hitherto seen only fig bushes. They said the fruit was of three kinds, but no samples were to be had. Somewhere in the neighborhood of Kirman excellent figs are grown because medium-sized, sugary, and nearly seedless fruits were found for us in the city, and we were assured there were even better ones. Figs are a popular fruit in Persia, and there are numerous varieties, both cultivated and wild. Some of the latter are as good as some of the cultivated kinds. Most of them are eaten fresh and only in relatively small quantities are high class dried fruits to be found on the market. From the neighborhood of Kermanshah come the greatest quantity of these, prepared by packing in a leather sack with sugar or flour sprinkled between the layers of fruit.

The houses of the village are small, well built, with nicely domed roofs and ceilings, and well modeled doors and windows. The rugs on the floor of our room were nearly worn out—of excellent colors, but as different in design from what we call "Kirmani" in the United States as is a Navajo blanket. It seems these rugs with the insipid flowery design are of a type that suits the luxury trade, and the people weave for themselves something simpler and more artistic. They took us to see the rugweavers at work on a pair of room-sized rugs that they said the Shah had ordered through a Kirman contractor. A design had been drawn up on cross-section paper, colored appropriately, and this pattern was now in the hands of three men

A Figtree at Deii Bala, Kirman. Figs are common in Persian gardens, even in the cold parts, and in places they grow wild. The fruit is variable in quality in these wild growths, often edible. Figs are usually bushes, and rarely do they grow to such trees as these. The large trunks in the background are mulberry. Walls are usually higher than these. They must be high enough to keep the goats from climbing over and are sometimes high enough to keep out men.

who were singing to two looms, behind which sat men, women, and even children, some of them not more than ten. We could see nothing but the back of the rug with its pretty vine design and the fingers of the weavers flying through the warp. On the ends where the weaving was most intricate sat adults. Not even Ali, our companion, could understand the chanting instructions to the weavers so we never found out how the individual sorted out his particular grain from the chaff of confusion, and we wondered no less how the reader followed the tiny squares of the pattern without a pointer to aid the eye. While a reader let me examine his script, a woman had to wait.

Then he asked, "Where was I?" The woman said something and he started singing again. A baby was asleep in a cradle and a granny was minding three others. They say a man can weave about an inch a day over the stretch of about a foot that is his field to weave on.

The wage they get for weaving is only enough to sustain life, and the misery of the creators is a strange comment on the beauty of the thing created. But the people didn't look unhappy and there came to mind a conversation I overheard once between an Irish girl and Rup Chand in America. They decided Tibet and Ireland were indeed poor, but said the lassie, "You didn't *think* you were poor, did you?" These people have handsome soft dark eyes and look as if they were capable of doing nice things.

We got off at nine, though we were ready at seven (no one would have been able to explain the two hours delay) and were soon at the top of the pass. From there the descent is continuous and rather sharp, and after about 10 miles we came to Mohamedabad where our donkeys were at home. The *qanats* were rarer today. Yesterday near Deh Bala they were running gristmills with *qanat* water. The water is led out of its subterranean channel to drop into a deep pit (*tanureh*), in the bottom of which the mill is built. In the Himalayas one would never have found such an ingenious application of water-power principles to these simple mills. Some of the Himalayan villagers are so stupid they haven't even thought of a hopper for feeding in the grain and do it by hand. The most interesting thing I remember anywhere else about mills is the practice of some Western Tibetans of using beef shoulder blades to make the paddles of their waterwheels.

Wangyel came down from the mountain and said there were snowcock here and sought to convince us with a handful of porcupine droppings! He has lived all his life among snowcock and porcupines and is a good hunter besides. Such stupidities as this and even more amusing and surprising ones he exhibits from time to time, but in dealing with people he has the uncanny sharpness that is characteristic of his race, from whom the human heart has few secrets.

January 8. There was a pair of bulbuls[1] (*Pycnonotus leucotis*) in the garden, which indicates a warmer region, and indeed though the day wasn't warmer than at Kirman, the night wasn't so sharp. Ali said his heart sank (in Persian idiom "his times got bitter") when the order came from

---

1. *Bulbul* is the vulgar term currently applied by ornithologists to some kinds of birds of the family Pycnonotidae. To the Persian the *bulbul* is the nightingale.

Dugout Homes of the Desert Poor in Kirman. Trees and stones are not always available for building in the desert, so these people have managed to make shelters with simpler materials. These houses that look like great termite mounds have two apertures, one for tenants, the other for the smoke. The desert vegetation is shrubby and abundant, but not abundant enough to support cows. They have a feeding place in the reeds lower down.

Tehran for him to escort the American scientist. Perhaps things turned out better than he expected, or he wouldn't have told me.

The way today, they said, was 8 *farsakhs* and added for greater lucidity that it would take from dawn to dark. There was a shortcut over the mountain that the donkey drivers didn't want to take, but I went that way along with Rup Chand and two of the three soldiers who were accompanying us. The mountain is of marble, nearly bare, steep-walled, and since we were headed for the date district, the descent was longer than the climb. A road has been made that donkeys apparently can go over, since we met two bringing onions. The soldiers weren't so surefooted as the donkeys and had some trouble going down. Fuz, at the foot of the steep descent, was the first settlement we came to. A wild rambler had crawled 10 feet up into a fruit tree. A boy said its flowers were yellow and about 2 inches across. In the gulches here we had seen bush-roses with still an occasional single pink bloom, but not since northeastern Afghanistan, where wild roses are enormously varied, do I remember having seen a yellow rambler, and the flowers of that rambler aren't much bigger than a dime. There were plenty of woodpeckers in the orchard, a black thrush, and numerous flocks of chukors (*Alectoris graeca*). The latter were fearfully shy, though it doesn't seem likely they are much hunted here. In parts of the Himalayas they are also inordinately shy in the fall but tame in spring. We often found even the small birds on the Tibetan plateau very wary, and almost everywhere in open country it was more difficult for us to approach birds than for the natives to whose style of dress they had been accustomed. Springs that rose in the village joined to make a little stream that received other reinforcements on its way down the gulch and soon made a pleasant rivulet bordered with oleander bushes and lofty clumps of grasses. In one of the earth walls of the gulch some caves had been dug and several donkey caravans were having lunch. The owners too were lunching and invited us to share their bread and tea and pipe. They might have managed between them to feed us without going hungry themselves, but in Iran the quantity or quality of the food has nothing to do with the offering of hospitality. I don't remember even one instance when a Persian failed to offer to share his meal with me, however miserable it may have been.

When the stream reached the mountain we left it and began to climb up the barren side of the highest peak. Dry rhubarb leaves were blowing about over the slope, and I wondered if it had the large heavy roots that in Afghanistan we sometimes used for fuel and that burned with such a beautiful blue flame. The descent from the crest of the pass is long and gentle through a deep gulch that permits no view till it opens on the endless vista of the Great Desert, the Dasht-i Lut, that stretches on for barren miles toward Afghanistan. The way all day had been over terrain harsh and bleak even for Iran and now in front of us in soft-hued haze lay the palms and orange groves of Chaharfarsakh, their flaunting fronds and sunsteeped foliage shielding the gaze from the awful sublimity of the infinite desert beyond.

We stopped in one of the gardens where some other travellers with their camels and donkeys had halted, and the soldiers went off to find some food. Then till dark we waited, watching the caravans that in the late afternoon poured steadily out of the gulch, hoping to see ours among them, or watching every speck on the desert for the foodbearing soldiers. At seven, Ali came along and at once set off to see what had happened to our foragers. The dear lad was office-bred and must have felt like doing almost anything but continuing his promenade into the desert. He didn't reappear, but sent rugs and a lantern, and we camped luxuriously under the orange trees in beds of petunias and gaillardias. We made a fire and chewed dates that we got from one of the camel drivers and waited. The soldiers didn't come back, but at eight our donkeys came tinkling down the mountain, by far the latest of the travellers. For all their hard day they were fresh enough and after a roll in the ashes of an old camp fire dashed off to graze in the garden. Food for us wasn't so easy to come by, so we ate cake and drank coffee and went to bed in the fresh breeze that slid off the mountain.

January 10. The gardens of Shahdad[1] have high walls and the passageways between them are narrow. In the gardens date palms are planted at regular intervals, and the remaining space is filled with a dense growth of citrus. Violets grow wild under the trees. There are a dozen varieties of citrus, most of them interesting and several such as I had never seen in other countries. The tangerines are of good flavor, sometimes with only traces of seeds and often with little rag. The sweetlime, the lime, the bitter orange, and the Valencia orange are good enough as such things go, but the most interesting things are of the lemon class. The *otroj* is a rough lemon, 5 inches long, with salmon-tinted flesh and a pleasant acid flavor, milder than a lemon. The *daba* is larger and smoother than the *otroj*, with a nice lemon flavor. The *bakh* is a grapefruit-like lemon, 3 to 4 inches in diameter. Then there is the common *limu khargi*, separable into segments, that we saw in the Kirman market. The dates are of a dozen varieties or so. The Shamsai and Basmuni which are the best, are of a quality I had seen heretofore only in the much larger Piyaruni that I found at Hajiabad on the way to Kirman. These dates are not at all sticky outside and can thus be carried in the pocket like nuts. They are of good flavor and of the consistency of a caramel. Another dry date, orange-yellow in color, with or without a developed seed, is strongly tannic and used mostly for cattle feed. It is supposed that the imperfect development of these fruits is due to some fault in fertilization. The fruit trees here all appear healthy. There are fewer dead palms than at Bandar Abbas, possibly because the groundwater along the coast is nearer the surface. They say that dates thrive better still and give better fruit at Chaharfarsakh on the slope at the foot of the mountain where it freezes and snow falls. The people carry torches of dry date leaves at night.

Toward sunset a storm rose in the west and in its struggle to put out the dying sun, piled up battalions of black and ragged clouds that towered jinn-like into the sky. The sun shot volleys of arrows into the monster that pierced his writhing depths and deepened his inky wrath. Higher surged his awful mass. For a few brief moments Light and Darkness thus battled and then the shafts fell faster, the apparition dimmed and faded, and the

---

1. Shahdad (30°18′N, 57°49′E, ca. 2000 feet). An important plateau city of the early third millennium B.C., it has been little more than a village in recent times.

storm spirit swept in empty fury into the desert, leaving the sun to set in fiery glory among the tattered banners of the conquered foe. Desert storms often are such fantastic and fearsome visitations that pass in the gale and spitefully spill a tantalizing sip to the parched creation. More generous are the storms that arise from great low-pressure areas that move slowly and may refresh large stretches. In the Himalayas, rains are often local and one may see the manufacture of the storm. A cloud wisp appears on the peak and floats forward, gathering volume so swiftly that it covers the sky as by magic and rain falls.

A big flock of goats came from the direction of the mountain at evening, tended by two boys. The shepherds are probably hired by the village goat owners and every morning assemble their charges and every evening bring them back. A young woman with a baby and a bleating kid came out on the plain to meet the herd, and when the kid's mother joined them, they went back again. I had never seen so many red goats in Iran before. In many desert places the goats are mostly black, though offhand it would seem that white would be a more suitable color in the heat. A flock of at least 50 ravens was busy feeding on the desert, but what the barren ground was yielding, I couldn't determine.

A man told us garlic was an excellent tonic for the eyes; Lahulis on the contrary positively know that garlic weakens the sight! Garlic is believed beneficial for malaria in Iran, but Lahulis again have the opposite idea. Garlic here and in Lahul has at least the same odor, and it is quite possible that it has no effect on vision or malaria. Then too, Lahulis are apt to have something against everything on their meager bill of fare, except mutton and roast barley flour (*sattu*), but so, for that matter, are the Persians. It is unthinkable that a physician in either place shouldn't rigidly restrict the choice of diet of his patient. Two children told us it was a sin to kill a woodpecker and then were frightened at their temerity; we might take it as a reproof. The people whistle while the donkeys and horses drink—always the same sort of trilling whistle. Lahulis whistle while horses drink but don't bother for donkeys. The children here have their hair clipped except over the front one-third, and the sun has often bleached to a queer red what hair they have. Those whose hair Time has bleached make their red too but with henna, which is a common plant in the warmer parts of the country. From India to Persia old age seems to be dreaded—something to be ashamed of in both sexes. Where the Mongol gets respect for the fruits of his experience, it seems his western neighbors get pity or contempt, and so even the commonest people seldom show white hair.

January 16. The weather looked hopeful this morning, so we got ready to leave Chaharfarsakh. By searching in the gardens here and at Shahdad, we finally got a collection of seeds of most of the usual vegetables. Many things seem not to be generally planted so one finds peppers only in one garden and eggplants in another, and nothing seems to be common but greens and what we call "herbs" and seldom plant. We got much help from a schoolboy who, tempted by an American jackknife, ransacked the village with good effect, and every evening delivered his finds on a handsome blue donkey. There are several woodcock here in the orange groves. They say their name is *khoftu* and that they stay the year round, but that can hardly be.

As we entered the *dar*, the gulch that leads to the pass, we shot a golden eagle that some ravens were teasing. As is often the case with birds of prey, even with apparently expert hunters like duck hawks, there was no trace of food in its digestive system. Golden eagles we have often found thus empty of food. From the fact that this eagle is one of the most widely distributed birds and in parts of Asia and America, at least, is a common bird of prey, it seems well adapted to survive and it may be abstemious by nature. In Afghanistan we used to take live chickens to the mountain tops to bait the eagles, but though they clearly saw the bait none ever attacked it. Other wild birds such as chukors and snowcocks I have often seen them chasing, once even a great bustard, but I never could be certain they ever caught one. On the other hand it seems that at times they get rather hungry. An old female was brought me at Karaj one summer by a peasant who said the bird had struck at some pigeons and had hit the ground so forcibly that it couldn't rise again. One dropped from the sky within a few feet of where I sat one day, attracted by the punch-bag we put up for our wild boar to exercise on. I have also frequently seen them sitting around or looking over carrion, though whether they ate it, I couldn't be sure. Smaller birds of prey like kestrels and harriers I have usually found to feed regularly, but the game they look for is of course commoner and more easily got.

As we started climbing, snow began to fall, soft, thick flakes, and by the time I got to the top of the pass at one, everything was white. The ravens and crows had flown high last night, circled and dropped and sailed again, and the natives said a storm was in the offing. The passage of the seasons alters little the face of the desert but the passing cloud had for a brief moment transfigured it, and I thought of the lines of Omar Khayyám:

> The wordly hope men set their hearts upon
> Turns ashes—or it prospers; and anon,
> Like snow upon the desert's dusky face
> Lighting a little hour or two—is gone.

A flock of fine donkeys reached the crest with me, carrying oranges to Kirman. I brushed off the wet snow that hung heavily on the uneven load

RUP CHAND AND A GOLDEN EAGLE NEAR KIRMAN. The golden eagle is at times a common bird of prey in Iran and Afghanistan, as it is in places in our own country. The largest of this tribe, it is also the most interesting and often puts on a spectacular act in the desert's show.

and their master told me, "You'll get your hands cold." The descent, in the slush and toward the retreating storm, was easy. The bare mountains, black in the heavy light, now looked wild and weird; the pleasant little stream below stood out swollen and muddy. A scrubby tree growing out of a boulder along the way had numerous rags tied to it—just as one sees in the mountains from here to Tibet—one of the relict customs of an ancient culture which the religions of two millennia have superseded but not effaced. In Tibet the rags are tied on with a prayer that the god of the region is besought to bring into fulfillment. Along the stream a sparrow hawk (*Accipiter nisus*) flew out of a bush with a red ball that looked like a pomegranate. He had captured and plucked one of the little mountain partridges.

Toward four o'clock we arrived at Pushte, a lone house with a little orchard and a few fields, the only stopping place till five hours' journey ahead. Room had been made for us, but we were a considerable party and the house was small, so there was evident inconvenience for the lone woman who ran the place and her assorted livestock. We seemed to have trespassed especially on the rights of a swarm of dapper parti-colored cockerels that, till dark, rasped the air with their amateur crowing kept up beyond their habit by our intrusion. Our baggage had been stored in the oven where they generally spent the night. The hostess had taken refuge with a goat and a calf in the other room and wasn't disposed to have any traffic with her lodgers, not even to supplying us with a couple of the supernumerary roosters. At last, however, she consented to give two hens, and even to give two eggs with each hen, if we'd take them instead. This struck me as the height of imprudence—to kill hens in the beginning of the laying season when there was this obvious plethora of unprofitable males. The root of the difficulty seems to have been that hen meat is "warm" and cock meat "cold," or perhaps vice versa. Ali probably thought my insistence on roosters was motivated by these considerations instead of economic ones and finally triumphed, but he had to give a letter saying that he had requisitioned the birds. Probably the woman would be held accountable to someone for the shortage.

In the fresh damp air today the whole route was perfumed, and I came to understand what the old poets meant when they sang of the fragrant earth of Iran. Striking fragrances rise from freshly plowed fields, due probably to the broken roots of scented plants. The *Artemisia* or wormwood freshened by the rain gave off its bittersweet odor, and at times on the slopes there was a strong smell like lemon verbena. In the valley along the stream some tall sugarcane-like grasses were redolent of honey. I may have been a bit fanciful because Rup Chand said he had smelt nothing but the "old house" smell that you get around the tamarisks.

One of our donkey men has a job, from which he was temporarily released to go with us, that pays him 2 rials (6 cents) a day, and food. What the food consists of he didn't say, only that tea wasn't included, so he drinks water. The people in Kirman are generally poor, even judged by standards of a country where almost everyone is poor. Fuel is a luxury and is seldom used for heating houses; one tries to keep warm with clothes. Not everyone can manage to buy fuel even for cooking and food is commonly bought cooked, or for a small sum you can have your dish of stew cooked by the foodsellers in the bazaar. One of the men thought Rup Chand would look younger if he'd wear one of their felt hats instead of his American straw one. I was a bit surprised at a suggestion of rejuvenating Rup Chand because he is usually taken to be fifteen years younger than he is and I fifteen years older.

January 20. Today is some kind of a holiday,[1] and the city is quiet as the grave. Accordingly I had Nikbur phone the mission hospital, which they said was run by Americans, to see if I might call. The hospital is on the other side of the city, and it took an hour to walk there. Afterwards everyone wondered that I had found my way back. They say there are two horse-carriages in town that haul people about, but neither crossed my path. I found a gentle, kind woman in charge of the hospital, who turned out to be British and not American, exceptionally observing and intelligent, and who of course liked the people. She said septic conditions were common, likewise deformed pelvises from rug weaving, that she had seen more hysteria here than ever she had seen at home. I had assumed that hysteria was an abnormal condition and that where every woman got a husband and therefore lived apparently more normally, neuroses might be less common. We generally feel sorry for the downtrodden females of the East but from what I have seen and heard, they rule the roost as effectively here as do their more enlightened sisters in the West, and the old girls are downright corkers. A young Persian woman has as wholesome a fear of her mother-in-law as she has of hellfire, and when I asked a friend once what was the trouble with her mother-in-law, she countered with, "Do your girls like them?" Then I asked what sort of life they had when there were a couple of wives in the house and was told the husband had to spend most of his time away from home if he wanted peace. The Persian woman impresses me as an intelligent, capable, and active creature. The man is likewise intelligent, but more the dreamer, and easygoing. I thought I noticed about the same difference between the sexes in our South and have read that but for their magnificent fire-eating spouses, the men would have thrown up the Civil War much earlier. Certainly if I wanted to do something in Iran, I should prefer to have a band of women to work with than their husbands or their sons.

My friend said there was no foreign parcel post, except sample post, but that there was a reliable parcel post for the interior. She thought I might find baking powder but dried milk she hadn't seen. She said there were so many beggars that they were forced to go out with empty pockets so they could truthfully say they hadn't money. A teacher had told her that the children had fine memories, but that it was difficult to make them reason. Since then I have spent two years at the government's agricultural high school and observed something of the educational system and its effects. I should have to say with the unknown teacher that logic wasn't the forte of the finished product of the Persian schools, but it seems I could understand

---

1. Perhaps connected with the Shia religious holiday celebrating the birth of Imam Reza.

that if a boy didn't learn to think it wasn't exactly his fault, since thinking is no more encouraged in school than, under the despotic government, outside it. Education in Iran, as in old Europe, is a stuffing of the memory, and agricultural instruction consisted in large part of memorizing scientific names of plants and animals, no matter from where, and if the teacher chanced to know them, the English, French, and German names as well, of endless morphological and physiological terms of botany and zoology and whatever the other sciences could yield in the way of polysyllabic words, so that for weeks before the examinations the boys paced the avenues mumbling their jargon in preparation for the ordeal. And ordeal the examination was, a veritable academic trial by fire. The victim might be made to sit a day, or even two, outside the examiner's room waiting his turn and then have his fate settled by a question, or maybe two, such as: "Name the breeds of French horses." One boy did especially well by being able to give the name of the elm tree in six languages and neither he nor I (I had had two year's experience by then) was surprised that he didn't recognize the tree itself as it grew in the avenues of the grounds. The fact that the names learned were sometimes partially or totally incorrect was a trifling matter because neither teacher nor student could believe that the correct scientific name of a Chinese plant or of the details of the digestive tract of some unknown insect had any bearing on Persian education, so the wrong one was no more irrelevant. Instead of showing the boys a cow's skull, the teacher described it; instead of letting them raise chickens, statistics were read on the status of French egg imports from Belgium, so it isn't strange you could find graduates who couldn't tell wheat from barley, nor a peach tree from a willow, nor was it an idiot either who having watched me dip water from the stream and put out the fire, asked if the liquid had been gasoline.

Let no one suppose from the foregoing that the Persians are feebleminded. I should rather say that they are mentally as agile as any people I have ever been among. Certainly for learning languages they have the extraordinary aptitude one often finds also among the Indians. One boy who came to me for English lessons after school could with ease carry on a conversation in that language at the end of eight months and had read with me all the reading material prescribed in the seven years of English instruction in the schools. Another student who studied German mostly by himself could converse with reasonable fluency after four months. And coupled with this remarkable ability one finds a keen appreciation of literary beauties rare among us. The amount of poetry most Persian boys know is colossal. A common way of killing time is a game called *moshaireh*. One boy quotes a line of poetry and the next has to quote one in return, beginning with the letter that ended the previous quotation. Such a game would soon be finished in the most intellectual group we could collect in the United States, but the agricultural school boys had sessions that lasted through the afternoon without any of the competitors falling out.

The Persian peasant, on the other hand, never goes to school and is by no means mentally constipated. He has to use his wits to wrest a living from a parsimonious Providence and a conservative landlord. He has observed and profited by his observations. He has seen that only certain lateral shoots of the muskmelon vine bear fruit well and he will show you on the growth rings of a stump that young trees need three years to establish their roots. The Karaj peasants, though my fame as a foreign specialist in agriculture was bruited abroad, didn't rush for advice till they saw results that they hadn't expected, and their discussion of world politics had more sound sense than an armful of *Reader's Digests*. I often recall a conversation I once had with a Georgia cracker. I expressed my surprise at the originality and soundness of his views and he replied, "You see, we can't read. We have to think things out for ourselves!"

My sojourn in Iran was prolonged always in the stimulating hope that I might be able to get some government interested in letting me try to do something for a people so worthy of a decent life. No Persian ever believed that I or anyone else would be successful in arousing such an interest in any government, and they were equally unanimous in blaming the blocking of all progress in the country on the British. The Germans, they said, had repeatedly made proposals for economic improvement, and foreign pressure had always effected their rejection. The strong pro-German sentiment in the country may have had its roots in such beliefs as this.

On the way home someone hailed me in the half-lighted street, and I found one of the young military officers who had come up with us from Bandar Abbas. He had had perhaps a glass too much and we hugged each other and exchanged vows of friendship.

The men were bargaining today for a piece of cloth, fine handloom stuff of cotton warp and cashmere weft, such as one seldom finds nowadays since there are weaving factories that reproduce foreign designs. They were ready to pay 65 rials against the asked-for 80 when a beggar gave them a wink and they got it for 60. Ali said that it was the right price and that the beggar added to his income by such hints to prospective buyers.

Children and youths here often have the whole side of the cheek a bright red, but for some reason they fade soon. The men gave the housekeeper's little girl some candy, and her father came with a slab of bread. They gave some to Nikbur who had wanted to bring us all supper from his own home the night we came back from Shahdad, a hospitality he could probably afford less than I could giving away an automobile, and he brought a plate of nice red apples. The aforementioned candy was enclosed in a sack made from an old rug pattern, a bright thing that I cut up and enclosed in letters to friends at home. Wangyel was met with hard scepticism when he described the potatoes in his country, and not till he cut the size to no more than twice that of the runts one sees here was it allowed to be likely.

January 24. We expected to leave Kirman for Jiroft today and got ready. Nikbur took home such things as we wouldn't need on the trip, and at 3:30 they took our luggage to the bus station and weighed it. We had been warned the bus would start at 4:00. Nikbur wanted terribly to go along with us because officials get a little travelling allowance, but the job fell to a youngster named Zand who had seemingly never undertaken such an adventure before. His friends came in hordes to bid him goodbye, and the garage courtyard showed scenes like those before the gangplank of an ocean liner, but still the bus didn't start and eventually the cold emptied the courtyard of all but the passengers. The last to go was one of Zand's relatives, a boy of sixteen, with the usual nice Kirmani smile. He knew some English and was delighted to talk in public in that language. We got off at six, well loaded with human cargo. We were given the "best" seats, behind the driver, but there were sacks on the floor so that my knees were wrapped around my ears. Outside the city, we stopped for the customary police inspection, and for an hour the passengers had their passes registered by a nice-looking youth who did his job pleasantly. We didn't have any passes, but there had been a telephone call about us. A lot more people got aboard at the police station, but I was too weary to see where they could possibly stow them, and a little farther on we picked up a couple more who hadn't passes and therefore were put to the inconvenience of walking past the police post. At 8:30 we got to Mahun and stopped for supper. They said we could have anything we wanted to eat which is the usual way of saying tea, bread, and eggs. An hour later we piled back into the bus and drove a bit to pick up one of the passengers who had gone to someone's house. He came out and said he hadn't eaten yet, might he eat. In 15 minutes he came, and we started.

There is a famous old mosque in Mahun,[1] the turquoise dome of which shone in the moonlight, the first impressive building I have seen since the Moghul remains of India. The road soon ran through a snowy landscape with low ridges on either side. At three we stopped somewhere for tea, about the first building since Mahun. There wasn't any place to wait except in the crowded "coffee house," as these places are called for some reason (Persians seldom serve coffee except at wakes), so we crawled back on our seats in the bus and crouched there benumbed till the driver came to start at half-past five. We got to Bam sometime after sunrise, too stupified even

---

1. This is the shrine of Shaikh Nimatulla, initiated in A.D. 1437.

to be bad-tempered. This was our first ride on the public buses, smart-looking light-blue glassed-in things that gave no clue from their appearance to what agony one might endure from a ride in them. I could never get any other reason for riding through the night than that it was too warm for the cars in the daytime. More enlightened comment suggested that since camel caravans had always set out at evening, folks had come to like night travel. With trifling added inconveniences such as derive from association with carsick or lousy neighbors, this trip was a sample of our travel in these vehicles while we were in Iran. One wonders perhaps that I don't mention quarrels and bloodshed, but the Persian is singularly patient and tolerant, and almost never anything but courteous, and it seems as far as is possible he disregards his own discomfort, perhaps since he doesn't have to look far to see someone obviously less comfortable than he. They said folks at Bam suffer much from malaria which they get from eating so many dates. At Bandar Abbas they also said that the disease was contracted from date-eating and that such a diet made the complexion dark. I had heard in India that malaria may result in a deepening of the skin color, and it may be that the swarthier complexion of the older Persians is due to malaria. It may be mentioned that the cause of malaria is ascribed in different places, to different things such as spring water, stagnant water, grapes, cucumbers, etc., and I don't remember ever hearing the right cause mentioned. Even at the Agriculture School at Karaj where solemn lectures were given the students on health, the mosquito-wrigglers waxed in the pools, and the doctor's assistant, who had his house carefully screened except for a hole that a dog could have gone through, slept outside without a mosquito net.

Persians have very mobile faces, and like us their mask is stiff and repelling. Tibetans, on the other hand, can make their faces such a blank that you are as unaffected by them as by a statue.

January 30. Deh Bakri[1] is in the foothills of the great Jamal Bariz range that forms part of the southern rim of the Great Desert, the Dasht-i Lut that runs for more than 500 miles to the north. We have come on foot from the date plantations of Bam to visit the more important and more extensive ones across the mountains in the Jiroft district that stretches off southward to the ocean. People here commonly wear for shoes a big piece of wood tied on with a string. One man has cloth *giveh* like mine, but he has reinforced the sole with a piece of heavy sheet iron. He said he couldn't be buying new shoes all the time. A nice purple *Colchicum* is blooming in the fields. One garden has a most attractive almond tree, much like our yellow birch, which they said had bitter nuts.

---

1. Deh Bakri (29°07′N, 57°59′E, ca. 6000 feet).

THE SHRINE AT MAHUN. There are countless shrines (*imamzadeh*) throughout the country in varying degrees of size and sanctity depending on the repute of the person whose remains they house. A few cities have superlative structures, and the great mosques of Qom, Isfahan, and Meshed might well draw to worship gentle people of any faith.

We arrived here day before yesterday in the rain that was heralded by a gale so tremendous that walking was difficult. The rain kept on for 36 hours, and we have been sheltered in the one-room telephone office, apparently the finest building in the village. It required a skillful comprehension of space relations to find room for everyone to stretch out his length at night among the piles of luggage, but sleep was another matter. The mud roof, softened by the rain, began flowing in trickles through the reeds that formed the ceiling and then dripped capriciously here and there over the helpless human carpeting. Three huge cats frolicked and yowled over belly and face till even the Persians lost patience a couple of times and chased them out through the windowless apertures. During the day there was no peace either. From time to time someone came to telephone and made his way to the instrument by stepping over us with an "Excuse me" apiece, as we sat huddled in the mud on the floor. For a few minutes he would shout at his distant auditor who seemed not to be giving full attention and constantly was admonished to "look" and "listen." After a brief interval of calm the whole thing would be repeated. Apparently they only wanted to see if the

MOUNTAIN FOREST NEAR DEH BAKRI IN KIRMAN. The higher mountains of the great Iran Plateau have or had forests of oak, and more rarely juniper growths that may properly be called trees. In much of the country the "forests" will be such growths as this, of almonds of several sorts, cherry, maple, and *pista* (wild pistachio). There is always game in such places, partridges and pigs the commonest.

line was working and thought it would be impolite to let it go at that. There are times in this part of the world when a simple "How do you do" won't do for a greeting. In Afghanistan the salutatory ritual was perhaps the most complicated. Both parties began the recitation simultaneously, and among certain peoples, accompanied it by a series of embraces. The performance is hardly less original than our handshake and exchange of trite remarks and has the advantage of having a prescribed and predictable end.

Our poor camel had to sit outdoors in all the rain because none of the doors of the buildings are over 5 feet high. He was heavily blanketed but nevertheless complained dismally to anyone who approached. Camels are said to be very intelligent. Their haughty bearing and measured gait bear this out, and I was always favorably impressed by the air of disdain with which they regard humanity. I am told if you load them too heavily they won't get up, and it is dangerous to mistreat them—they keep it in mind. Their incredible hardiness and their uncanny skill in finding their way through trackless wastes are proverbial. I learned here that in places they are stimulated on hard journeys by tobacco smoking. People have also told me of tamed sparrows, foxes, pigeons, and other animals that became tobacco or opium addicts and came regularly at smoking time. When there is a particularly long waterless stretch ahead, the drivers inform the camels at watering time by a special song so they will drink more heavily. The Tibetans have a special song they sing to their sheep while loading them to remind them there's a hard day's work ahead. The plowing cattle are also encouraged with a song that urges them to make just one more round and calls them pleasant names like "drinker of the snow water" and "eater of the lovely flowers." Unlike the noble horse, the camel isn't greedy. A caravan of these great animals kneeling shoulder to shoulder around their meal of shredded herbage, served on a cloth like their master's *sufreh* and munching in dignified silence gives a chastening air to the camp, and whether from association with their magnificent beasts or from their life in the solitude of the desert, the camel drivers are a manlier group of human beings, simple creatures with more sense of human dignity. The tree of the windswept plain takes a different form from that of the sheltered forest.

I found three magpies dead, apparently of exposure, under a tree. The other magpies seemed none the worse for the protracted rain. At Karaj I occasionally found corpses of magpies that seemed to have died of intestinal troubles. Other birds were seldom found to have died except through violence.

We started on our way through the long stretch of broken ground that separates us from the coastal plain. For most of the day the road ran through rocky ravines rather densely grown up to scrubby trees and bushes of wild *pista (beneh)*, maple, and almond. In places there were large and very dense trees of *beneh*, and in them for the first time we found a curious grosbeak (*Coccothraustes coccothraustes*). Goldfinches and chickadees were common; there was one blackbird (*Turdus merula*) and a flock of serins (*Serinus pusillus*), and we collected a golden eagle ready to lay. Since our stage today was to be only 12 miles, we didn't take much lunch, but when at half-past three we arrived at Maskun, the rendezvous, no one was there. Luckily we met a traveller who said our things had gone on to Mohamedabad, so on we went in pursuit. Mohamedabad is off the road, and we passed it without knowing it, but no matter, since the next person we met said our caravan was still on the march. His neighbor joined him now and urged us to stop and rest a bit while he made tea for us, and he'd find out something definite about the travellers ahead. A man came just then and said that they had made camp at a settlement 3 miles farther on. It was now five o'clock and near sundown, and it was always possible that the distance might be more than 3 miles, so we sent Wangyel on to find them. Our host sent a man to accompany him and to bring back our bed. Us he took into his dugout—he had three in a row; he had two wives, he said—and got out his lantern. One of the wives was told to get ready bread of the best white flour, to make tea, to kill a chicken. This last was a remarkable order since Muslims in these parts don't kill things after sundown, but we saved the chicken's life. We had shot two partridges on the way, and these we roasted over the charcoal—a popular form of preparing meat in Iran and called *kabob*. Our host's brother and son and a couple of neighbors sat with us. The boy was a nice lad of about fifteen but for some reason they insisted he was twelve. It seems the official birth records are somewhat lax and on the identification cards that every male has to carry the recorded age is, for one reason or another, likely to be incorrect. Many don't know their age or their birthday, and many have registered themselves as older or as younger, probably with an eye to the compulsory military service law. The boy had just shot into a flock of partridges with an ancient homemade shotgun, but without effect. I remarked that if he'd got a bird with his shot we'd have had a nice meal. The uncle observed if he had got two, if would have been still nicer. I said how nice that they had so much wood, and they answered that that was about all they did have.

To approach the partridges the boy used a screen made of a sheet on which were painted in various colors, dots, bars, and other figures. Such screens are used from here to the Himalayas to delude the chicken tribe that seems especially fascinated by strange sights. Himalayan hunters often use leopard skins for the purpose. We tried such screens on the great bustard, cranes, and other wary birds but they only fled the sooner. The boy brought out his geography book and took a look at the map of the United States; what did we buy from Persia; what was the news of the war? Tibetans always like to have war news too. When the bed came, we went out and slept in the alfalfa field, to our host's dismay. They had sent a sack of candy with the bedding, and this we divided among the small crowd that had collected to help put us to bed. The man who had brought the bedding got the biggest share, but he promptly distributed what he got among the poorer lookers-on.

There are apple trees here 3 feet through and peach and apricot trees up to 2 feet. Usually apple trees and peach trees hardly get larger than posts in the desert regions we have visited. They have a huskless barley (*jau khilu*) that looks like wheat; it isn't glutinous enough for good bread, they say.

February 3. Tomogaon lies several miles beyond the foothills at the edge of the great plain in a landscape that is reminiscent of the Punjab. Half of the fields are planted to grain now beginning to head, and the rest are fallow. Apparently there is plenty of water for irrigation. Outside the fields are large patches of grass and tamarisk bushes. A few miles below there is a "jungle," all of grass and bushes, where fires are burning here and there. The word 'jungle' is Persian in origin, and here or in India does not mean necessarily a dense forest, as has come to be its signification with us. In fact, outside of the narrow Caspian coast strip, Iran has no forests worthy of the name. In India, the term may be applied to a stretch of wild grass without necessarily a tree or bush in it, while Persians call such places *besheh*. Across the river to the west in the desert are patches of green—villages lying in palm and orange groves. Those nearest the mountain have best citrus, they say, while Dusari,[1] 6 *farsakhs* below, is recommended for its dates.

The houses here are mostly built of cattails on stick frames. Last night when we arrived, we camped under a large *Zizyphus* tree in which the birds were busily eating the fruit and raining the pits down on us. Then a thunderstorm came over the mountain below and looked so threatening that we carried our things into a house. Earlier, it had been cleared for us of all inhabitants except two hens and their chicks. The mothers were distrustful of the foreign infidels, and until we put out the lantern they croaked and squawked alarms to their unconcerned and drowsy family.

We paid the horsemen, but they decided they might as well take us back to Bam; so we engaged to board the donkeys till the return journey begins. They could graze during the day on the edges of the fields and in the desert, and at evening we'd give them some grain and some grass to keep them occupied through the night. (Cattle have to be brought in at night everywhere on account of the wolves and leopards.)

Seed collection went on briskly all day. Such an enterprising lot as these villagers we hadn't seen in a long while. They ransacked their fields and their houses to get what we wanted and even found a few wild cucumbers (they call them "devil's cucumber," *khiyar shaitan*) that have long since been out of season. These wild cucumbers are the size and shape of an egg and keep well, but seem to be eaten by wild animals, probably for their seeds, since the flesh is bitter. Edible sorts, of the size and shape of a football, that are cultivated in parts of southern India, keep for months hung up in the house. India has many varieties of cucumber; another remarkable one doesn't run like the rest of its tribe but stays bushy. Eggplant, cucumber, carrot, squash, and onion seeds have been rare; leek and pepper have not yet appeared. There is a curious long white and purple turnip as long as an icicle radish, the like of which I had never seen anywhere. The foliage even is different from that of orthodox turnips. Peas we find for the first time in Iran.

---

1. Dusari (28°25′N, 57°59′ E).

KIRMAN AND THE GREAT OASES

REED HOUSES IN TOMOGAON, KIRMAN. The people of these parts make shelters of grasses of one sort or the other that grow abundantly in the undrained parts of Jiroft. The air circulates through the walls, and the shelters can be cooled by water. The strangers have just arrived, and the populace has not yet collected to admire their funny things. Someone will move out to give them his house.

Birds, as birds in desert places go, are common. On the river are some waterfowl, and the grainfields provide forage for many others. The fields are especially the haunts of two kinds of partridge: *Francolinus pondicerianus* called *karmanzil*, and *F. francolinus*, or *toraj*. The former sings in the morning from 6:15 to 6:30; the latter from 6:30 to 8:00. Without a dog they can't be flushed from the grain, and outside the grainfields they are very shy. Our host—a nice boy—said he could get them for us, but we didn't take the promise seriously since they wouldn't dare use guns in front of our soldier-escort, and even if they had firearms they would hardly be equipped for partridge hunting. In India these birds are often netted, but here folks had a different way of hunting. They got them with sticks! In the evening they brought eight. A crowd of men and boys having flushed the bird hurl their sticks at it and if they miss they rush to the spot where it alighted and try again. The price we paid for the birds was so tempting that a protesting hen was brought afterwards with the assurance that she too was a *karmanzil*.

The ladies of the community gathered to watch us eat breakfast, and then one asked for a taste of the funny-looking cake. A good Moslem would never think of eating anything a Kafir cooked. There might be a dozen reasons why it would be unclean, none of them of course having the remotest connection with actual cleanliness. A Hindu goes the Moslem one better— he not only won't eat anything an unbeliever touches, but what's more, not what lower castes of believers touch, and I am told the matter has been carried to its logical conclusion by one sect. Its members eat nothing that anyone touches—each member of the family does his own cooking.

A bee-eater is boring a hole in the wall of one of the few mud houses. I wonder if he will make his nest before he bores through. Some of the women in the mountain above here blacken their teeth with something they call *ahmen* and here to enliven their tea they add a mint called *alale* or *aglale*.

A goat got caught in the thorns of a wild *Zizyphus* bush, and the shepherd found him by the crowd of vultures and a golden eagle that had assembled for the end. There seems to be only one cat here, but dogs are plentiful. One poor puppy got a lot of beatings for trying to steal his living, so Rinchen Gialtsen has been feeding him and the yelping has stopped.

The women all appear to be pregnant, and most of the birds seem to be breeding: duck hawk, barn swallow, shrike (*Lanius lahtora*), dove (*Streptopelia decaocto*), pipit (*Anthus decaptus*), etc. The women spin cashmere thread very fine (I never saw such skillful spinners anywhere) and they weave beautiful cloth from it. Its width is only about 6 inches; I don't know what they can make of it. The goats here seem to have heavy loads of "cashmere" under their hair; they say a goat may yield as much as 2 pounds. Tibetan goats have a much scantier growth and probably a dozen wouldn't yield 2 pounds.

The Governor at Sabzwarun sent a stone jug with about 10 pounds of Murdasing dates preserved in date syrup, each fruit separate and sugary, something quite new and nonpareil in the date line. The date syrup, or *shireh*, is in itself a most delicious thing, though it is but little known outside of the date-growing regions. When the date bunches are cut and hung up to dry, the juice that drips from them is collected and made into *shireh*. Grape *shireh* made by boiling down grape juice is found everywhere, but always has a cream of tartar tang that limits its usefulness as a sweetener. The earliest ripening date, they say, is the Alimeteri that ripens about the first of July; the latest the Halili, in September.

At night a little boy came with a *karmanzil*. He could hardly contain his joy at the prospect of the 25-cent reward he would get. He had caught the bird himself and probably was getting the first money he ever had, and such a lot of it too. There are a few pairs of mongooses about camp, but they never come near. In India they sometimes came into the tent after meat, and at one place in the Himalayan foothills a pair stayed with us and came regularly for the discarded birdmeat of the taxidermy operations. An enormous lizard was likewise attracted by the meat and took up his quarters in a hole nearby. He came to blows with the mongooses one day and for a few minutes there was a bit of an uproar, but the encounter didn't excite him enough to disturb for long the nap he was taking at the mouth of the hole when the trouble began. I had expected from what I remember of *The Jungle Book* that a mongoose would make short work of anything in the reptile line. It is said there are in the mountains two kinds of wild grapes with large berries. I had noticed vines with huge trunks in the ravines on our way down.

Chapter III

ISFAHAN NIM-JAHAN[1]

February 20. Yezd[2] is a nice town with the neatest mud walls around the yards that I have ever seen. The streets and roads are clean, and the white-vaulted bazaar is well kept and colorful. They are just now engaged in tearing it down to modernize the city. The houses have small towers like large radio cabinets on the roof to catch the breeze—a device I have also seen in India where winds from one direction prevail. Though in the midst of the desert, I hear there is nevertheless much malaria here, as there is in most Persian towns. Everyone if possible has a water storage tank, which of course breeds mosquitoes.

We put up in the *mehmankhana* (hotel) and have a nice room with a huge Kirman rug that we share with two dozen long-haired Persian cats; the rug and the cats are all colors. This seems to be the headquarters for such beasts. The landlord warned us that they'd steal and pointed out a couple as more adept at thieving than the rest.

In the market we found a small orange-colored gourd; some candy called *gaz*, made of eggwhite, sugar, and *pista* meats said to be from Isfahan; a butterscotch in pancake form called *sohan*, delightfully flavored with saffron and cardamoms; another sweet called *pashmak*, a taffy perfumed with rosewater and cardamons and pulled into fine needles, so that when it is finished it looks like a horsetail. This is broken up and packed in tins in a

---

1. Persian saying: "Isfahan half the world."
2. Yezd, or Yazd (31°53'N, 54° 25'E, 4100 feet). A city of about 60,000, Yazd existed in the Sassanid Era, and is to this day a center of the religion of Zoroaster, as well as of the Bahai religion and conservative Shia Islam. Parts of the fourteenth century town wall and several outstanding mosques survive. At the time of Koelz's visit the town was an isolated oasis, watered by *qanats*, or underground water conduits, famous for its candies and fruits, and a center of cloth weaving, dye manufacture, and glass production. It was connected by direct roads to Isfahan and Kirman, but the railroad had not yet reached the town. There was a hospital, several banks, and one garage. Shirkuh southeast of the town reaches 13,000 feet providing a less arid, cooler area of productive agricultural villages and summer homes.

mineral-wooly mass that dissolves like snowflakes in the mouth. There were very large and sweet seedless raisins, better than any I ever saw anywhere; several sorts of heavy silk in natural color, for which the place is noted. In the streets one often sees handsome, gaited donkeys, elegantly caparisoned—quite the proudest donkeys I know. The air is spring-like, and the sun is bright. The peasants are busy spading. Keeping cattle for plowing is an expensive matter in the desert. Groups of men, up to a half-dozen, can be seen working side by side, driving the long spade deep into the earth, their strong legs bare to the hip.

The Yezdis are well known in Iran for their thrift and their industry and also for their bad Persian accent. Many of them are still Zoroastrians whose priests were the Magi of the Nativity and who worship fire as in the days before the Arab Conquest; in fact about all the survivors of this ancient religion inhabit this area. One group, the Parsees, is found in India, mainly in Bombay. Though according to Islam they are as much heathen as Jews or Christians, they are not persecuted, and I never heard anything of them but praise from Moslem Persians. Like Jews and Christians, they have a sacred book, the Avesta. This, along with the Talmud and the Bible, the Moslems recognize as legitimate (though they are more or less mistaken sources of spiritual guidance, since unlike the Koran they didn't fall from Heaven). Everything to the eastward in the way of religion, book or no book, is classed as plain idolatry.

A curious turnip called *mandab*, with large white to purple flattened roots, 9 inches across, mild and firm, is now in fragrant bloom. They say it is planted for the oil of its seeds, which is used to grease the skin of camels. Camels need greasing in summer.

I saw a caged nightingale which its owner said lived on mutton. Though nightingales are common birds, I never saw one caged before. In fact, caged birds aren't seen nearly as often in Iran as in Afghanistan, and seldom does one see anything but canaries. The Afghans don't seem to care much what kind of bird they keep. I have seen golden eagles, owls, ducks, nuthatches, and once a shopkeeper in Kandahar had a half-dozen wagtails that were busy catching the flies that filled the shop.

The lofty Shirkuh rises nearby to over 13,000 feet. It is still snow covered. Deh Bala, the summer retreat of rich Yezdis, at its foot, can be reached in a day. In orchards of cherries, apples, pears, and other such fruits, there are pleasant houses, and straight above tower the walls of the mountain.

February 26. We chugged on with the usual tinkering into the small hours of the morning, when we ran out of gasoline in the desert near Nain.[1]

---

1. Nain (32°52′N, 53°05′E).

ISFAHAN

I rolled up on the ground in a strong wind and got two hours of sleep before another car came along and gave us fuel. Nain is a nice little desert town with the highest garden walls I ever saw. To find out what was inside such walls, I shot a raven on the top of one 10 feet tall that had plants of camelthorn (*Alhagi camelorum*) growing on it. This is a nearly leafless, thorny, dense, green plant that is common in arid Iran and not rarely is seen growing on the sunbaked mud walls that enclose the gardens. The plants of the arid steppe are of three kinds: (1) small annuals that complete their growth-cycle quickly and lie dormant as seeds, (2) plants that have bulbs or fleshy roots and green in the wet-season, and (3) perennials that send roots deep into the earth where they find moisture in the summer when no rain falls. Water storage arrangements above ground are found for the most part only in the halophytes that are most often seen in very alkaline soil, and water-storing plants such as cacti that are so common in arid America and depend on summer moisture are not found here. When I finally got over the wall the proprietor of course was expecting me and had recovered my bird. No one is surprised at your shooting a raven since they have well known medicinal value, and in any case I had long since learned better than to say anything so incomprehensible as that bird skins had scientific interest. The gardener was busy uprooting his almond trees, some of them 8 inches through. There seemed to be nothing the matter with them, but he said they were too old; they had exhausted the available nutrients. The almond-growers at Taft, near Yezd, claimed too that orchards needed rejuvenating. There were two nice fat dogs in the garden, one black and white with some large brown splashes on his face that looked like mud, and since their master was friendly, they were too.

After Nain there is a slow ascent taking a couple of hours to reach the broad pass near which are scattered villages with a few trees. The descent is the same gentle grade to the great Isfahan Plain. Rain began at the bottom, and at noon while we were at lunch it soaked the engine so it wouldn't run. Meantime the roof began to leak and the passengers tried to protect themselves with whatever makeshift devices and draperies they could lay hands on. A little boy got violently carsick. The father got nervous, slapped him and then picked a quarrel with his wife, a good-natured fat creature: she should have known better than to give the boy anything to eat. A passenger said one shouldn't strike small people. A gay blaze was made under and around the engine, and thus treated, it began to run again. At each fresh start, the Yezd passengers shouted out some blessing on Mohammed and his descendants, one leading and the rest answering. Whatever good it brought to Mohammed and his descendants, it obviously brought us none. To be sure these invocations may have kept off real misfortune, since except for the rain, the rest of the vicissitudes were those normally to be undergone by anyone foolhardy enough to travel in a bus.

Down on the alkali plain for several miles there were large marshy ponds with water running under the roads in large culverts. Perhaps the pools were recently formed, since there were no waterfowl. Ordinarily wintering ducks are to be found collected throughout Persia wherever there is standing water, even in small puddles or streams. Sometimes these congregations cover an acre of ground or more. The commonest ducks thus found are mallards, teal, and shovelers, but in migration, gadwalls, pintails, baldpates, and othern northern species pass through to winter in the south. There are also a few kinds that breed in this country, of which some do not go far northward. About 10 miles from Isfahan, near the ruins of an ancient city, cultivation begins, and soon low, fat towers are common. These towers are built for the pigeons, the common blue rock pigeon that is found wild in all the country and semi-wild with us at home. The pigeons are not molested in the towers; their squabs are not wanted but their manure is, and precious as it is, one wonders how the balance sheet finally reads, since the birds have to get a large part of their feed from the fields. Especially at sowing time they take heavy toll from the seed. At that time the fields can be seen blanketed in blue as hundreds of pigeons fill their crops with grain that the plow hasn't been able to hide. At other times they glean, and such grain would for the most part be lost, but it may be that they learn to thresh the heads as do the choughs and chukors. At least they are credited with remarkable enterprise in one place in the Himalayas: they told us there they dig up wild tulips—bulbs of a species that grows below the reach of the plow. But the Isfahani has proverbially the shrewdest head in Iran, and he undoubtedly weighed the matter well before he went to the trouble of making these towers. The Tibetans say, though, that the greatest follies may be expected from the wise, or those who pass for wise, but the adage is probably intended only to explain occasional inconsistencies.

Certainly the Isfahani is wise in wanting manure. Manure here, as everywhere else, is the basis of agriculture. In the desert where fuel is scarce, most of the dung of the larger animals is used for cooking. It is made into large flat cakes, pasted on the wall to dry and then stored. What isn't needed for domestic use is sold. That leaves ashes and human excrement for fertilizer, and often the latter isn't used. It is surprising then that anything can be grown. In America it would be interesting to know what his special circumstances were if a farmer should sell manure,[1] and certainly without fertilizer no farmer would last long. But in the desert often only a fraction of the land can be plowed each year because there isn't water enough to irrigate it all. Fields are thus left fallow to "drink sun" for a year or two, and then a crop of grain or pulses can be grown (the agricultural produce of most

---

1. Since writing this, I have found farmers in the U.S. who will sell manure. They have been taught, I am told, that manure is detrimental to the soil.

of the country is mainly these). What manure there is is used first for cucumbers, melons, and opium—products which have an important place in the national economy. Vegetables as we know them hardly are important. There is no class name for them even, *sabzi*, "green things," is the only term of the sort and is applied to the scented "greens" that are mostly eaten raw to flavor bread. Most vegetables can be found in the markets of the larger towns to be sure, but in comparatively small quantities, and the bulk of the population has no place for them in its diet. For the peasant to grow them moreover, would require manure, and it is hardly likely the absentee landlord would allow the cultivation of a crop from which he could derive no benefit. The condition of fruit culture is much the same. Only grapes and mulberries are at all common, and these are important in the general diet. They are eaten fresh as an accompaniment with bread; they may be dried or be boiled down as *shireh*, a pleasant thick syrup, used as a sweetening or as a spread. In places wine is made from grapes, and native wine is a common item of sale in the larger towns. The grapes are rich in sugar and are of unsurpassed flavor so that superb wines can be made of them. Sometimes such wines can be bought, but too often the produce offered for sale has been spoiled in the manufacture or subsequently adulterated.

From the foregoing the reader may wonder what the Persian eats. For most of the people, there is wheat bread (in places corn, millet, and other grains are used as supplements), pulses, cheese, a little meat, tea, and sugar. The bread is seldom spread with butter except by people rich enough to use it in that way, but anything in the way of pungent or aromatic greens that comes to hand is used to increase its palatability. Such things as leek leaves, dill, and the various garden herbs are found in every market for this purpose, and in summer from time to time a bit of fruit or a melon provides a welcome change. It will thus be seen that bread is the important element in the diet of most Persians, and it can then be imagined what the nation suffered when it lacked bread during the occupation years of the war, when sugar sold at a dollar or two a pound.

Nearer Isfahan, especially along the small river that flows through the city, many fields are given over to the cultivation of poplars and other timber trees. They say it has rained two days and nights, and the town floats in mud. The police spent half an hour with our passports after they finished checking the rest of the passengers. Those that had no papers got out before the police station and walked past to rejoin us beyond. This greatly added to the discomfort of travel, since it was next to impossible to wade in the sticky mire—the soil in Iran is often a heavy sticky gumbo that makes a mud as difficult to walk through as so much cold molasses—and then hardly had we left the police post than we ran out of gasoline again. For three-quarters of an hour we sat in the dark and mud, and at 7:30 got to the garage. A couple of two-horse carriages called *droshkes* took our things to the Hotel Ferdosi in a broad three-lane street. Ferdosi was a celebrated epic poet of a thousand years ago, and he is often commemorated in the naming of hotels, streets, and the like. I don't remember ever hearing of Shakespeare Avenue or Hotel Shakespeare, so our people apparently don't honor literary eminence in that way. We were shown into a pleasant room, and a cheerful maid came promptly and lighted the fire, while a youth put in a stronger light bulb. This was the greatest comfort we had had in many months. It will be supposed we were full of gratitude to a benevolent Providence for thus having brought to end our 24 hours of travail, but 10 years of vagabonding between here and Tibet in every wind and weather had made us as indifferent to the smiles of Providence as to its frowns. Rup Chand had expressed our common philosophy when he said it was pleasanter to bear misfortune than monotony. The Tibetans have a proverb that conveys about the same idea: "Chewing a turnip is better than doing nothing," and the Indians say, "Carrying a forced load is better than going empty." Kurds say, "War is better than idleness." Americans have outgrown such ideas by a hundred years, if they ever had them.

February 28. We searched the bazaar and found plenty of large still-fresh muskmelons, in form and size much like those that are sent from Kabul to India, but these are sweeter. They are a common item of the fruit trade in the capital, and every Tehrani will accordingly tell you that the country's best muskmelons come from Isfahan. Anyone who has ever been in Khorasan will have quite a different opinion. There were goatskins full of half-dried yellow plums that are said to be from Kashan and like the melons arrive in most of the large bazaars of the country. Persians like acid things for flavoring and besides vinegar, use large quantities of limes (dried and fresh) and also lemons—of which they have a greater and better assortment than I have seen in any other country—sumac fruit, and extract of green grapes, apricots, plums, dried green mangoes from India, etc. They make quantities of pickles, usually in simple acid medium, flavored with garden herbs, but often they sour them by allowing them to ferment in a salt solution on the principle of sauerkraut. The Indians make better pickles by a more elaborate process using oil, mustard, and other spices abundantly in the preserving mixture. In addition to the above-mentioned flavoring agents, quantities of tomato and pomegranate "paste" are used. The tomatoes and pomegranates are boiled down and in the case of tomatoes, the residue is heavily salted. Both kinds are to be had in the bazaar under the name of *"robe."* Canning is an almost unknown culinary operation, though tins of fruit of a mediocre quality can be bought in the bazaar, prepared by small factories mostly in Meshed. Canned goods are of course of less importance in the domestic economy of a country where winter is so short as in most of Iran, and where semitropical areas line both the northern and southern boundaries. Almost everywhere pomegranates, citrus, melons, apples, quinces, and even grapes in the way of fruit, and hardy green stuff in the way of fresh vegetables can be found throughout the winter.

The market also has handsome fragrant quinces, 4 inches through. Quinces are generally beautiful things in Iran, of two kinds, sweet and acid, and probably more commonly used than with us. The Isfahan quince is, moreover, famous. From the south had come bouquets of narcissus, a 6 inch pomelo called *fatabi* and a few kinds of dates. There was a tin of Italian sardines that they priced at 50 cents. The police escort who went with us to Shirkuh had told us of a wonderful apple here that has powerful medicinal qualities, but we didn't find it. From here to Tibet and no doubt till land ends in the east, one constantly hears of vegetable and animal products of remarkable virtues. The Asiatic seems compelled to feel that the various flavors of his foods must have special effects. Where we look to the prosaic carbohydrate, protein, and fat content, he is impressed by the more poetic volatile oils or psychological intangibles. There would be no use trying to persuade any Asiatic I ever saw that the physiological results of eating a banana and a potato, or tiger meat and donkey steak would be much the same, and no one would undertake it after he had got used to hearing that a certain kind of snipe-meat turns your teeth to gold; the juice of a certain mango makes so much blood when eaten; the fruit of a certain tree held in the hand a few minutes has a laxative effect.

We were sorry we hadn't bought some of the heavy silk shirting in Yezd. In spite of all our searching here, none of the best quality was to be found. The antique shops are the most interesting we have seen since Agra. Apparently customers are rare and the proprietors were correspondingly vivacious and put us to bed at night and got us up in the morning. The commonest item is brocade, mostly as small scraps from the seventeenth and eighteenth centuries, though occasionally even older. Sasanid seals in stone; glass money; silver coins of various periods from Alexander down; shawls of the quality we had learned in India to regard as Persian; Persian porcelains of a hundred years ago; modern bracelets and lockets made of pieces of mother-of-pearl on which miniatures had been painted; incised silver articles—these are the chief stock of them all. One of the most enterprising of the dealers located for me a magnificent Koran with a dated cover and dated text of the early eighteenth century that had inscribed in it the vital records of some of the bygone great. As it was customary to record births in our family Bibles, it was also often done in the Koran by Persians. It is one of the few valuable books I have ever been able to buy in India or here. With the book was a queer Persian cloth print showing seventeenth century European figures and a gorgeous Bakhtiari *abba*, a sort of cape-cloak worn by the Bakhtiaris, Lurs, and mullahs, woven of softest brown cashmere with a pattern on the back in blue and threads of gold. Indian prints of a century ago are not uncommon but old Persian prints are very rare. They make plenty of modern prints in the bazaar now, and there are numerous shops where men and boys are making boxes, trays, vases, and other things in silver with incised designs. The poor devils' eyes must soon suffer from the strain of cutting the minute lines which constitute the drawings.

The city of Isfahan[1] itself is one of the sights of the world. The Maidan Shah (Royal Square) is one of the finest plazas that any city has to show. On one side is the "Palace of the 40 Pillars" of Shah Abbas, 1587-1627. The portico has 20 wooden pillars which, reflected in a large pool (now dry), gave the palace its name. The interior decorations are still fairly well preserved under a coating of whitewash with which some successor of the incomparable royal patron of art had bedaubed them and which they are now engaged in removing. The so-called music room has curious incised plaster decorations all over the wall, and people who ought to know better tell you the musicians played in the room, and when later the king wanted to hear the music, he opened the door and it was echoed back to him from these concavities. The knack of performing this remarkable feat seems to have been lost. From the palace opens a royal view. The eye gazes over gardens of budding and blooming trees of almond, plum, peach, and other fruits of temperate climates, and grainfields in the lush green of spring, to the white caps of distant purple mountains beyond which lies Kashan, or to the lower pink and hazel hills that bound the great plain on the east and west. On a wall nearby, two storks were busy on a huge nest of sticks.

On another side of the square are the royal mosques constructed with colored and figured tiles of the elegant style of the period of Shah Abbas—jewels of fancy in which the dreamers of the past embodied their sparkling visions. For, as the forces of Nature arrange the simple and common elements to make the dazzling diamonds and serene sapphires, so the artist has the power to make of these same elements the jewel crystals of human thought. In these great constructions are reflected the grandeur and symmetry, grace and splendor in which the artistic soul of Persia bursts into bloom. Through the long spring the oft-frostnipped bud had swelled and now in flower revealed its golden heart. Spring passes and the time of roses;

---

1. Isfahan (32°40′N, 51°38′E, 5800 feet) was a city of 205,000 ca. 1940. It existed in the Sasanid Era if not before. It reached its zenith during the sixteenth and seventeenth centuries, under the Safavid Shahs whose many palaces and mosques stand today. It is a center of traditional Shia, Jewish, and Armenian communities. By 1940, Reza Shah had restored many buildings and encouraged both a modern weaving industry and many traditional crafts such as brasswork, blacksmithing, hat manufacture, brocading and pottery and candy manufacture. There were all-weather roads to Tehran and Bushire on the Gulf Coast. There were several hospitals, banks, foreign consulates, garages, and an airfield.

STORKS ARE A COMMON INHABITANT OF MANY TOWNS IN IRAN. This one's nest seems to rival the mosque dome in antiquity.

the petals fall and with this burst of blossom, decorative art in East and West passes into Fall.

In the great mosque one of the domes has a yellow ceiling, so made that it looks flat and not concave, and if you stand in the right spot a sound will reverberate several times. At other places there is no echo. A staircase 10

THE SHAKING TOWER AT ISFAHAN. The towers can be made to shake to a startling degree.

feet long and fountains 5 feet high, carved out of single pieces of marble, along with other details compel admiration, even from those who do not read the divine message of the genius that created it.

In another part of the city is the amazing Shaking Tower. The building is small and is said to have been built 640-odd years ago by Amir Abdullah, who lies buried in it. There are two minarets on either side of the front of the building, about 15 feet high. A man climbed into one and as he rocked to and fro the tower swayed perceptibly. They said the other used to rock in sympathy. I could see no cracks in the baked bricks of the wall.

The Customs in Bandar Abbas, in registering the amount of money in my possession on my entry in the country, recorded $24 as $2400, and the bank here said I'd eventually be required to account for that sum. An American in Afghanistan told me of a traveller who had been sent back to Tehran from the Afghan border—the terrors that such a trip might involve I now appreciate—because a £ sign had been written instead of a $ mark in a similar registration performance.

March 3. We took a horse-carriage with two plump iron-grays and went down the river to inspect the cultivation. The almonds are in bloom and the apricot buds are crimson. The early plum buds are pink, but they open white and give off a fragrance, not that stinging wild smell that ours have. The season is later here than at Yezd; there the almond petals were already falling before we left. Birds are common: white herons, cormorants, and ducks on the river; woodcocks, magpies, and finches in the orchards; rooks and crows, even a pair of ravens in the green fields, and on the fallow, the desert sandgrouse. There are trees wherever there is room to plant them: poplars (*tabrizi*), elms (*vesk*), ash (*zaban gunjishk*) and planes (*chenar*), for the most part trained to grow straight and tall to provide beams or boards for building. Nowhere in all Asia had we seen such care of trees. The fields are well laid out, and the peasants look sturdy and healthy. They often wear coarse blue cotton homespun made into a long loose blouse and full pants. Many are busy weeding the poppy fields. The pigeon-towers we had seen on the day of our arrival are built of blocks of sundried mud, a block missing wherever possible so that the birds can nest in the holes. The towers are 30 to 40 feet high. Some have a door near the ground; others are entered by a high ladder. Though the pigeons aren't disturbed in these towers, many prefer to nest in the deep wells, as in India, where they find some cranny or ledge to hold their flimsy nests. How the squabs ever get out of the well I can't imagine. To rise even 10 feet in a well-shaft is a great accomplishment in an adult bird and theoretically impossible for one that never flew before. The immunity from hunting they have in the towers—and I believe they aren't shot at in the fields—is not shared by the well-dwellers. They are trapped by putting a net over the mouth of the well and driven up into it by a man at the bottom. The wells mentioned are the shafts of the *qanats* and are connected with one another by the hollowed out water channel through which a man can crawl. Some men were thus engaged in pigeon-catching today, and we bought a few of the captives. The carriage hire had cost us a pretty penny, and since ostensibly our aim was hunting, the four sparrows we brought back amused the horseman considerably. He told us we could have bought as many hens for the money we had spent and asked in conclusion, "Do you want me again tomorrow?"

On the way home we crossed the famous Pul Si-o-Seh, or "Bridge of 33 Pillars," of Shah Abbas's time, to visit Julfa. The bridge is a picturesque thing of two stories, nearly a thousand feet long, that spans the Zaiendeh River. Closed-in passages for pedestrians flank the main way, and there are rest rooms on the side and stairs that descend to the river. Julfa is an Armenian town said to have been named for the city of old Armenia now on the Russian border. Shah Abbas, who encouraged all artisans, brought skilled workers from Julfa and allowed them religious freedom. The churches there, done in the style of the great king's time, except for their Christian paintings, are a part of the sights of the city. One museum has some nice seventeenth century embroideries, cotton cloths printed with gold, a Bakhtiari rug, and some European-style paintings. —The drinking water here is very alkaline, and they say it should be filtered. —The office boys of the Agricultural Department brought over a big Osage orange and wondered what it was good for. I had often wondered, too.

Chapter IV

SHIRAZ, JAHRUM, AND NIRIZ

March 6. I took leave of the Rais of Agriculture and thanked him for his favors. He is sending one of his staff to accompany us to Shiraz. The bus will leave at 4 p.m. they said, and they wanted our luggage at noon. It got to the station at 5 p.m. and as usual we didn't start till near dark. I never found out why all public conveyances had to move at night. Varied explanations were proffered, the only plausible one that travel out of sunlight was pleasantest, especially when transport was by caravan. To change the schedule in cold weather has not occurred to anyone, if such is the basis of these nocturnal arrangements. I wonder whether they will be influenced by our habit of turning clockhands back and forth to suit the calendar. An officer went to the Shahrbani to get a pass so that the police at the checkpost outside the city wouldn't have to worry over our passports or the gun licenses. The hotel clerk presented the bill in an attempt at Latin script. The figures were clear enough, but there was an addition of ten percent for an illegible item. He identified it as "service" which he said was "for the management"; "no," he corrected, "for the servants." In case the first assertion should be the right one, the servants were tipped individually too. This morning the Jewish traders who wouldn't take my offer last night came and took less. They are uniformly well-mannered and pleasant to deal with. Across the street from the hotel, Yadegar brought a nice seventeenth century Koran with lovely lacquered covers and an old cotton print of the same period and said it was from a bank official, so I went there and paid the asked price in dollars.

We finally left at 5:30 and arrived with exceptional speed at Surmaq at 1 a.m. We had gone 268 kilometers, they said, when the car stopped for the night. The night was snappy, but we found a depression on the plain, hidden from view and went to bed.

March 7. We found here a splendid large green (sundried) raisin, *askari*, very soft, tender and sweet, a first class product. There was a larger black one with a more conspicuous seed. Hazelnuts were of good quality, but smaller than those seen heretofore. A nice soldier, pink-cheeked so that he could have passed for an English lad, accompanied us in our search in the village. He spoke English well and said he was Armenian. The gasoline seller over filled the chauffeur's gasoline tank. The driver protested with, "I told you how much I wanted. Should I have told you in Arabic or Russian?" Donkeys were easily found for our trip. There were lots of them at work carrying desert topsoil to the fields, virgin soil in lieu of fertilizer.

Iqlid, we hear, lies 4 *farsakhs* away against the foothills of a white range with the lofty Kuh-i Bul[1] as its peak, behind a low range just ahead of us. The path runs over a barren plain with vegetation greening here and there. A flock of gazelles and an occasional sandgrouse in addition to the everpresent larks, the usual desert wildlife, were met on the way. As we approached the hills, tops of trees were visible a long time before the first village came into view. The distance turned out to be the 4 *farsakhs* they said it was when we started. Measurements of distance in Persia and Afghanistan were generally elastic, especially when we were on foot, and we were given low estimates, so we never knew when we started how long we'd be on the way. Once in Afghanistan such a trip, plausible in concept, engaged us from daybreak till far into the night, with no possible stopping place en route. Even if we'd been willing to halt, feed and water for the animals had to be considered. And anyone you are likely to ask on the way how much farther it is to your destination will never discourage you, saying "It's only over the hill you see ahead." If you are being told the truth, they'll hold up a finger to show how far you've yet to go, in proportion to the distance you have already covered.

The donkey driver, dear soul, instead of dumping our baggage at the village and going home in peace, said there was a fine spring farther on where we could camp pleasantly. On we went along a good road with cultivation and houses in small groups for a good *farsakh*, with fields and gardens all the way, till finally we came to several strong springs coming out from under houses. The environment wasn't especially pleasant, and some women said farther on were other springs. Some boys came along just then and urged us to go farther; there was a fine place to camp beside a great spring. They led us to a stream coming down from a cliff with several ancient *chenars* (sycamores) along it. The stream flowed from a beautiful pond to which great blue herons and cormorants came in the evening and on which three grebes were swimming. The great plain stretched out, well cultivated, with no sign of the alkali so often present on the shores of water bodies in the desert. The only drawback I saw was the chilly wind, but the

---

1. Kuh-i Bul (30°48′N, 52°45′E, 15,600 feet).

children said the wind wouldn't reach the nearby cliff wall. This was true. Wangyel detained a donkey laden with an artemisia-like brush from a flock carrying the fuel to the village. A man from the village came to inquire what we'd need. Our Persian companion straggled in a little later, very tired and flushed (we had travelled from ten to five), and we persuaded him to make himself comfortable in the village. We kept warm by burning the brush which blazed hot for a few seconds. There are nice walnut trees in the cultivation, some pears, plenty of sour cherries (often as thickets of small unbranched trees), quinces, apples, apricots, plums, and plenty of vineyards with the grapes cut back to stubs, 2 feet or less high. People were busy weeding and thinning the opium, often six to ten folks in a plot.

March 8, Surmaq.[1] They said there were snowcocks, *kabkedari* or *kidari*, the magnificent huge grouse-like bird we had found in the high Himalayas, but Rup Chand found no traces of them on the mountain slope. Horned larks and a duck hawk were something we hadn't seen on the desert. In the way of vegetables there was a yellow pumpkin; a red squash with brown seeds and a similar one with white seeds; tender purple carrots; flat, white, strong-flavored onions; top-shaped red beets; tender, mild black radishes. There were still grapes of several kinds: *mansuri*, round, green, tart; *shahani*, elongated, black; *askari*, green; *kishmish siya*, small, black; *nabati*, round, green; *kishmish pilaui*, seedless, 5 millimeters in diameter, red-black. The last is the variety that I found also in Northern Afghanistan and is the substance of our culinary dried currants, the name said to be derived from Corinth—no relation of course to the seedy red currants of Europe. In the gardens a lavender crocus-like *Merendera* and clumps of *Muscari* are in bloom and in the desert a lovely mother-of-pearl iris with purple bars on the falls. They raise two kinds of alfalfa, or *shabdar*: one they cut once, the other seven times. *Yonge*, the annual clover with the pretty flowers is also a forage crop. —The sand grouse is called *bagna kara* the same as in Afghan Turkestan, or *sinasiya*. —The edges of the pond froze last night, and there were 3 inches of ice in the waterpail. —The doctor had come two days ago, and three women were in the seedshop getting prescriptions filled. One with sore eyes got some fluid in a little bottle and had to pay 1 ½ kran (a few cents)—or 1 ½ kran more than she had.

The dried apricots are sweet, slightly sour with kernels, some edible and some bitter. Dried peaches are 3 inches across, white, sweet, and there was a can of Meshed peaches put up in Isfahan: white, 3½ inches across, freestone, of a pleasant taste, different from our canned peaches. Potatoes can be 6 inches long, yellow-fleshed, like the "salad" potato of Germany. —

---

1. Surmaq (31°03′N, 52°48′, ca. 6800 feet).

Some men wore nice *nimda* (felt) coats made of *kurk* (cashmere), said to be from Yezd. —A blind woman spun cotton faster than I ever saw anyone spin. For a loop to hold the reel, she had a watermelon seed with a hole in it.

The Blind Spinner at Eqlit.

March 10. We got to Persepolis at midnight. We had quit Surmaq at 5 P.M. and had been promised arrival at Persepolis by 9. We had to go over the mountain and had stopped at all of the few villages on the way. Usually there were a few passengers to get aboard. Sometimes we took them but only after bargaining, fortifying our stand by starting and then waiting while they brought their luggage. The bags were never visible during the negotiations and probably would have weakened their bargaining position by exposing too much eagerness to go. We had a bottle of wine that Wangyel had provided for our journey, and we made coffee before going to bed. We got up this morning, as usual half-dead, and went about the landscape.

Takht-i Jamshid (Persepolis) is built against the low black marble mountains and faces the great plain, hemmed in by similar ranges; some 10 to 15 miles away to the west, and to the northwest there is snow on the crests. The whole plain is green and looks like a field of sprouting grain. We made some fifty collections, tiny plants of families common to the north temperate zone, hurrying through their cycle in the few days they have before the earth about them dries up. In another direction over a ridge were different plants, all an inch or two high like the first; often the species were rare. A black spaniel that lives in our quarters has adopted us and came hunting with me. He can climb like a squirrel and likes the birds. The first meal we provided of fried egg and bread, he left to come over to thank us, then grabbed the egg. Now that he isn't hungry anymore, he despises bread unless we take it off our own plates and dip it in egg. He got locked in inadvertently today when we went to the ruins, but he didn't disturb anything, though bird skins and food were all about. There are a dozen barn swallows like those we have in the U.S.A. that sleep in the rooms at night, a pair in each, resting on a reed splinter that hangs down from the ceiling thatch. They are unaffected by the light or our activity beneath. There are plenty of birds about on the desert—desert larks, wagtails, wheatears, rooks, ravens, blue pigeons (like ours), desert partridges, chukors—and in the ruins dozens of kestrels (*Falco naumanni*) resembling our sparrow hawk are apparently nesting, likewise a few little grey owls (*Athene brama*). The ravens come to the plains and carry mouthfuls of caterpillars to the mountains.

The ruins of Persepolis are among the most impressive architectural constructions of all time. They arise on a platform hewn and leveled out of the rock and display a conception of grandeur in design and fitness of ornamentation even in decay and neglect. Begun by Darius I and enlarged by the succeeding Achaemenid rulers, Xerxes and Artaxerxes, the palaces were destroyed with Alexander's conquest of Persia two-and-a-quarter millennia ago. The wanton destruction of so much magnificence has clouded the repute of the great conqueror. What can be deduced from the character of the man—and from the high regard in which he was held by his companions and no less by the conquered Persians—precludes acceptance

PERSEPOLIS OR TAKHT-I JAMSHID.

of the theory that the act was in retribution for vandalism of Persian armies in Greece. Fancy lightly reconstructs the splendor of the royal city, but from what foundations this splendor sprang is in these days nowhere in evidence. All Persia, except the Caspian littoral, is a desert, in great stretches virtually waterless, and elsewhere with precipitation sparse, totally absent in summer. Some six hundred years ago Marco Polo found agricultural capacity greater by far than it is today, probably under political conditions no better than they now are. One must conclude that the power of the land to sustain life has declined. Cultivation exists in small islands where a limited supply of underground water is available. No army could operate in Persia today, as did Alexander, living off the land.

SHIRAZ, JAHRUM, AND NIRIZ

March 13. On the way to Shiraz[1] this morning we passed the sugar factory[2] where the locally raised beets are processed. Then we passed a large lake that shrinks or disappears in the rainless summer as do the numerous bodies of water on the Indian plains; it is right now a pleasant, green place. Birds in abundance frequent the lake: storks, white herons,

PERSEPOLIS OR TAKHT-I JAMSHID. Detail from the previous photo.

---

1. Shiraz (29°36′N, 52°32′E, 5000 feet). Shiraz is in a high valley well watered by several streams. The town of about 129,000 people, perhaps founded in Sasanid times, was the capital of Karim Khan-i Zand, ruler of much of Iran in the mid-eighteenth century. He built several mosques, the bazaar, and gardens—including those within which are the tombs of the poets Hafiz and Saadi. It has a community of the Jewish religion. It serves as a market center for several Zagros nomad groups including the Turkish speaking Qashqai. The town has been a center for carpet manufacture, silverwork, glass production, and products of the grape. Koelz arrived here just before Nowruz, the Persian New Year, when businesses are closed and the countryside is in full flower. At this time there were several hospitals, banks, foreign consulates, a wireless station, and an airfield. The all-weather road between Tehran and Bushire passed through the town.
2. The sugar factory is in the town of Marv Dasht (29°50′N, 52°40′E).

PERSEPOLIS OR TAKHT-I JAMSHID. Detail of the wall ornamentation.

pelicans, coots, and ducks. The road goes over low dry hills, and suddenly through a gap you see Shiraz below, a large town with open fields around. We went to the Mehmankhane Saadi, but they didn't like the look of us and gave me a little room in a corner which the sun hadn't reached at noon. It had no stove, and the day was bitter cold. They had no place where the men could cook, so when the driver of the truck that brought us said he knew a garden a kilometer away, we reloaded our effects and drove off. It was a beautiful old garden, laid out in the style of days gone by, called the Bagh-i Safa and occupied only by a few women, a gardener, and dogs. A man from the town had come with us and went back with Rinchen Gialtsen to get supplies, but as he started he sneezed—but only once—so he had to stop. It was a bad sign. If he had sneezed some more it wouldn't have mattered. After smoking a cigarette they went on. Our Persian friend came back in the evening and said he had made the necessary arrangements with the garden owner and the police. The police had been here during the day and made the usual inquiries: did we photograph and what, etc. The dogs have apparently never had much to eat, and the puppies get very thirsty. The garden has a few walnuts and quinces, lots of pomegranates, almonds (these nearly out of bloom), apples in bud, and stately cypress trees. There are no orange trees in the garden; they say it's too cold here, though there are trees in the Agriculture Office, one-quarter mile away, and there were large trees in a garden along the Isfahan road.

March 14. Two of my men came at 4 P.M. They had been arrested and kept in jail for two hours because they didn't have a passport. I don't know how they got out of jail, and our guide went to see about the matter. He came back, much disturbed, saying, "The police knew nothing about the business"; "it was all right," etc.

THE BAGH SAFA AT SHIRAZ.

Two sorts of little owls (*O. scops* and *O. brucei*) were very vocal last night. The first sings at two-second intervals, a short high metallic "uh," the other at half-second intervals, a distant-sounding throaty "puk," continued 261 times without stopping. Ice froze in the pond last night. The wind has moderated today, but it is still cold enough for an overcoat. The people here don't think much of my dress, I suspect. My Parisian sandals with crepe soles and my white socks do catch their eye, but the rest of my outfit is too sombre. They like felt hats of atrocious shapes and foreign-style cloth of nondescript patterns, though usually not loud. In large markets all over Persia very fine imported woolen suit-yardage can be found, as fine as any to be found in the U.S.A. and very much cheaper, likewise the best Italian and German felt hats. —The town is decorated in the national flag of red, white, and green, and rugs are hung on gates and doors in honor of the Shah's birthday tomorrow. —The dog buried a piece of surplus bread, and a magpie dug it up at once and carried it off.

March 15. It was cold, and ice formed again last night. The almond and apricot blooms froze, but not flowers of a plum that was growing against the wall. The plum flowers have a sweet fragrance, not the bitter fragrance of ours. The garden walls are protected from the weather by a roof made of sticks laid side by side and covered with earth. On this earth, now on the wall around the adjacent Bagh-i Aram, patches of *Muscari* are in bloom. Flocks of chaffinches roost in the cypress, also crows and several flocks of some fifty wood pigeons (*karkaftar*) fly over low or stop. The crows come near dusk and leave before sunrise, with great clamor at each event. Lashkare, our guide, came with us to the mountain, a not very pleasant exercise for him, a pampered city boy who could hardly imagine a reason for the undertaking. The youth said he had spent fifteen months in Egypt as a government scholar, studying cotton. He had been back a year. He regrets he didn't get to Europe. Such subsidized boys most often went to France in the old days and, more recently, to Germany.

The mountain was bare of all woody growth and had few plants of any sort so early in the season, but a pretty yellow anemone, washed red outside (*A. bicolor*) had hurried into bloom. The birds on the mountain were of course other than those we had seen on the plain: ravens, rooks, a pair of golden eagles, blue rock thrush, rock larks, a pair of rock nuthatches and an owl (*Athene*) or two. On the way we passed through unirrigated (*daimi*) vineyards in the torrent bed. The vineyards were being spaded up, having been pruned a week ago, we were told. The pruning seemed severe. The trunks were up to 6 inches in diameter, and the surviving stub was a foot, or at most 2 feet, high. Some of the plants, they said, were 80 years old and were of different varieties from those that grew under irrigation. A good plant would bear 6 pounds of grapes. Some 20 varietal names were mentioned. I have heard that in some localities there are 50 or 60 such grape varieties.

March 18. The car jumbled along all night, stopping only once somewhere while we got a little tea. In the morning at 7:00, we were outside of Jahrum[1] but ran out of gasoline, and it took an hour to get some from the garage or somewhere. No one in the car was in the least cross, nor impatient, and most of them sat in the car to wait. A poor little girl with a fresh baby must have had a bad time but took it for granted. Her husband had on a schoolboy uniform and was probably fifteen or sixteen. Arriving at the garage, Rinchen Gialtsen made coffee and we went to sleep on the roof. I hear they cut the barley here, never wheat, twice: first for fodder and then to get a little crop of grain. The air is cool and pleasant in the daytime but chilly after sundown. Our guide had coffee with us.

March 19. Today the civil authorities sent a handsome soldier, such as are known as *amnieh*, to take us to a pleasant house in a garden of date palms, with a pool in the patio with goldfish and another pool inside the house. In the town I found a variety of citrus, some such as I'd never seen anywhere: (1) *Naranj*—a Valencia type commonly grown elsewhere. It is said to be the most cold-tolerant sort and grows at the limit of citrus culture. (2) *Naranji*—another orange type. (3) *Otroj*—3¼ inches, rather rough orange type, gold in color, seedy, acid. The peel is said to furnish an extract. (4) *Balang*—fine, smooth, gold lemon, 5 inches long. (5) *Batabi shikan*—top-shaped, 5 inches high, color like grapefruit, smooth. (6) *Shahpasand*—pyriform, smooth, 4½ inches high. (7) *Batabi*—fig-shaped, rough, 7 x 8 inches, navel area indented. (8) *Turunj*—rough, orange-colored, 3 inches high. (9) *Betkani*—orange-shaped, gold, rather rough, 2½ inches, acid. (10) *Limu shirin*—yellow, with a navel, tender skin and flesh, insipid sweet. This is much esteemed here, as in India and Afghanistan. (11) *Batabi misri*—rough yellow grapefruit type, 4 x 5 inches, seedy, acid. (12) *Kadumul*—top-shaped, 5 inches high, texture and color like grapefruit. (13) No name—rather rough, yellow, 3 x 5 inches. (14) *Limu khargi*—orange-colored lemon, as at Shahdat.

The dry plain around the town is green with tiny plants, as at Persepolis. Around the town is a dense plantation of dates—we were told twenty-thousand of them; our guide thought a million. They say it freezes here, as I'm told it does in other localities of the country where dates thrive. I well believe that it freezes; I need to wear woolen clothes. They are beginning to pollinate the date blooms. The flower clusters are then wrapped well for

---

1. Jahrum (28°31'N, 53°33'E, ca. 3800 feet).

protection against frost for some two weeks. Today is the New Year, and everyone is out-of-doors and with friends. We passed a group of men who invited us to picnic with them. One was carrying a sausage grinder, such as we have at home. The lads were gathering flowers, the small ones getting them in the grain fields, the older ones going to the mountain for tulips and anemones. There is a pretty liliaceous violet-colored flower in the grain called *shir-i berinj* (*Ixyolirion*) that we can buy from bulb suppliers in the U.S.A. Pear trees are in full bloom as are fragrant pink-bloomed apricots; there are lots of plums, quinces, and apples. The grapes are trimmed to a 3-foot height. There is also the magnificent rose, first seen in Afghanistan—the bush is rounded, 10 feet and more high, covered with large fragrant single white flowers (*gul-i nastaran*). The nightingales sing all day in the gardens. When we ask questions and write the answers, folks don't like it, and finally they say there are only two kinds of anything and that neither of them is any good. They probably feel that evil consequences may come from our incomprehensible scribbling. In the Asia I have seen, it is safest to do nothing; thence you can incur no blame. Or if your conspicuous activity is obviously profitable, you might be subject to appropriate tax. The silversmith in India who did considerable work for us had a heavy tax levied by the Rajah; Wangyel said he heard it was all our fault.

They are making the second cutting of barley. Since we buy seeds and birds for our collection, the children bring us cats also. In the cemetery are man-size slabs on the ground, usually dated and full of writing, with a nicely incised figure of a man and horse, or two of each. The guide says these mark the graves of young people. A few others have only a carved figure of a roundheaded animal, big as a large dog, that may represent a lion. It stands on a low pedestal, probably over the grave. At the garage when we were ready to leave, there were in the yard huge bundles of rags that were being loaded on donkeys. They are used to make soles for the *giveh*, the distinctive Persian footgear. The sole is made of these rags, strung on two thongs, beaten tight, and thereby forming a hard durable cloth layer an inch thick. On the sole, which can be shaped at will, is crocheted the upper in white cotton thread. The result is attractive, comfortable, inexpensive, and serviceable.

March 27. We got to Istabanat[1] (Shabunat) at 1:30 A.M. and went to bed on a roof under huge walnut trees, 3 to 4 feet through. (The two names given are the new name and the name it replaces. In the course of reforming the culture of the nation it has been deemed necessary to make changes in names, mode of dress, town-planning, and related matters.)

---

1. Istabanat (29°08′N, 54°04′E, ca. 5700 feet).

AN OLD TOMBSTONE. Such tombstones may be seen in parts of Iran and Afghanistan, dating from the last period of the Moghuls. The slabs are of marble. Nowadays permanent markers are not seen in Persian cemeteries, and no effort is made to decorate such places. They might, viewed without prejudice, be considered more proper locations for disposing of objects past usefulness to the Body Social than Christian cemeteries. There is no flaunting Eternity with an ephemeral flare of marble and metal but a resigned return to the elements, to be forgotten only a little the sooner.

The road we travelled ran by scattered walnut trees among gardens of almonds (*badam*) and a patriarch sycamore (*chenar*) 7 feet in diameter. The town lies in a narrow valley, some three-quarters of a mile wide with a high mountain wall on each side. We still had, we were told, 12 *farsakhs* to go to Niriz, our destination. The country on our way was faintly green with the usual tiny plants of the short spring in these parts, and soon we came to a great lake against low rough mountains. For some 20 miles the road runs beside it, and some 4 or 5 miles beyond is the town of Niriz. Sandgrouse were seen along the road, and on the lake were a few white pelicans.

A Grave Marker in Jahrum, Fars. Apparently it represents a lion and is nearly life-size. Such markers are now rarely seen in Persian cemeteries, and graves are ordinarily left unmarked.

We got to Niriz[1] around noon and were put up as usual in someone's garden. It had great cypresses (*sarv*) like those of our Shiraz *bagh-i safa*, also four huge *Celtis* (*saya khush*) 3 feet in diameter with beautiful soft purple-grey branches. Everywhere were almonds, now past bloom, plus a few pink-flowered apricots, some citrus trees, and a half-dozen full-grown date trees. There were still pomegranates from the fall crop, half dried with delightful garnet-colored juice that tasted like overripe cherries. Woodpeckers and crows nest in the garden, and at night a couple dozen kestrels (*Falco naumanni*) come to roost in the cypresses. Our guide considers magpies to be young crows. A policeman stays in the garden to keep out sightseers. The owner of the neighboring garden said he would have liked to house us, but he lost out because he hadn't accommodation for the guide. He could have got a pair of pants then for his eight-year-old boy who now has a castoff pair of his father's. He brings us chickens, nice fat ones, but not so big as the Plymouth Rock type of Jahrum.

The grapes here are trained as sturdy climbers. They say there is also a wild sort, of which Wangyel got some nice seedy raisins in the bazaar. — Our guide telephoned home and heard his poppyfield had been frozen, causing 1000 tumans damage. There are snow flurries here and it is bitter cold. —The people here won't talk to you unless you're looking at them. They usually grab your sleeve to get and hold your attention. They'll start to say something and if you don't say "yes, go on," or look with evident interest, they'll pull your sleeve.

March 29. We went to the mountain and climbed to the top. Rup Chand got lost before our very eyes. We waited two hours and got home at five, and

---

1. Niriz (29°12′N, 54°19′E, 5350 feet).

WILD ALMONDS AT DEHDISK, JIROFT.

he came an hour later. The culture of almonds that begins at the foot of the outwashed fan continues to the mountain cliff. They have grafted principally onto the wild brushy species (*barshik*), but also onto a tall scrubby sort with large pink flowers (*arjan*) that grows higher up the mountain. The cultivated almonds are of several varieties: *shalal, turshan, meshi, bawarjan, gizarjan, dana safed* (white kernel, the largest sort), *monacha* (paper shell), *lingekaushi* (long hard husk, 3 to 4 inches), *salbi* (round), *name shahanjir* (large but inferior), *suja, sozu*. They cultivate figs commonly as short trees (5 feet), some showing fruit. I hear at Shiraz they eat the *chogol*, the marble-sized unripe almonds now on the trees. They rub off the fuzz and eat them with salt. One *arjan* had a plum graft, 10 feet high. A few grapes and pomegranates are scattered among the trees, and on the mountain, untended, was a thrifty apple tree full of pink buds, with a 6 inch trunk. On the mountaintop also are small wild almonds and little roseflowered cherry bushes in abundance. A few cedars and junipers also occasionally occur, obviously relicts. Most of the shrubs are in bloom, a few almonds are in fruit. They say they will graft almonds in about two weeks.

Among the few other flowers was a striking bulbous violet-blue iris, with a yellow spot in the falls. There were birds on the mountain we hadn't found below: *Phoenicurus ochruros, Oenanthe melanoleucos, O. picata, Syvlia crassi-rostris, Serinus pusillus, Emberiza cia, Phylloscopus neglectus, Carduelis carduelis.* A bitter wind blew all day, but the night was quiet with a hard frost. The almond grafts are well tended, with usually a pit dug around each tree. Often the parent stock is blooming below the graft.

We get little help in our collecting in camp because of the guard at the gate. Some few get by and more climb over the wall between us and our neighbor. A little boy brought a chicken and asked 7 kran.[1] "What was the last price your ma told you to take?" "5 kran." There are no mosquitoes yet, but any standing water is full of "wigglers." Day was quiet and cool. All the almonds of the garden, even those in full leaf, froze as well as the blooming apricots. Found some nice *naranj* and *madeni* (sweet limes) to send to Washington for frost-tolerant citrus study. Rinchen Gialtsen bought all the neighbors' chickens as provender for the journey back to Shiraz tomorrow. Our helper got the price of one hen as a tip, and with this and with the "profit" derived from our custom, he intends to go back to the chicken business. —The bread here is good even when cold, and without grit. —People wear nice sleeveless capes of felt.

March 31. We had engaged passage to Shiraz on a truck, which came at 7 A.M. loaded with asafetida (*anquze*) or *hing*, as I knew it in India, where in our cooking it was always used to flavor lentils (*dal*). This substance is a resin obtained from a plant, or plants, of the genus *Ferula*, robust desert plants of the parsnip family. Parasitic on some such plants is one of the world's best mushrooms. It is called by the Tibetans *moksha* or *shamok* (false meat) and is at times available in dried chunks. The truck was too full to take our party and had to unload part of its cargo. When we finally finished this and police formalities it was near ten and we started, still well laden with other passengers and a few live chickens. We could have gone on the mail vehicle last night and blundered through the dark till next day, as we have done so generally, and this truck would no doubt have gone last night too if it hadn't been bribed to wait for us till morning. The road goes back along the lake, as we came, till within some 5 miles from Istabanat it turns north into a narrow valley like the Istabanat Valley, with scrub trees and snow patches on the hills. The trees gave way to shrubs. Before we came to a road from Fasa, there were several large springs on the roadside. One was some 30 feet across, a lovely clear blue. The chauffeur told our friend something, who

---

1. The *kran* was officially replaced by the *riyal* in 1932, but the term is still used. Ten of these units constitute a *toman*. Unskilled day laborers in the 1930s received only 2 *kran* per day.

relayed to us that so far no one had been able to ascertain the depth of this spring, but he added his opinion that it couldn't be more than 18 meters. You could see that it wasn't even 18 feet. At Miyan-e Jangal is a fine growth of the wild almond, *barshik*, in bloom, some trees like a peach in bloom at home, and also a small forest of *beneh*, wild pistachio (*pista*) that stretches to the pass before Shiraz. We were told of the horrible slaughter of the natives in an uprising against the government, probably a reference to the Qashqai trouble. None of the wild almonds had been grafted at Niriz, but at Istabanat everything at the periphery of the habitat had been grafted. A police post here cost the driver a 5 tuman fine for carrying passengers. Otherwise police ask only small favors and are very polite, but here the captain was a nasty-looking man of thirty, whose counterpart I had seen only among the few foreigners in civil service here. At half-past nine we were 8 *farsakhs* from Shiraz, and I began to worry about the police who had given us some unpleasantness on our previous visit, but when we finally reached the police post at midnight, everything passed off smoothly. Outside the city we had met two men on bicycles to whom the driver gave some small change, and all passengers but us were unloaded. There was only one carriage at the post, so it took two trips and 3 tumans to settle us in our former garden, a sort of homecoming. We were ready for bed at half-past one.

April 2. Today is the thirteenth day of the New Year and a big holiday. Everyone is out calling on friends and picnicking. Our garden is so full of people that we had to move out of the way, but still some of the women couldn't resist taking a look at the queer foreigners and chatting vigorously with Rinchen Gialtsen. Sometimes he gets cross, but today he was pleased with the attention. White violets are in bloom in the garden; they said they were purple and fragrant earlier, most likely an earlier sort, not a transfiguration as the informant implied. We hear too that at nearby Darab there are citrus: (1) *Shamani*: shape irregular, medicinal, tree tender; (2) *Naranjdotai*: orange in color, with a broad navel, acid; (3) *Naranj golabi*: pear-shaped, and at Sultanabad a huge fruited thing nearly as "large as a melon," and also bearing date palms. —I sent to Washington several parcels, including fruit and seeds of Niriz and Jahrum cold-tolerant citrus. —Supper consisted of the desert "thistle" (*kankar*) and truffles (*dumbala*), a tasty dish. The *kankar* is often met with in the desert areas. —The men have enlisted native help to clean the seeds we have gathered for shipment home. The help is effective but has to be watched to keep them from eating certain samples or throwing away things like onion seeds that are hard to clean. They usually divide up the troublesome samples, so that no one is stuck too long with a tedious job.

I got two fine Sasanid seals from a dealer. He had waited for me and it had grown late. The gardener's wife expressed her uneasiness: "It's getting dark and I don't know you; you'll have to leave," and it cost him a tip to soothe her fears. —They say that it is forbidden to grow rice here because it competes with the northern rice, but that the queen is trying to get the embargo removed. —We plan to go to Bushire tomorrow, to the regret of the garden owner. He offers to rent us the garden as long as we want, after some polite adjustments to his figures as to period of stay, rate of agreed rent, etc. The gardener had apparently expected to make the collection himself and was displeased that the boss had beaten him to it and rather irrationally, it seemed, called him a beggar. He said the owner beats his donkey, which he shouldn't do, because "the donkey has no speech." The auto driver yelled to a man to stop beating his donkey.

Chapter V

KHUZISTAN

April 7, Dasht-i Arjan. We arrived at Dasht-i Arjan[1] at 6:30, some two hours on our way to the coast. Toward the last of the journey wild almond trees were common, the tall shrubby one in showy pink bloom. The village lies against a limestone cliff out of which poured a great spring of roaring water. A dozen other smaller springs came out below, and all joined to make a stream too deep to wade that flowed through a great plain into a big lake edged on the Shiraz side with the tall reed, *nai*. The mountain slopes have abundant trees—oaks, almonds, maples—and the great Imperial Fritillaria in bloom is common in patches among the trees. The landscape is rich in birds—water birds like herons, rails, cormorants, ducks, even a small flock of cranes, with warblers in the reeds—and in the woods habitat are nuthatches, chickadees, woodpeckers, little owls. The great owl, *Bubo*, was heard, as also at Niriz and Shiraz. The plain is water-soaked, like the "pang" of Tibet, and large herds of cattle and horses are grazing. Charcoal burners' fires are visible on the mountains. There are still patches of snow on the heights, but the days are warm and quiet. Most of the birds are getting ready to nest. Frogs make a magnificent chorus; snakes are common, sunning themselves when it gets warm. A tortoise, a foot across, was in the woods. He had a big scar on his shell where something had tried to eat him. I recall seeing an otter once in Assam trying to eat a turtle. He tossed the turtle into the air and caught him in his jaws only to have him slip out unharmed. His tries were so persistent and noisy that I was attracted to it, as were three peafowl, who were so rapt in watching the exhibition that they didn't notice me. It's the only time I ever saw feral peafowl (except occa-

---

1. Dasht-i Arjan (29°39′N, 51°58′E, ca. 6500 feet) is a high valley of the southern Zagros which remained little damaged into the 1970s and was made a protected game preserve during that time.
2. In the desert snakes are rarely seen. I once saw a huge specimen of the common viper waiting for game at a spring, and once a smaller one had somehow crawled to the end of a then-horizontal limb of a dead tree, 10 feet above the ground, apparently in wait for wheatears that like to perch on such sites.

LIFTING WATER FROM A WELL AT AHWAZ BY CATTLE TEAM.

sional roosting specimens in some lofty forest trees at night). Peafowl of course are common in some Indian Hindu villages, where they are protected; Moslems eat them. I recall, too, stalking a fighting pair of pheasants in the Indian jungle with a leopard for an audience. It's the only leisured view I ever got of any big cat in all my jungle life, though one night in a mountain village a leopard carried off a dog that had taken refuge beside me, sleeping in my bed on the ground.

There are wild pigs in the rushes, and when I ran into a sleeping boar, he got up, looked at me and walked off. A sow with seven striped light brown piglets was walking in the woods. They say that pigs are hard on the pomegranate crop and that jackals like the watermelons. —A half-frozen lad of eight came with a few fish, cyprinids (our minnow group) some 2 pounds in weight, which he and his father and the dog got out of the streams, and we bought them. They were boney of course, but firm, not at all fishy, and quite edible.

April 10. A string of camels, a half-mile long went by today, headed toward Shiraz. Some of the animals were white. I never saw such in India or Afghanistan, nor for that matter do I remember ever seeing so impressive a caravan. The villagers decided if we were fool enough to pay for fish, which apparently aren't generally considered articles of food, we could pay 10 kran for chickens, instead of the regular price of 3 or 4 kran. A hawk (*Circus aeruginosus*) caught a bird in the rushes late last night and came back early to finish eating it, but he couldn't find it. A little owl I collected had a maw full of cockroaches.

We left at 9:30. The road winds up to a dip in the Pir Zan Mountain and then gently descends to a flat valley, full of oaks, with some dry fields in the openings, these often with green unheaded grain. The opposite wall has the low Dukhtar Pass, the crest straight and evenly sawtoothed. The strata dip at right angles toward the valley floor. The view from the pass is impressive: down into the Kazerun Valley, green-carpeted, with a big lake at the upper end. On the valley side are leafing oaks. Grain here is beginning to ripen.

We passed through Kazerun,[1] a rather ruinous village, with houses of limestone or lime-mud, and went to a garden a mile or so below, Barkatak. The garden had dates principally, with some citrus in bloom, heavily fragrant, with weeds, *tuleh* (*Malva*), 4 feet high. We got a raven here and learned afterward it had a nest nearby. The gardener said it was a shame to kill birds now since they were nesting. Even his little son expressed regret. They said the bile of a raven and something from a pig were good for the eyes. Swallows are God's birds. The black partridges here, though they differ slightly in external characters from those we know elsewhere, have a different song. It lacks the sharp introductory "click," has an extra note, and

LIFTING WATER FROM A WELL AT AHWAZ BY CATTLE TEAM, ANOTHER METHOD.

---

1. Kazerun (29°37′N, 51°38′E, ca. 2800 feet).

a reedier quality. —They had a pet wild piglet here that went to sleep in my arms, first complaining pitifully of the treatment he'd had.

The bus driver "shsh's" the car on a steep descent. That's what they say to donkeys on descents, so it seems appropriate for the car. In Afghanistan I have seen the auto entrusted to divine manipulation. The driver in a tight place may raise the hands high above the wheel, whether in invocation or to clear the field for celestial help.

April 25. We have left Dizful[1] along the turbulent Diz River that runs through a gorge, bringing cool water from the north. It had already become warm here and later, we were told, the heat becomes terrific. Fortunate people have shelters against the heat, deep underground. At the village Sar-i Beshe, folks wear the *aba*, a simple sleeveless cloak, roughly described as two squarish sheets, joined, with aperatures for neck and arms. One we bought in Isfahan was elegantly decorated with designs in gold and colored threads on a rich brown fabric of fine wool. The people are nice looking and friendly, and there is such noise and bustle with dogs, chickens, cows, donkeys, and people. They get up here at three to turn the cattle to pasture and then bring them back to milk. Pasture is abundant, the herbage tall. Fields of grain are common, mostly wheat, some man high. They summon the chickens with "chabi-chabi," or less often "chiky-chiky," as we called them at home. We left at eight for the journey into the Bakhtiari country, and soon came to the foothills: jumbled low sandstone ranges, the strata tipped at about a thirty degree angle or worn into narrow topped buttes. The path wound across streams with pockets of clear water in which were crabs and fish, through rich pasture and occasional patches of cultivation, but no settlements. There was a small flock of gazelle (*ahu*) today and a few ibex on the hills. A huge Gila monster-like lizard was bathing in a pool, as if he were a turtle, and another in copper sulfate-green was lying on a rock. Small black ants have clearings 2 to 3 inches across in the herbage and a half-dozen highways leading out. There were very fragrant pink and cerise oleanders and some tall reeds along the stream today. Last night at Sar-i Beshe were the smallest fireflies I ever saw, half the size of those at home. The night was cool here, decidedly cooler than below, with a gentle breeze; below it was often gusty. A big-drop rainstorm came up in the night and soaked me, but I slept on in the wet blankets.

Stone and brush piles, such as one sees from here to Tibet, are met in places along the road, particularly on high places. The headman, *kat-*

---

1. Dizful (32°23′N, 48°24′E, ca. 400 feet).

STILL ANOTHER METHOD OF IRRIGATING. The peasant is pouring water lifted from a lower source into a channel higher up. The weight on the pole helps to raise the loaded bucket. The hookah or waterpipe in the foreground is a common article in the Middle East. On embers in the top cup is scattered tobacco, and the fumes are strained through water in the bottom bowl.

khuda, came back from a pilgrimage to Kuh-i Haft Tanan,[1] the nearby snowy peak. He had a sick baby, and his sacrifices to the orthodox deities

---

1. Kuh-i Haft Tanan, "the mountain of the seven prophets" (32°34′N, 48°44′E, ca. 5200 feet) is one of several mountains so named in Iran. In 1973, a spring high in a mountain cleft was said to be the place where three pagan wise men—disgusted with the wantonness of our world—entered the mountain. Local Chahrleng Bakhtiari herders said that prayers at this spring could cure illness and bring fertility.

being of no avail, influenced by an old woman's dream, he appealed to the mountain. The child was cured, and the debt to the mountain deity was paid. —The road is becoming very rough. For the twentieth time, one of our mules slipped today and was saved by the watchfulness of one of the men. —There is such pasture as I have never seen in this country, grasses and clovers, burnt in the lower stretches by the growing heat. I found 16 species of trefoil in one field.[1]

April 27, Lab-i Sefid.[2] Last night people in the village had what you might have thought was a fearful quarrel. Everyone seemed to be screaming at once, so they relieved their feelings without hurting the feelings of anyone else. The women were in mourning because the men were taking the flocks to the summer pasture in the distant mountains today. We sat under the only tree, a *Zizyphus*, and waited two hours while Rinchen Gialtsen went for rice and flour. One wasn't ground and the other wasn't husked. Our guide to Lab-i Sefid was a nice simple sort who asked if we were *kafir* (heathen) and was pleased to hear we weren't. I'm sure to the unsophisticated native a *Kafir* is anyone who isn't Moslem, though I have heard from educated friends in the country that religions "who have a book"—Christians, Zoroastrians, and the like—are regarded on a higher, or perhaps less low, plane.

April 29, Cheshme Shirini. We saw on yesterday's journey the snow-peaks we hope to reach. Two men who were going to the *yelaq*, the summer pasture, with provisions from Dizful, said it was two days more to the snow. Perhaps realizing they might be in trouble for bringing strangers into the pasture land, they then denied everything and advised us to go to the right, away from the snow. We went on and soon came to an encampment of animals and human families on the way to the grass. They said we could get to the snow easily in three days but that our mules, being townbred, couldn't travel the rough road. They couldn't be bothered with us, but maybe some neighbors farther on could help, and they'd send on to ask. Our horseman then said he'd pull the shoes on three mules, and we'd leave the rest here. They said we'd find plenty of snowcock, *Tetrogallus*, on Kuh-i Nō.[3] They called it "Kinu." They speak a dialect here that I understand poorly; the last two consonants are often inverted, as in the Kuluese of the Punjab foothills. —The birds are now varied, of familiar sorts: swallows of the species *Daurica urbica*, *D. rustica* and *D. riparia*; a couple species of shrike; swifts; the great vulture (*Gyps fulvus*); the white vulture; the

---

1. This is probably Sar Dasht (32°33′N, 48°46′E, ca. 700 feet).
2. Lab-i Sefid (32°34′N, 48°42′E, ca. 800 feet).
3. Kuh-i Nō (32°37′N, 49°28′E, 12,200 feet). The party is here encamped along the Balut River, near 32°40′N, 49°10′E and ca. 3800 feet in elevation.

A Roadside Cairn in the Bakhtiari Oak Forest.

lammergeier; several species of warblers and of sparrows (*Emberiza*). The wheatears (*Oenanthe*) are rare now, and the corn crake and *Circaetus gallicus*, a rare Indian eagle, have been seen for the first time in Persia. — The horseman's helper says his expenses are ½ kran for meat, 1 kran for tea and sugar; flour he has—a total of about 4 kran a day (or 2 cents at my exchange rate).

April 30. Our neighbors left early. We packed up the minimum for our three onward-going mules, reducing even bedding, and sent the rest back with the head horseman. He didn't know what to do with the hand I proffered in goodbye, since of course hands aren't shaken in the Asia I know. Among the Lahulis, not even a son touches his mother's hand after puberty, much less kisses her. There is required instead a show of respect, perhaps a more wholesome and sincere exhibition than affection.

The road goes up the limestone slope. The mules slipped badly and often had to be unloaded. Our fellow travellers didn't unload, only beat and yelled. Near the top we overtook a very old man who had been at our camping place last night. His skin was like the leather of an old waterbag, stretched over his withered frame. A young woman, carrying water, accompanied him. The road is plastered with the manure of straining animals and splashed with the blood of their wounds. The climb finished, we passed for some 3 miles across a wooded plateau overgrown with stunted oaks and found our friends of yesterday beside a cool spring. We had of course found no water on the ascent, and animals and men were parched. Our friends had sent a man with water from the spring, but he had somehow missed us.

There are new birds now: cuckoo, oriole, crow, nightingale, jay, kite, woodpecker, and other kinds of shrike and warbler. A few orchids, pink and purple, and a white violet grow under the oaks.[1]

May 2, Pashm-i Shurun. The night was cool with enough mosquitoes for a net. We camped at Tazeh[2] at 12:30, in a torrent bed that leads to the pass. There are herds of all sorts of animals all about ready to leave for the crest around dawn. There is no grass left except on the ledges high above us, and they bring down loads so the beasts can have a bit of breakfast before they leave. A nice dog had a piece of bone from our camp and wanted to stay with us. His folks had a bad time getting him away. His name was Khali. Two others found a dead donkey and intended to stay there to eat it. Their masters came back 4 to 5 miles to recover them. A poor baby donkey got lost and will starve. We should have shot the poor thing, but there might have been trouble. Women carry their babies in cradles on their backs, the feet often sticking out. An old woman had a kid for her load, and one husky red-cheeked young woman had a baby donkey loaded with her own baby. One white-haired mother assisted by a little girl and a piece of dry brush performed the job of bringing along the kids of the year.

May 3. The horseman kept our poor animals in the grassless camp all night, so that even the neighbors protested. Grass could be seen a half hour above the river, and he left for grass only when I told him we wouldn't move till the beasts were fed. Wangyel went with him at 5:30, and in three hours they came back with loads of grass they had pulled. Our neighbors, some dozen troupes of donkeys, cows, horses, sheep and goats, had mostly gotten ahead of us, but others were still coming up from below. A little beyond the mouth of the ravine the walls narrow, and the floor is filled with a jumble of boulders and rockpiles. Up over these goes the way. They have made some crude paths with brush and stones, but for a few hundred yards during which the traveller climbs a hundred feet, the way is nasty. The animals slip and have to be pushed and pulled. Ours had to go unladen over the final stretch. Everyone yells to encourage the animals, the children cry, the women scold, and it all reverberates in the canyon with awful effect. In all their calling there is a wild fearsome quality, even when they shout to one another on the hills. The call is high and wavering and ends with a "hi-hi-hi," and you're sure something terrible has happened.

---

1. Koelz is following the Chahrleng Trail described a few years before by J. V. Harrison in "The Bakhtiari Country" (*Geographical Journal* 80, no. 3:195-98).
2. Tazeh (approximately 32°43′N, 49°22′E, ca. 7000 feet).

MARKET DAY IN KHUZISTAN.

Once through the canyon, though the valley is still narrow with not much room on the slopes for trees, the road isn't bad. The climb to the crest is steep, and when we got to the top a snowstorm dropped huge pellets of soft hail on us. The guide wanted to join the swarm of travellers in some caves but we went on up a ridge that looked lush and green with some groves of oaks. The herbage, however, was comprised of *Colchicums* that aren't edible, so the camp was made at Damavar beside a stream from the melting snow. There is a nice red tulip with long and pointed flower parts and three to five shiny leaves; a large rose purple onion with a 3 inch head of flowers and broad leaves, very common; a tall white flowered one with two-ranked

TRUCKING IN KHUZISTAN. There is an old tale that the camel was made of the leftovers when the rest of the animals were created, and the tale might have added that the Creator displayed well in his final job the results of his abundant practice. There are handsomer beasts but none that combine so many special features that fit animals for the part they play.

leaves, very pungent, eaten by the people; a nice bushy cherry, 10 feet high with racemes of cream-colored flowers and cordate leaves, the fruit of which, they say, is eaten by the wood pigeons. On the slope in front of us, midst patches of snow, are pink-flowered almond bushes. —Rinchen Gialtsen asked the guide's name and was told that since we had been together ten days without knowing his name, it could hardly matter now.

May 4, Damavar. The men ascended a couple thousand feet to the crest above us. They could look across to the snow-covered Kuh-i Nō we have seen ahead for days, no higher than the peak they were on, and down onto a great green plain with a lake a day's journey away. Tree-filled ravines open into the plain. Our journey began in a landscape burnt and bare that will not green again till autumn brings it rain. We look down now into a Promised Land. Through the ages man and beast have here satisfied their primal needs of grass, wood, and water. Once more they have reached the Place of Plenty over the harsh and weary way.

Chapter VI

DORUD AND TI

May 20. Dorud[1] lies at the edge of a great green expanse where two rivulets join. The name means "two rivers." Tibetans call such places *sumdo* meaning "three directions." Huge patches of heading wheat carpet the valley floor, and here and there splashes of darker green mark marshes, while the whole is reinforced by the heavy green of the invasive licorice-root that, immutable and resolute, still keeps the valley green when the summer sun has seared the wheat and scorched the marshes. The Bakhtiari tableland stops short in its advance on the great plain in embattled ranks of cliff-faced snow-capped peaks that soon shut out the setting sun. Across the valley, so far away that the watchtower of Tanurdar on its earthen mound can hardly be discerned, a chain of rounded and uneven hills rise step-like and retreat into the eastern sky. Here and there high earthen cones dot the plain, monuments of some vanished race, now appearing out of place on the level valley floor, as if they too should have been swept back into the jumble of the distant wall. Both the rivulets alike are full of sullen silty water and reach the town in channels drab and bleak, as though their courses had been laid out for them by some highway engineer. The smaller Marbur that draws from the snows of the nearby Ushturan creeps along the foot of the Bakhtiari front, through thin thickets of blackberry bushes and other thorns and scattered patches of scrubby trees. The Tireh Ab that comes down from Borujird to the west cuts its way through the plain in a shallow bed with dirt-cliff walls, and no vegetation aids the eye to trace its course. Where the waters join, the stupid streams become a foaming, frenzied torrent that rushes through a boulder-blocked rock-walled bed grudgingly granted for its passage by the majestic Pariz and Bahur that stand guard on either side.

---

1. Dorud (33°28′N, 49°04′E, 4770 feet). A new town at the southeast end of the broad Borujird Plain, not far from the all-weather road from Hamadan to Khoramabad to Ahwaz and the Gulf ports. Here there was a railway station with coal and water facilities and a telegraph. It was easily reached by railroad from Tehran.

The town of Dorud is a forlorn agglomeration of a few wretched structures slapped together of mud, sticks, tins, and whatever else, that stand in ridiculous contrast to the pretentious railway station to which, so to speak, they owe their being. The magistracy and the post office have taken shelter in some of these architectural achievements, and the rest house the few shopkeepers that supply the simple wants of the outlying villagers. Years ago, they say, there was no town here and the marauding Lur tribes used only to camp long enough to divide their plunder. The stopping of the upbound and downgoing trains in recent times has somehow fostered the eruption of a settlement.

They said an Armenian keeps a hotel in the place, but without investigating it we camped in a vacant field, now full of blooming plants, and got ready to sleep in the freshness of the herbage and the cool breeze that slid from the Bahur.

We are tremendously happy with the prospect before us. We must wade in those distant marshes, explore those thorny thickets, reach those glistening peaks. We didn't yet know that lapwings nested in the marshes and the great bustard fed at their borders, and we only guessed that wild pigs hid in the thickets and that tulips and *Colchicum* bloomed along the snows.

Through the years, my Tibetans have taught me to view the landscape with a special eye. As the fish sees his element from his particular view, so the jewel of Nature turns to us a special facet. And I often recall a Tibetan friend's delight with one of our Indian camps. "What a lovely place!" he exclaimed. *Chhu mangpo, tsa mangpo, shing mangpo* ("lots of water, lots of grass, lots of wood"). But for Lobzang's praise I should hardly have noticed the charms of the place we were in just then: a drying-up pond on the bleak Punjab Plain. But a diamond is a diamond; the fault is in you if you mistake it for glass.

May 21. We climbed the Rangi that shoulders against the snowy Pariz.[1] A rich spring green clothes the mountain almost to its bare and rocky summit; a deeper green lies at its foot where the soil layer is thicker and the vegetation denser, and in large patches where oak bushes grow are second-growth remains of the outposts of the Bakhtiari forests. Conspicuous stripes of richer color also mark the course of spring streams that in varying length streak the sides, while in places great splashes of purple lie in the verdure where grows a lush vetch (*nojivar*) that is gathered soon for winter hay. Two species of wild wheat and a wild barley are headed.

Flowers are everywhere, and as we climb, the roster changes: pale blue hyacinths, wine-colored gladiolus, and purple *Colchicum* bloom along the

---

1. Pariz is probably the main peak of Ushtarinan Kuh (33°21′N, 49°15′E, 14,200 feet).

rills that wash the base, and violet gladiolus, red tulips, Star of Bethlehem, and purple iris flower on drier ground nearby. Honeysuckle and roses line the higher streams, with now and then a wild apple and wild pear, and blots of color mark beds of huge-flowered purple onions, giant red-belled fritillarias, pink sweet peas, yellow snapdragons, and rose-purple mint, *Nepeta*. On the summit that looks bare from below, flowers are even more varied and of rarer and brighter hue. A creamy black-eyed asphodel, a white tulip, yellow *Eremurus*, plum-colored gladiolus, onions in pink, purple, and white, pink *Dianthus* and also other bright gems that our gardens do not know sparkle from the rocky setting. A herd of ibex that had been lying on a ledge retreated slowly before us. Each had pawed out for himself a little platform on which to rest. Over large stretches, bears had upturned the stones seemingly in the search of roots. A herd of last year's pigs sauntered past in Indian file, young bloods with no family cares, just killing time. From time to time one would try to advance himself in the rank, to be balked in his efforts by a "waugh" and a sideswipe from the first of his buddies he tried to pass. Chukor partridges (*Kabk*) were everywhere, and a golden eagle was in sight overhead most of the day.

A husky youth came singing over the peak with some women and children and urged us to let him show us where to hunt pigs. The sight of nice guns always puts the native in mind of pigs—they are the commonest game and the easiest to find. But the ladies protested, and he looked after us for a long time as we descended.

We reached the ford of the Marbur just as two men and a donkey came out of the water, and Rup Chand hastened to bargain for the donkey to take him across. The men were unwilling—the ford is a long one, waist-deep in ice water, and they were already benumbed from their crossing—but for a day's donkey hire they would go back, with the stipulation that the donkey needn't go an inch beyond the opposite shore. Then both plunged again into the stinging current, one on each side of the donkey and executed their bargain.

May 30. We came on down the river a day's journey from Dorud into the valley on the other side of the Pariz, and we have travelled for another day along the boisterous little river that bisects it. Our snowfed spring stopped flowing at 11:00 yesterday morning and began again at midnight. It stopped at 6:00 this morning. The day before, it was off at 2:00 P.M. and on at 9:00 P.M., and the day before that the time was 3:00 P.M. and 5:00 P.M. The stops are getting longer every day: 2, 7, and 13 hours. Off and on while the water is gone, one can hear toward the mountain a distant roar like an approaching hurricane. At the spring it sounds as though there were an aeroplane underground. When the water comes, there is a strong flow, and all the birds and even the butterflies come for a drink. The large white butterflies often spend the night nearby, ten to twenty of them roosting together on a single branch. The pigs have found it more convenient to drink here than to go to the river, and a herd or two has disturbed the camp every night. They don't worry us, but our horsemen have great fear of bears and are always in dread that it is a bear this time instead of pigs. For our part, after all these years of lying about on desert, plain, peak, and jungle between here and Tibet, we are only concerned that it is not men that come to camp in the night. We were flattered when the bison and the tiger came at Jagalbed.

The oak forest has been cut off in large stretches, and everywhere charcoal-burners are at work cutting up the trees with handsaws, making charcoal in deep pits, for sale at Dorud. One of the horsemen blundered into such a group and lost his coat and shirt, but the thieves gave back the things with apologies and kisses when they were convinced that he wasn't alone and had armed support at that.

The valley here is so narrow that Pariz's snowy cap is invisible above its palisaded walls. Over a stretch of miles there is only the naked cliff and then a break through which none but men and goats can climb the mountain. A swarm of bees has a home in a cleft near that path and, they say, have occupied it for years, just out of reach of the cupidity they constantly whet. A pair of golden eagles in aerial dominion over this rugged realm from time to time ring out their eerie cries, and mimicking jays echo them, as if it were the sound that suited best the rocky solitude.

We moved camp up to Tī,[1] a few miserable huts in a beautiful spot along the river. On the way we passed a rude shrine, a pile of stones where all sorts of articles were hanging: lanterns, teakettles, feedbags, blankets—at least five horseloads of the most tempting things, their allurement not to be measured by their value in our market. Local people said this was the safest place to leave things that you didn't momentarily need. The valley here is so notorious for its robberies that we were warned not to come, and it seems curious that valuable property should be so safe as it apparently is, hanging on bushes along the roadside.

The people here are Lurs, probably the most primitive of the Persian tribes. Physically they are inclined to be strapping, often blue-eyed, often handsome—at least to the x-ray eye that can penetrate the obscuring film of dirt—and almost invariably of pleasant manner. They seem always to have been marauders and were one of the last tribes to be subjugated in the regime of Reza Shah. It is said much blood was shed in doing it. The

---

1. Tī (approximately 33°20′N and 49°10′E, ca. 5800 feet) has not, so far as the editors can determine, been described by any other traveller. Koelz's description appears to be a unique ethnographic record.

A Lur "Village" in Luristan. The Lurs are naturally nomads, and though their country is one of the most suitable in all Persia for agriculture, and wheat and barley grow wild there, acorn bread is a common article of diet. It is no more palatable than it sounds. The Lurs have permanent settlements that in architecture are hardly more graceful than those of prairie dogs, and not nearly so well equipped to afford shelter from the elements. They are favorable to flea culture, and Luristan is famous for its fleas. The structures shown here are of reeds and goat hair weavings, the last often too sleazy to shed water. The elements of structure are easily packed and easily transportable.

territory they occupy, like that of the Bakhtiari, their neighbors, is mountainous. (Actually we are now in Bakhtiari country—the Dorud River is the boundary—and these few people in our valley have invaded the fringes.) These people exhibit no agricultural aptitude. From the oak forest they get their bread of acorns, and from their flocks, that in summer find abundant pasture in the mountains and in winter are driven to the warm deserts in the south, they get the rest of their simple needs. Charcoal-making from the oaks and collecting the gum of the *beneh* tree (*Pistaccio*) and the wild shrubs called *gavan* (*Astragalus*) provide a little cash to oil the domestic machinery: to buy tea and sugar, and maybe kerosene, to furnish the boys with the means of buying a wife, and to purchase the sundry other little luxuries of existence. The word Lur then has come to be an epithet of contempt, and these people in our valley insist they are Bakhtiaris.

At Tī there are a few worn-out fields, the best of them ridged to hold water and apparently devoted to growing rice. Others have been planted with grain. There are more people about than in the villages below, and most of them are busy in the fields. At my approach, two girls fled from the rice fields into a nearby hut but soon came out again, shaking their shoes and clothes, swatting, slapping, and scratching, and ran off. Rup Chand stopped to rest on the roof of the hut and in a moment found out why the girls had fled—the hut simmered with starving fleas. Luristan is noted for its fleas.

Tī lies in the beautiful valley like a gravel set in platinum or an inkblot on a brocade. High cliff-fronted mountain peaks wall in the valley. Above, the canyon opens and the view stretches into the distance to a white-clad range

TENTS OF TIBETAN NOMADS. The difference in architecture that has evolved on the Tibetan desert at 10,000 feet elevation and on the Persian plain a few thousand miles away would probably not be appreciated by the American house-dweller, but the arrangements serve their purpose. They provide the sort of shelter the inhabitants require.

that sends down its melted snows in a turbulent, rock-bedded stream of silvery water. In front of the village, a grove of primeval plane and walnut trees cover the slopes from the rivulet to buttress the opposite cliff. Here, cradled in blooming roses, a great spring takes its source, and its crystal waters roar down over mossy rocks through the Druid wood to augment the foaming flow below. At the edge of the grove in the halo of its chill freshness we made our camp.

A villager brought us a bundle of snowcock (*kabk dari*) feathers and said the birds lived nearby. A Russian discovered this bird in the Bakhtiari mountains and named it *Tetraogallus caspius semenowtianschanskii*. Few people have ever seen one. The feathers show that it is paler than the birds of the northern mountains, just as Sarudny affirmed.

This evening in the oak forest a fox was catching crickets, the big black and yellow ones that were such a scourge in Bakhtiari. They seem to be emergency rations—he chewed them with teeth and gums exposed as dogs do when eating something they don't like. After a few mouthfuls he yawned, and looking around, caught sight of me. He suspected I was a new item in the landscape, but since I didn't move, he was finally reassured and went on catching crickets. After a moment he gave a jump, barked, and ran off up the ravine. The chickens here feed on the crickets, too, and have almost doubled their weight with fat. The fish in the stream, all of the Minnow family, the Cyprinidae, are likewise gorged with crickets, and only with the exercise of all our cunning did we at last hook a few. Plenty of them weigh two pounds. Farther down in the Ab Diz there are monsters, even to man size.

In the grove beside camp is a crude shrine that hardly seems to have anything Islamic about it and recalls those of the Himalayan villages. A platform 6 by 4 by 3 feet has been built of flat stones, and on it are teakettle tops and small tins, empty or containing buttons and glass beads strung on safety pins. When one of the horsemen reached the shrine along the path today, he rubbed his palms on the earth and then, facing it, went through the prayer movements.

June 1. We came up the valley as far as the animals could carry us and dug out beds for ourselves on the slope, as do the ibexes. This morning I met a caravan of cows and donkeys coming down from the summer camps near Qadi Kuh, the white-patched range above, to replenish their stock of acorns. In one place along the stream a basketful of crushed acorns was being leached by means of a little current led to bathe the top of the unattractive mass. The leaching seems to be a relative matter since the dismal slab of bread they gave me to taste was still bitter enough. In places in the Himalayas they treat horse chestnuts in this way, but there the leaching was so thorough that the bread looked as if it had had been made of ashes, felt as if it had been made of rubber, and tasted like nothing at all.

The country is now rugged and paths are few, so I followed the cattle trail to reach the snow. It brought me against a wall; it would hardly have entered my head to try to climb it, but the cows had indisputably traversed it, so up I went, wondering no less at the surefootedness than at the steady nerves of the cows and donkeys in these parts.

To one side now, a little stream comes down through dark bare walls in a niche of which a few primroses are pasted. On the other side are earthen slopes nearly as steep and as bare, except that some rhubarb plants, each with two gigantic short-petioled leaves a yard, or even four feet, across lend an appearance of fertility that the sterile ground ill deserves. In the floor of the gorge are scattered skeletons of ibex, probably killed under avalanches of snow. One with teeth not yet worn down had horns that measured 49 inches. In the Himalayas, wild animals often perish in the snowslides, and the carcasses are sometimes recovered, well preserved in the natural refrigeration.

Nearer the crest another stream descends, this one softly over the earthy slope, and a broad band of green marks its course. In places a wide lawn of short sedges borders the water and in others a meadow of tall grasses, with scattered rose bushes burdened with heavily-scented pink blooms and

Our Persian Escort, A. Mighnat, and Rup Chand with a Leaf of the Wild Rhubarb that is Common in Iran and the Afghan Mountains. The "stalks" are not so long as ours but very much more robust and usually of milder and more pleasant acidity. Such large leaves (they may be 4 feet across) I have regularly seen only in the Bakhtiari country. This was common around Galegahar, a great freshwater lake of lovely blue icy water a few days into the mountains from Dorud.

great patches of tall rose-purple onions, white orange-anthered *Eremurus*, and the gorgeous imperial fritillaria in an abundance I had never seen. On the crest in trickles of melting snow are carpets of little pink primroses and blotches of white tulips, washed outside with rose, and lavender colchicums. Among them are feeding flock of serins (*Serinus pusillus*) as bright-colored as the flowers, and round about are the other birds of the high mountains. Snowfinches (*Montifringilla nivalis*) with their young flutter from one snowbound rock pile to the other, flushing the grasshoppers from the sun-warmed stones. Small groups of stone sparrows (*Petronia*) too are there, busily searching the gravel as other sparrows (*Emberiza cia, E. melanocephala*) sing round about. Chukors flee clucking to the summit, and overhead soars the golden eagle and the circling yellow-billed choughs give their friendly cry. To the left on a dry rocky slope is a small grove of cedar trees (*Juniperus*), primeval patriarchs 6 feet in diameter, and to the right the plateau I am on terminates in a cliff against a lush valley that extends out of sight behind the Qadi Kuh. Far away beyond the valley, the horizon ends in a lofty tableland crowned with chilly gloomy peaks, more forbidding and mysterious even than those around me, like Cosmos rising out of Chaos.

All at once at my feet, among the lichen-splashed limestone rocks, a flower took form, floating out of the tones of dove and purple in which it blended, like a fairy thing called up by the spirit of this enchanted realm. It wasn't a thing of fancy but an iris. The mystic flower, 6 inches across, borne on a stalk of less than that dimension, was evenly toned by close veining in dull shades of purple, except where on the falls huge spots of velvety black guarded its heart. Only a few small plants of it grew on that barren spot, and long afterward we searched the hills for more. It was Rup Chand and Wangyel who found the flowers again, and when they bloomed we went on a pilgrimage to see them. Rinchen Gialtsen, who always stayed to do the work in camp, and Piggy, the wild boar, who was still too small to take long journeys, on that day came too.

Rup Chand and Wangyel also had a tale to tell. They had climbed the precipice where the snowcock stays, and across the summit they found a bear and her cub amusing themselves by sliding down a snowbank. When Wangyel first saw them the bear was rolling down the snow while the cub stood watching, and Wangyel called to Rup Chand that a bear had met with an accident! The cub liked the fun best and slid down sprawled on its belly while the mother looked on. Then both would coast down together, the mother on her haunches and the baby hanging on its mother's neck.

The great crickets have taken to eating our clothes and bedding. They ate Rinchen Gialtsen's hat, the horseman's coat, and one of my cashmere blankets. They have eaten the green pears on a tree near camp and chewed a hole in the almond sack and carried off the kernels.

Chapter VII

THE CAPITAL

July 8. The train brought us from our happy valley in the mountains of Luristan, across the mouth of the furnace into which summer has transformed the Great Desert, to the flea-bitten Capital of the King of Kings,[1] heir of the world-embracing empire of the Medes and Persians. Let him describe this modern Persepolis for whom it is the hand of Progress that sweeps out a place among the mud hovels of the wretched for grandiose agglomerations of concrete and stone or that clothes the infirm Body Social in the cast-off finery of a foreign and moribund civilization.

I am not condemning Reza Shah. On the contrary. He did the best he knew how, and like many who preceded him in high position mistook form for substance. His government was a despotism succeeding anarchy—anarchy and despotism seem to have been the normal cycle of Persian history—and that he restored order none will deny. The cost may have been as heavy as it is claimed and the advantage as light, but from my experience the Persian was still better off materially than his Indian and Afghan neighbors, and it would be difficult to prove that his government was worse.

---

1. Tehran, or Teheran (34°40′N, 51°26′E, 3750 feet). The nineteenth and twentieth century capital of Iran lies at the arid southern foot of the Elburz Mountains. Though only about 300,000 people lived in the city itself on the eve of the World Wars' convulsive impact on Iran, little more than other plateau cities, the capital was the city most affected by the modernization efforts of Reza Shah and his immediate predecessors. The walls, previously rebuilt around 1870, and much housing, had been leveled to provide broad avenues transecting the town. The water system still depended wholly on *qanats* and small open conduits, but surveys were taking place for several diversion schemes and reservoirs. Tehran was the center of the network of "all-weather" roads radiating toward Russia and the Caspian Sea to the north, Afghanistan and India to the east, Turkey to the west and the Gulf and the Arab countries to the south and a parallel network of railroads, still under construction. Several hospitals, a medical college attached to the new university, and the Pasteur Institute producing and administering vaccines were all available. As many as one-third of the modern factories encouraged by Reza Shah—including those for armaments, chemicals, tobacco, foodstuffs, soap, matches, and many other goods—were in or near Tehran. Embassies, banks, and wireless facilities provided international connections. Above all, Tehran was the center of Reza Shah's centralized administration.

THE PEACOCK THRONE. This can be seen in one of the palace museums of the capital. It was brought from India by the last enterprising Shahenshah Nadir Shah who in the first part of the eighteenth century extended the ancient imperial power far beyond its present limits. The throne is of enameled gold heavily inset with stones, which from the casual guarding the palace gets may be assumed not to be the original ones.

The lands under royal control looked far and away happier than those of others, and I heard from a fellow countryman, who ought to have known, that they were the best managed in the country. Reza Shah was a simple, unlettered man, I understand, who seized the throne of a country that was in greatest part a barren desert, with only the most primitive agriculture, no industrial development or highways, with a priest-ridden population, fatalistic and ignorant, socially in feudalism and surrounded by powerful and hostile neighbors. Against the organized opposition of the best of his own people—the priests, nobles, and landlords—this iron-willed man began his hopeless, thankless task, and his partisans may well find gentler condonements for his failures and even brighter commendation for his achievements if they examine them in the light of the background and accomplishments of contemporary dictators.

Someone has given all the ant colonies near the American Legation a handful of wheat, and they are busy in the morning carrying it in. The afternoons are too hot for even the ants to work; their Bakhtiari relatives always took the afternoon off too. They work on one side of the nest and clean up the grain there before beginning elsewhere. I never saw anyone here feeding ants before nor have I ever observed the interest in watching them work that one often sees among our people. Indians like ants and commonly feed them.

In the bazaar the little seedless currant-grapes (*yaquti*) have been available for two weeks. They differ from those of Baltistan in being of nearly uniform size—in Baltistan the bunches often had a few large seedy berries. There was a clingstone apricot, the first clingstone I ever saw, of good size and flavor but heavy-skinned.

The antique shops are interesting. Old rugs and pictures are nonexistent, and very few old *ghilims* even are to be seen. We thought we had found a picture, a simple ink drawing with gilded figures, of the style of the seventeenth century, but it had been drawn on a page of an old book from which the writing had been erased. Coins of silver and glass, seals (of agate or other forms of quartz; sometimes of ruby, or of bronze) of the Sasanid period or older are not rare, but these too are seen in modern imitations. There are fragments of various weaves used as dress, the best of them silk brocades of the seventeenth century, but the most interesting items in the shops are the porcelains. Persians apparently have always liked nice china, and wares of the best English, Russian, and Chinese factories of a century ago and even earlier are found in many of the shops. A few dealers specialize in antique pottery and porcelains; these have interested us most. In Afghanistan we found only small sherds in the ancient ruins of Balkh and Kandahar, but here we could even find unbroken pieces that had lain hundreds of years under the desert dust.

Rinchen Gialtsen has recovered from what we suppose is the sandfly fever, one of the curious fevers foreigners contract in these parts. For three days he has had hard pains in head and limbs with intermittent fever and once or twice nausea.

For two weeks we have been trying to get our arrangements made to leave the city and continue our explorations. For two weeks I have been going from pillar to post. At 4:00 I have been told to come at 11:00, and at 11:00 to come at 4:00. Today the American Minister said he had been informed that the matter must go to the Prime Minister and that he would see the Prime Minister today. Later, a phone message from the Foreign Office informed the Legation they had told the Police Department the matter needn't go to the Prime Minister. At this point a car came for me from the Department of Agriculture with two men who took me to the Police Station with a sealed letter marked "Urgent Confidential," said to contain a royal order to let me go. We took it upstairs and then downstairs and were told to come at 4:30. At 4:30 they said there was permission for me to go all right, but not for my men, and to come back at 6:00.

A Street Restaurant, Such As Any City of the Mid-East Can Show. This one serves a popular meal. The boy has wrapped meat fragments around an iron rod which are put for cooking over a charcoal brazier. The proprietor is fanning the embers with a palm fan. The meat will be wrapped in a slab of bread such as the man third from the left has his hand on and then eaten *in situ*. There is little overhead, though nowadays most governments manage to tax locations of such institutions.

We hadn't much hope now, especially since the American Minister was uninterested. He said he had told a subordinate on leaving the Prime Minister's office to phone him unofficially if they had anything against my travelling, and he'd let the matter drop. But at 6:00 the police said everything was in order, so we engaged four droshkes for 5:00 in the morning to take us to the train that leaves for the Caspian Shore.

Rinchen Gialtsen wanted to buy some wool yarn and inadvertently spilled the proprietor's cup of tea. No, pay wasn't wanted for the tea, and no other damage was done, but there was no yarn for sale. The cartridge seller refused to have anything to do with us because he had seen us coming out of his competitor's shop, and vegetable sellers have once or twice had the same reaction.

Shops in the city are closed on Friday, Juma, the Moslem holiday. The Jewish shopkeepers close on Saturday and the Armenians on Sunday. The Legations keep their own religious weekly holiday. According to the Buddhist religion, Lahulis have certain days of the month, not fixed days of the week, when one may not work, ride horses, cultivate, etc.; namely, the first, tenth, fifteenth, twenty-second, twenty-fifth, and thirtieth. Observance of these rest days has, however, relaxed nowadays so that most people pay no more attention to them, except they don't do butchering on such dates.

There is considerable excitement about the German military successes. I recalled a little note in a Georgia newspaper of March a year ago quoting Poultney Bigelow who had just returned from Europe. He said nothing could stop the German advance to the east, and if the British and French were "fool enough to make war, the Germans will be in Paris within a year." It took them considerably less time to get there. The people I have talked to might be considered pro-German, but they aren't outspoken. I gathered from certain diplomats' conversation that the government is considered anti-German, but that there are enough Germans in the country to overthrow the government.

Chapter VIII

THE CASPIAN SHORE, FROM BELOW SEA LEVEL TO ABOVE THE CLOUDS

July 11, Gurgan.[1] From the terminal of the Trans-Iranian at Bandar Shah we were carried in trucks to Gurgan at the eastern horn of the forested crescent that cradles the Caspian Sea. The town has stucco buildings, and orange trees are planted in the streets. Steep wooded slopes rise at the back, and in front there is a gentle green-clad descent to the Turkoman steppe. We camped in the Agriculture Department's garden, in a grove of small mulberry trees thick with an undergrowth of annual wormwood. There are 270 American plows and a couple of tractors standing about, and under a shed is a grain separator or two. Weeds apparently grow well, and a crowd of women and girls are hoeing away at them without apparent effect, except that immediately behind them there is a temporary clearing. They hoe till 7:30 P.M. with two and one-half hours off for lunch and were hilarious with their monthly pay envelopes today: 9 tumans ($3.00). They wanted us to change the bills for them, probably by way of displaying this wealth. Persians are fond of carrying money and seemingly like to flash bills. It is no uncommon thing to see a wad of currency in the hands of people who obviously have no immediate need of large sums of money, and often I have been asked for a large bill I 'chanced to have, whereupon the solicitor would pull out his roll and give me part of it in exchange. Rinchen Gialtsen was touched by the poor women's simplicity and bought them a sack of candy. At first they were puzzled by the gift, but when they saw what it was they fell on each other's necks and squealed.

Near us a workman has a nice one-room house of the usual stucco, in which he, his wife and baby, a horse, a sheep, and a goat find ample accommodations. The family has one end of the room and the animals the

---

1. Gurgan (36°50′N, 54°29′E, 240 feet). At the northern foot of the Elburz, this town serves as a market town for Turkoman farmers and nomads of the Gurgan Plain to the north. Its population was about 15,000 in 1940. It could be reached by motor roads from Tehran via Demevand and Sari or by Shahrud and was only 20 miles from the terminus of the railway to Tehran at Bandar Shah.

other. They own a dog, too, but he stays outside. I wondered what use a horse was to them, but it seems they always had wanted one and with the abundance of weeds about it doesn't cost anything to keep it. The goat is kept tied up because his predecessor walked off and went back to the mountains where he came from.

The wild pigs come to our garden, and pheasants and black partridges are common there. Wild blackberries seem destined by Providence in these parts to inherit the earth and if vanquished in the fields establish themselves in formidable thickets at their borders, reinforced by another savagely-armed thorn (*Paliurus*), wild pomegranates, and grapes. In the fields thus freed, wild carrots and thistles grudgingly give room to the crops.

The muskmelons are beginning to ripen. We got 35 kinds in the bazaar today, which is as much variety as we have seen in the Turkoman countries to the east, but the quality is much inferior to that of the unsurpassed melons of northern Afghanistan. These, however, are not well ripened. I gave our neighbor's horse a piece of watermelon, but his master snatched it away and said watermelons are bad for the stomach (they are in truth virtually inedible here, but I shouldn't have suspected they'd injure a horse); muskmelon rinds the horse could have. Some children had some large cucumbers 13 inches long and 5 ½ inches through, larger than any I had seen till now, but not till I had bid them up to a dizzy price would they part with two of them.

Wangyel discovered there was a spring within walking distance and went for water. In spite of our many years of living among people who drink from gutters and puddles, we still adhere to our first principles, and spring water failing, we drink tea. The spring water we must fetch by ourselves. Lahulis find nothing strange in my ideas of germ-spread and in the matter of food preparation take even squeamish precautions in food handling. The cook would never put a spoon he had used to taste his mess back into the cooking pot, and food is not touched by the hands unless necessary. The highland Tibetans haven't these ideas, and I suspect the Lahulis take them from the Hindus, their neighbors to the south, for whom the essence of religion is cleanliness. The Moslems take a liberal view of sanitation. Ablutions are prescribed for the excretory regions, a bath after copulation, and washing of hands and feet at prayer time (though this may be effected symbolically), but in the matter of food hygiene fundamental principles aren't observed: two may share a glass of liquid together; the company may eat together from the common platter with their fingers, and if the cup is too full the servant will more than likely sip the surplus before serving it. As careless as we apparently are (and we have agreed we look dirtier always than any of the natives we chance to be among), our food is strictly clean. Consequently, we never have had any of the diseases of the digestive tract that most people seem to take as a matter of course.

Wangyel took an eight-year-old boy as guide to the spring, and since it

THE CASPIAN SHORE

A MUSKMELON COLLECTION SUCH AS CAN BE MADE IN THE TURKOMAN SECTIONS OF IRAN AND AFGHANISTAN. The Turkoman melon unlike our cantaloupe never separates from its stem and keeps much better. Some sorts can be stored for several months. The quality is far superior to our average, and the best are superb. In places the flesh is dried. I assembled all varieties of muskmelons for the U.S. Department of Agriculture, since they always had a potential value for breeding for disease resistance. On occasion, I had a donkey load of samples to carry home from the farmers' market. I was once asked what possible use I could have for such quantities of melons, and I thought I was making a joke when I answered I was going to dry them for winter. My friend told me I had bought the wrong kinds. In parts of Iran and Afghanistan, they do that very thing, and candylike strips of dried muskmelon can be bought in the markets.

was a long walk the wage was fixed at 2 rials, a half-day's wages for a man. I asked if he had been paid and he answered: "Not a stiver." "Well, if he forgets to pay you, let me know," I said. His "Bali" (yes) was said in a tone that was understandable as "I certainly will." *Bali* may mean "maybe," "I don't know," or "of course," depending on the intonation. With his money he went to the bath, gave ⅒ rial to a beggar, and bought himself a melon.

Some soldiers gathered at our garden, and an agriculture officer gave them a fluent lecture on how to grow cotton. The days are hot in the sun but the nights are pleasant, especially if there is a breeze. The frogs in the rice fields make such a din at night that you are hardly aware of it. The rooks in the Legation garden at Tehran also kept up such an even-toned and sustained tumult that we soon ceased to notice it.

July 15. The frogs stopped abruptly in the night and some katydids took their place. All the plants of the fields have aestivating snails that have glued themselves to the leaves. We started off up the mountain at quarter to nine with five horses and soon entered the wood through a fringe of bushes of blackberry, *Paliurus,* and even wild quinces and plums. The trees, mostly oak, were large and gave the atmosphere of a virgin white oak forest. Green woodpeckers, chaffinches, and wood pigeons (*Columba palumbus* and *C. oenas*) were the most conspicuous birds. For most of the day the way ran along a little stream. After about eight miles we came to a small clearing in which was a "coffee house," called Garmab Dasht (Plain of the Warm Water). Springs were numerous now that we were near the foot of the mountain, but none of them as far as we could see were warm. The owner was out inspecting his potato patch to estimate the damage of the latest porcupine visitation. Porcupines are common animals in most parts of Iran. They are much like ours in appearance, get to weigh some 50 pounds, and make good eating. They are nocturnal, live in holes in the ground, and are so shy and secretive that they are seldom seen. They like melons especially and do much damage tearing them open and eating out the seeds. One plundered my corn patch in Karaj for weeks, and though I slept there, I couldn't kill him. At the first motion I made he was off. The gardener said there were five wild bison on the cliffs above, but all day we saw no game, though pig-diggings were common. They had set a two-springed trap for them, but it had been sprung.

About 2 miles beyond Garmab Dasht the road abruptly begins a steep ascent of several thousand feet to Gozlu, a place like Garmab Dasht, with a magnificent spring. Rank growths of weeds more than man-high walled in the few fields that had been wrested from the forest, and crowding them from behind were thick growths of holly—rioting in the freedom from the forest shade. The forest now is of many species, primeval growths of linden, beech, maple, oak, ironwood, also yew and ash. Among the new birds the brown creeper is the only one we have at home, though the golden-crowned kinglet may occur.

July 16. The night was cool and pleasant. A wood owl sang. The ascent continues steep for several thousand feet more to a lone house, called Dimalu, near the top of the mountain. Here the forest, which has taken on the character it had when it began below—of great white oaks—ends abruptly, and the ground for a stretch is covered with juniper bushes of two kinds, one like our common juniper at home, and both old friends of the high Himalayas. In the forest are growths of holly bushes and wild peonies. The junipers end as suddenly as the forest—against a plain full of huge pincushion growths (*Astragalus, Acantholimon,* etc.)—and then begins the finest forest of juniper trees (red cedar) I have ever seen. The botanist

TEA ON THE CASPIAN SLOPE. The Persians learned to drink tea in recent times and now are addicts. Reza Shah introduced the culture of the tea plant on the Caspian slope where the climate, unlike that of the rest of the country, is tempered and humid. Chinese specialists were imported to manage the new industry and a creditable product is marketed. Everyone will offer you a cup of tea in Persia, served always with sugar, seldom with other accompaniments. Loaf sugar is preferred. The lump is kept in the mouth and the tea drained thru it. Handsome brass samovars from Russia are seen in many households.

may look down from the crest at Dimalu over the deciduous forest of the declivity onto the rice plains of Gurgan and over to the steppe that stretches into the northern haze. Then turning, he beholds the transition of wet high mountain growth to high steppe, to juniper forest and beyond on the southern horizon to the high dry mountain zone of Shah Kuh.[1]

Below the cedar forest on a green plain supplied by abundant springs is a small settlement, Karimserai. Thrifty fields of wheat and rye, still green, are the principal marks of cultivation. The Serai, they said, was one of the numerous caravanseries built 300 years ago in the reign of Shah Abbas, and like many of its fellows is still in good repair. Shah Kuh[2] is a large village a few miles farther on across a rough plateau, nestled at the head of a dry gulch. We passed through the village on toward the mountain that was our goal and camped on a pleasant spring meadow where a few primroses and

---

1. Shah Kuh (36°35′N, 54°45′E, 12,800 feet).
2. Shah Kuh, the village (36°34′N, 54°29′E, ca. 8000 feet).

Pedicularis were still in bloom.

On the coastal plain below here, the people in general have nice clothes, often of homespun silk, and their houses are, from the outside at least, better than those in most parts of Iran. But here the hand of improvement has left no visible mark: Shah Kuh is just such an agglomeration of mud walls as you would find anywhere else. I have heard no one expressing thanks for what the king has done below; instead, they complain of the taxes and that the royal landlord is worse than his predecessors. They make, however, much less noise than American businessmen do about the New Deal, and for my part I saw nothing to complain of except that the government officials were as impudent as one would find anywhere on earth. —The horsemen went home a roundabout way, else they said they'd have to take down a load of cedar telephone poles.

The water here is salubrious, as it generally is in limestone regions. In many parts of the country it is notoriously "heavy," *sangin*, as the Persians say, and in some individuals causes acute constipation. As is to be expected in desert regions, all the waters carry a heavy mineral load, and plants and animals have to adapt to it. There have thus been developed remarkable alkali-tolerant strains, especially of melons, and even wheats.

The sheep are already going down from the mountaintop to their winter pasture on plain and steppe below. In the forest there is grass of a species or two that seems to have high food value. The cattle that graze on it look plump, and I gathered seeds in the hope it might grow in our southern pine forests where a Georgian friend said pasture grasses were needed. The sheep, however, find no grazing in the forest and pass on through.

The nutritive quality of pasture plants varies with the locality. In the Himalayas the most striking differences are to be seen. On the monsoon side in the lush growth of the summer rains, animals don't thrive so well as across the mountain where the rains are slight and the herbage is short, while higher up on the Tibetan plateau, where one wonders what the animals find to put in their bellies, they remain in fine condition. It is due to the high nutritive value of the plants that livestock can be kept at all by trans-Himalayan peoples. Where half the year is winter and where hay is to be had only on the lands too poorly drained or too dry for cultivation (and such a thing as a cultivated hayfield is virtually unknown), the householder can give a winter ration of but a pitifully small quantity of fodder and is thankful to keep his beasts alive. Cows get only straw, which too is more nourishing than it is on the Indian plains; sheep and goats get the wild hay, which by the way is cut late when all seeds are formed, not in its prime, as we cut hay. Horses and donkeys get straw and the heavy stalks that the sheep can't chew. (In places west of India the donkeys get thistles for winter food, but they are often shredded before feeding.)

Chapter IX

THE BORDERLAND OF THE SOVIETS AND GENGHIZ'S HORDES—THE TURKOMANS

July 31. We are on our way to Meshed. There are two routes—one around the eastern end of the Elburz to Shahrud and then along the northern edge of the Great Desert, the other farther to the north and along the Russian border. We have chosen this latter route, and since traffic is light we have had to hire a car of our own to obviate an indefinite wait till passengers or cargo enough are assembled to start a vehicle on the way.

The Gunbad-i Qabus[1] is one of the noteworthy architectural remains of antiquity. It stands on the plain at one side of the town, an obelisk-like tower of brick, over 150 feet high, reminiscent of the Qutub Minar at Delhi. Its basic form is a cylinder capped by a cone, but ten two-sided buttresses give an interesting variation to the surface. A door is the sole opening. Two inscribed bands, one above the door and the other around the top of the tower, give information about the structure. The date is 397 Hejira or A.D. 1006. The tower is still very well preserved.

In places on the steppe, they are burning grass to get ready for the fall wheat. Stacks of grain stand here and there, and from one we got a black barley and the curious small-grained red-black wheat that we have seen only here. A Turkoman family has the finest cotton field we have seen in the country, and three generations are at work tending it. The children are shooing out the huge brown katydids (Rup Chand from a distance thought they were sparrows), and the grandfather is pulling the occasional weeds that have been overlooked. The middle generation is irrigating.

In the town there are few fruit trees. The Agriculture Department garden has a thrifty orchard of small, newly-planted trees. The shops have some small-seeded yellow prunes, a round black-purple plum, and a nice red-fleshed crimson sweet-apple, all said to have come from elsewhere, probably from Shahrud on the other side of the mountain.

The days here are hotter than at Gurgan—we are farther from the tempering effect of the forested slopes of the Elburz. We should accordingly have liked to start early, but the driver had drummed up some

---

1. Gunbad-i Qabus (37°17′N, 55°17′E).

passengers whom he couldn't manage to collect till near noon. He had a little freight, too, which he said he was taking as a favor for a friend and which would make the car ride better. Two of his passengers didn't like our looks and tried to get us out, maybe so they could sit on our bedding, but we pretended we didn't understand Persian. At last the driver told them something that quieted them, perhaps that we were paying for the hire of the car.

The road runs along the spur of the Elburz range that soon melts into the jumble of nameless hills that separate the mountains from their near neighbors to the east. The forest growths climb higher and higher as we go eastward but send a long tongue down into the ravines, and when at last they disappear from the hilltops altogether, there are still seen groves fastened onto the upper walls of the deepest valleys. In places the boundary of the forest meeting the steppe is as sharp and straight as a line drawn on paper—trees, not bushes, meet the grass—like that between the forest and the junipers on its upper border, as if Nature too likes to see things neatly done. The steppe vegetation varies as we go along, for no apparent reason, but the frequency of the plowing may have an effect on the nature of the plant growth. Perennials of the steppe are in general little affected by ordinary plowing since their roots go deep and suffer little from the plow. Near villages where fields probably are fallow one year and cropped the next, the fallow fields have a good hay growth, mainly one kind of grass (*Phalaris*), so that the large herds of cattle and camels we often meet are fine, fat things. Rich as is the plain, on the hills the vegetation is much richer, and when we crossed the spur at Kotal Yek Chenar, there was lush grass, untouched because of lack of water for the herds. This belt of dense vegetation ends almost as sharply against the sagebrush steppe to the east as does the forest against the grass steppe to the west.

Near dark we reached the little settlement of Garmab in the midst of the sagebrush desert. We camped beside the lukewarm spring that gives the place its name and the water that fertilizes the fields of its dozen families.

August 2. Bujnurd[1] lies in a small valley surrounded by the conventional dry mountains. The shop district is also the regulation street prescribed for modern Iran, in this case about one-quarter of a mile long, filled with very ordinary merchandise among which the only interesting items were a sort of baboon tied and muzzled outside one shop and two baby hoopoes bathing in the ashes of the corner fireplace of another. The rest of the town is no more picturesque than tumbling mud walls ever are. There are orchards

---

1. Bujnurd (37°28′N, 57°19′E, 3400 feet). This town in the Atrek River Valley was long a center for Kurdish groups, moved here from the Zagros in the eighteenth century to keep in check raiding Turkish nomads. It had a population of about 10,000 at the time of Koelz's visit. The area is one of successful dry-farming, but other manufacturers are not notable. From Bujnurd, a road of sorts goes east to Meshed and west to Gurgan.

with well grown trees of the usual temperate fruits, but fruit itself is scarce. There were late frosts, they say. In the orchards, they are cutting the heavy undergrowth of herbage for winter fodder. In the agriculture garden, they have a yellow carrot with wooly leaves much less dissected than those of the common carrot. We sleep on the roof of the office, and two peafowl roost beside us. They stay late in the morning and aren't disturbed by their unusual bedfellows. The nights are so cold that I sleep in my featherbed. — The gardener has a nice puppy with ears and tail cropped as usual. In Afghanistan too they cut off ears, and the reason given is that otherwise thieves can catch hold of them! I have also been told if the puppy is fed its docked parts it will be a good watchdog. —The agriculture director was a helpful, friendly person who seemed much interested in my herbarium, having, he said, a collection of 4000 species of Persian plants of his own. He instructed his assistant to watch me prepare bird skins so that he could make an exhibition collection for the office. The heart and brains, he supposed, were taken out in the process.

We have made arrangements with our truck to take us back to the Kotal Yek Chenar (The Pass of the Lone Plane Tree). Since there is no settlement there and probably no water, we have been busy cleaning out gasoline tins for water and gathering necessary provisions. The office assistant is going along, much to the disappointment of the gardener's helper who said he would be of some use to us, while the other would have to be looked after.

August 5. We gathered up 15 watermelons at Garmab on our way to Kotal Yek Chenar, most of which turned out to be green, but even so were more pleasant than the lukewarm water of our tins. Here the fields are irrigated and the melons have much larger air cells in the flesh than the dry-grown (*daimi*) ones of Gurgan and Bujnurd. The gasoline tins were filled with the warm water of the spring there, and the hole in the top ingeniously blocked by a piece of leather filled with earth and kept from falling into the water by being fastened to a ring of twigs. We made camp on the crest of the pass in the midst of the dense hay.

A flock of five small bustards, *Tetrax*, probably a family party, came out at evening and began flying about on the hilltop. Other birds were common too, especially seed-eaters like goldfinches and *Miliaria*, and what with them, the grasshoppers, and the ants there was hardly a seed of any kind left. The grasshoppers had chewed up the flowers and the unripe pods, and the ants had carried off what portable ripe seeds they came across. In Bakhtiari I often made good collections from the anthills: the insects had hauled home hard seeds, and finding after some days they were not what they had supposed them, they carried them out again. But here they had not reached such decisions as yet, and with great effort I got seeds of the fine alfalfa, a bush 2 feet high, an onion 18 inches tall with a flower head a foot across, another with yellow flowers, veined brown, that had buds, blooms and ripe seeds all in one head, and a curious two-leafed iris. The wooly-leafed pink that we have in our gardens is wild here, as is anise, and the only raspberry I have seen since India is just in bloom. Much of the herbage is already sere, but some late-flowering groups like Composites and Umbellifers are still fresh. Game is common. On the slopes, where the grass grows waist- or even shoulder-high, is the little barking deer, and among the thickets are plenty of pigs, so unaccustomed to human intrusion that they have no fear and barely allow us to disturb their nap. In making his way through a tangle on hands and knees, Rup Chand came face to face with a pig coming from the other direction, and at a distance of 10 feet the pig gave the right of way. On top of the ridge the ground had been torn up over large stretches, probably by bears in search of tulips and other bulbs. A lost camel stays out of our way more carefully than the native game and is verily in clover.

There are family parties of pheasant in the thickets, and wild pigeons, and on the rocky places chukors. A brood of longeared owls had been raised in a small grove of huge oaks, and I found the remains of two little owls (*Otus scops*) that they or some other night-flyer probably killed. Though we are perhaps a few thousand feet higher than at Bujnurd, the weather here is much warmer; in fact, the days are almost uncomfortably hot.

Today we went to explore the ridge, and I got separated from my friends and returned home alone. The region is said to be waterless—the camel always heads for the spring at the foot of the pass—but I found a small spring where the pigs wallowed and all the wild things came to drink. At three I reached it, half dead from thirst and drank till I shivered. When at six the men still hadn't come, I set out to look for them. An accident could hardly befall two people in such a country, but they had carried no water and didn't know about the spring and must have been suffering from thirst. At seven they came to camp, and a man came to find me. They had found my spring at five by following the mud marks on the trees where the pigs had rubbed their itchy backs when they left the mudhole, and had fallen asleep there from exhaustion. Such privations as this deeply affect what we call humanitarian impulses in the Tibetan, who is brought up under the doctrines of Buddhism which even yet have not wandered from the original principles of the unity of Creation: Man is but a link in the chain and shares the earth with other beings—quite a different concept from the one that makes him the Crown of Creation. The epithets of "ass," "camel," "pig," and "dog," which fall so hard on the ear of other races and other peoples, carry no connotation of abuse to the Tibetan. His kindly feeling toward his fellow creatures is also reflected in his dealings with his own kind: he has no religious prejudice; he may pity you for being so benighted as to have other religious views, but you are never an object of disgust or hate on that account. He comes nearest to anyone I have ever seen to ruling his life by the maxim of "Live and let live." There is moreover a natural evolution that changes a man from the destroyer of things to their preserver. Though I am so destructive to birdlife as to shock and amaze many Asiatics, who in general haven't the "sportsman's instinct" we condone or laud, I rarely kill for food, and from day to day the list grows of birds that sentiment prevents my killing for even scientific purposes, and I can forsee the time when the thrill I used to have in hunting things will give way to the quieter pleasure of being regarded by them without fear.

The view around us reaches far on all sides and presents a scene of contrast like the two faces of a mirror. To the north sweeps an arc of harsh and barren mountains, colorless and bleak, till the setting sun fills the pockets of their jagged sides with shadows in weird shapes and lends tints of red and purple to their cloak of weary gray. The disk reverses, and the horizon is bounded by rolling grassy ridges, with their black-green blotches of forest, which swing in a broad band to the east to join a lone and lofty peak bestrewn with cedars. Everything is inviting and friendly even in the sharp hard light of summer, but clothed by the eye of Fancy in the veil of Spring, the scene allures with its strange and varied plants that the plains, slopes, groves, and meadows then harbor. For me the Persian landscape has the same fascination as the stupendous landscapes of the high Himalayas, which in the same way show animate Nature in such varied guise. Nor is the pull on the soulstrings so very different. There is the same longing: in the one, upward where the eagle soars, "to the hills from whence cometh my help," and in the other, forward where the gazelle roams to distance-steeped barriers, beyond which surely lies Eternity.

Our three Persian companions are not seemingly bored by having to wait for us. They like to talk to each other, and if they maintain through the day the rate of volubility that I witness the few hours I am in camp, a great deal of information is exchanged during its course. The conversation seems most often to concern the everyday life of their several villages, with interspersions of those fanciful and hackneyed anecdotes that simple people the world over like to relate. Though all three belong to the artisan class, they are still too simple to be profane or obscene. In fact, profanity and obscenity I have never met in Asia, and the languages have no machinery for its expression. In the Asiatic languages I know, I have had to resort to literal translations from the English to try to make myself emphatic but with no success. "Go to hell" rendered into Persian or Urdu loses all its expressive finality and only puzzles and amuses the person you intended to crush. In Tibetan, there is no equivalent for the intended destination. Some of the tales the men told each other had as classic a foundation as those of devil's darning needles sewing up your ears, snakes' tails not dying till sundown, and toads making warts, though they are told by people who (like us) aren't afraid of dragonflies and toads. One involved an American

A Mulberry Tree in the Himalayan State of Chamba. Its size can be judged from the child beside it. Trees so large of any sort are now rare in India. Mulberries are far more generally grown in Iran and Afghanistan than in India, but I never saw there examples even approaching this in size.

woman whom a Luristan bear had carried off and kept as a concubine—bears are notoriously fond of women. She had been rescued after some months, and our friends had an altercation as to what the bear could meantime have fed his guest and in their dispute showed a sad lack of knowledge of the plant geography of their country. There is a kind of spider that is extremely dangerous if it drops on you. It may crawl on you without unpleasant results, but if it falls on you the consequences are serious. One of the narrators had seen a Turkoman who perished in this fashion, the man's legs were enormously swollen and evey bone in his body was dissolved. There are people who have such a deadly glance that they don't need a gun when they go hunting; one look at the game knocks it dead.

Last night there was a bit of excitement in camp. Two men passing on foot woke us up for a drink. They had a weary and fearsome walk, for settlements are far from us on either side, and after drinking they took a nap. We had nothing worth stealing and trustingly went back to sleep, but not so our companions who understood better the potential danger. When finally the travellers went on their way, they became vociferous with threats, warnings and protests, and through the rest of the night I heard snatches of their conversation. —The head of a tick that broke off in my leg made a nasty wound that lamed me for a few days, but today it cleared, leaving an impressive pit. —The Milky Way here makes a great blotch across the sky.

August 6. We were sorry to leave Kotal Yek Chenar. Below the pass a golden eagle was chasing the chukors that collected to drink at a trickle that came from the rock wall. It seemed to like to see them scatter and time after time swooped down at them with a tremendous roar.

We stopped at Garmab and had lunch. The muskmelons are getting ripe, and we bought a few from an old man who was guarding his little patch against the pigs. He knew each melon it seems and quickly selected the few he said were ready to eat. The Turkoman melon is of a different sort from our cantaloupes. It does not separate from the stem when ripe like ours. The Persian *garmak* does separate from the stem. It is generally much earlier than the *kharbuza* or Turkoman melon and usually of a quality inferior to our best, while the Turkoman melons are superior. We had lunch beside the spring, and a colony of crabs promptly gathered to pick the chicken bones. With the two fingers of its pincer, one would seize a drumstick bone, and sober and glassy-eyed, like a Chinaman with chopsticks, raise it to its mouth.

The plain beyond Garmab is strewn for miles with the huge leaves of a Cousinia-like plant, which the wind has torn from the roots that bore them. When evening drew near, we turned off our road into the village of Karak and camped at the edge of the green garden from which an old man was cutting ten-year-old poplar poles. Most of the orchards of Iran are planted to poplars. Planted as twigs, they are left to grow into trees large enough for building uses, and an income is derived with the minimum of risk and effort. Fruit trees are susceptible to more disease, and frosts often destroy the crop; in most places the market for fruit is limited, and the landlord cannot control well the marketing. Canning is possible only in the few places where there is enough produce to warrant a factory, and for the rest, whether marketed fresh or dry, the demand is restricted. The quality of fruit in the country is potentially higher than anywhere I have ever been, but the prime factors of marketing are ignored, and consequently the money value of the crop is only a fraction of what it might be. In the first place there is no standardization of varieties in the country. Nothing is named, or if perchance there is a name, it embraces so many different varieties of varying qualities that it has only a generic meaning. Thus there may be half a dozen sorts of grapes known as *askari* in one community, or the name *shahani* may be applied to any blue grape. In grapes, of course, the matter is relatively simpler since propagation is by cuttings, but in stonefruits there is often endless diversification, since many trees are pit-grown. The crop of apricots in a place then, to take an example, may consist of a dozen or several times that number of varieties, differing in size, quality, or time of ripening. They are fit, therefore, only for eating fresh, since in canning or drying, uniformity of product is desirable. Their fitness for eating fresh is moreover materially impaired by the methods of handling. They are gathered green, knocked from the tree, carried to market in sacks on donkey back, most likely with the owner riding on top. In drying, the same careless methods are employed. In a few places reasonable care—from the Persian point of view possibly extreme care—is taken in the preparation, but the best results usually fall short of American standards, and the average would hardly be acceptable in our market. Well-camouflaged gravel does much to discourage a consumer with poor teeth, even if he doesn't mind the unequal quality, dried stems, dust, and unmentionable articles apt to be swept up with the fruits after having been dried on the ground or on the roof. Our host wanted medicine for a three-year-old child with a bad diarrhea. The child was being fed on melons, which seemingly was not the most salubrious diet but maybe was the most available.

The men in Karak are often tall and handsome and speak a language I don't understand. They are said to form one of the numerous Kurdish settlements in these parts established in the region by Shah Abbas and exiles from Kurdistan. I shot a bird on the opposite bank of the stream and asked a youth to toss it to me. Instead, he waded across and soaked himself to the waist. Persian men and boys are usually very careful not to show themselves naked. I have sometimes seen women bathing together naked but only once men, and these were Lurs, the primitive mountain people of the South. The boy told me that in the hills there is a bird called *takhleitob* that when killed in the morning, weighs 1 ½ man, at noon 1 man, in the afternoon ½ man. Morning seems then to be the best time to hunt them.

We got two new passengers from here, both villagers, one, in spite of the summer heat, dressed in a long black overcoat, vest and sweater, the other in pants that reached to within a few inches of his armpits. Clothes in most of Persia, even among the enlightened of the capital are worn with somewhat a disregard of comfort, which isn't of course the original purpose of clothing after all. A Persian lady walking in the street on a summer's day in her fur-trimmed winter coat is as incongruous to me as a European sweltering in evening dress is to an equatorial savage. But this Persian conventionality also has an aim to clothe unseemly nakedness and extends even to children and youths. A young man would be about as likely to go without his pants as without his coat. The Afghans are similarly modest, and we heard that the mullahs protested against Afghan youths appearing at the Olympic Games in shorts. The Turkomans of Northern Afghanistan affect heavy wraps in summer too, but not primarily to hide sinful flesh. They wear thickly quilted chintz cloaks to keep cool and were always surprised that I could stand the heat in only a shirt, since they felt hot even in all their wrappings. The heat they try to protect themselves against is hardly so oppressive as that of Detroit. On the other hand, the Arab with his burnous has a sensible arrangement. It is of hand woven wool, not clasping, and allows air movement and acts as a parasol.

Chapter X

HOLY MESHED

August 9. We left Bujnurd at half-past seven in the evening, 36 of us plus a lot of uncounted children, packed into a bus that had the usual official notice up in it; "Capacity 23 persons with the driver's assistant." A vulture-faced old fellow in the attire of a man of God of these parts spread his shanks across my lap and stuck his elbows into my ribs and complained to the passengers that I was crowding him. They told him I seemed to be a decent person, and he quieted down. We solemnly crept out of the garage desertward and safely cleared the town before a wheel came off. From that time till dawn when we got to Shirvan, some 40 miles away, the night was spent stumbling out of the bus over each other's carcasses, lying in the thorny and now icy desert, and squeezing and shoving ourselves back in the bus again.

Shirvan[1] is a neat little place with the usual setting of low dry hills. A nice round park such as they have in most of the newly reconstructed towns had a lot of morning glories and hollyhocks, and we sat and waited in the freshness of the little oasis while they pounded away at the bus. A family of Turkomans with little children and two grandmothers had to wait too for their bus to resume its journey in the other direction. They had apparently been in Meshed and had bought a sieve, a gay porcelain bowl, and some apples. The father and mother were pleased with their purchases and fondled them appraisingly, commenting from time to time and smiling at each other. The grandmothers showed only an indulgent interest and the children none at all. They probably didn't know what apples are. At breakfast time each of the little children got a cucumber and a piece of bread. Something about it displeased the smallest one, a girl of three, and she had a tantrum in the dirt. Neither of the grandmothers paid a bit of attention, and at last the mother picked her up and carried her off.

As the morning wore on and the pounding grew no less, we sauntered off into the town but were at once spied by the police and had to go back and get our papers for them. That took half an hour, and by then the car was ready to start.

---

1. Shirvan (37°24′N, 57°55′E, ca. 3600 feet).

The country to Quchan,[1] the next town, is a broad plain with a high dry mountain wall to the left, at the base of which are patches of fields and trees, marking the place where some spring drains off a bit of the mountains' water-hoard. I couldn't see to the right but it seemed drier in that direction—low rounded hills intervene between the plain and the higher rocky mountains from which springs might be expected, and they hide from view the settlements that probably lie beyond.

On arrival at Quchan, it took half an hour to finish with the police. After writing down all the information that the passengers' passports afforded, they read the roll and asked questions. Everyone passed the examination satisfactorily. A youth aboard had a dozen gasoline tins of butter that took him 10 minutes at each stop for taxpaying and explanations. Our luggage was a matter of concern, probably on account of its bulk, but thanks to its dingy and worthless appearance they let it pass. Persian luggage is often wrapped in a nice *ghilim* or other special bit of weaving which if we owned we would carry carefully inside, not outside. At the other end of the town the same police ritual started over, and again a half-hour went by. An officer from the other post bicycled over with the document he prepared on our entry, but another was made up just the same. The passengers now began to get hungry and one by one slipped away. In spite of the driver's promise that he'd take them to a better place for lunch, the bus was soon empty. A few came back promptly with bread, cheese, and grapes but it took three-quarters of an hour to round them all up—a job which the driver deputized a passenger to do while he took the car out of sight in the desert. At half-past one the fold had been brought in again and off we went. We didn't get far till we were stopped by a half-dozen soldiers with a colossal pile of tents, rugs, bedding, and other camping paraphernalia. There began a genteel fray between them and some of our male passengers, during which voices were raised dramatically and arms carefully waved. At the proper time it all was appropriately ended by a woman who rushed into their midst with arms raised heavenward and in theatrical tones bade them peace. It seems the soldiers wanted to get in our bus with their impediments though I thought we were already loaded in a fashion that would have given pointers to a sardine canner. But I was mistaken. They found a place on the slopes of the mountain of luggage we had on the roof for their mound of baggage and even room for one of their number inside, and off we went again, leaving the other five in the desert. But rubber and iron could bear no more. The car stopped dead a few hundred yards farther on in the midst of the Persian Army. A mass of men, mules, and munitions were gathered together in the

---

1. Quchan (37°06′N, 58°30′E, 4260 feet).

waste for maneuvers, they told us, and mercifully they were all so busy with their own affairs that no one noticed we were foreigners, else someone would have suspected we had stopped on purpose to collect military information.

People in Asia suspect every stranger and all foreigners of being spies, even where to a normal mind there would seem to be no information of possible interest to anyone, and the more experience one has in that part of the world the more one sees that this point of view isn't so absurd as it at first appears. In India, especially, one is soon reconciled to the fact that his servants and every foreigner who calls on him makes a report to the Criminal Intelligence Department, to say nothing of the friendly railway employees, fellow passengers and whoever else crosses his path and stops to chat with him. Sometimes the overzealousness of these people causes some minor difficulty with the regular authorities, but for the most part nothing worse happens than that his dossier with the secret police gets bulkier. After a while one realizes his life is as public as that of a lion in a zoo, and for self-protection he takes care not to speak to people he doesn't know. There again troubles may arise, especially among sensitive people like Persians and Indians, who it seems would rather you quarreled with them than ignored them. In Iran we were always escorted by a government officer and as far as we knew his report of our activities was adequate for what corresponds to the Indian C.I.D.

We expected to spend the night where we were, but soon a nearly empty car drove up and in a little while we were packed into it more solidly than before, and at 7:00 started off for the remaining 50 miles to Meshed. We didn't tarry on the way this time except that once some police officers detained us for 10 minutes. They had a corpse—someone killed in a traffic accident during the day, they said—and probably had thought of putting it in with us. At 9:45 we got to the police post of Meshed and duly thereafter were deposited in the garage. Here they had to weigh our things and it turned out we had 70 pounds less than the estimate we had paid for at Bujnurd, but they said they didn't care about that—they were only weighing to see how much they had carried in order to settle with the broken-down car. It was now too late to leave the garage, so we climbed onto the roof, off into a corner where the odor of the privy was faintest, and went to bed. This institution in Iran is one the foreigner won't forget even if he has been brought up in the United States in the days of the back-house. The arrangement is a little sink that leads through a most inadequate tube into a cesspool which isn't as large or as deep or as far away as it should be. In the hotels the sewer gas is often stifling, and in many private houses even when this convenience isn't beside the gate as you enter, its whereabouts is no secret.

The Lovely Mosque of Hazrat Masumeh at Qom, One of the Holy Places of the Shia Muslims. The mosque is sacred to Fatima, the sister of one of the 12 Imams, and is as sumptuous as the artistic canon allows. Such places attract wealth, as do the holy places of the world generally, and formerly among their treasures were numbers of rare and costly objects of art. The great carpet of Ardebil in London is one of the better known of these things that found their way into profane hands. Only the mosques at Meshed and Isfahan in Iran rival this in beauty and splendor.

HOLY MESHED

August 10. The main part of the city of Meshed[1] has newly been laid out in paved streets, much wider than need be, as usual, and the improvements have been made at the expense of everything that was old. In one street leading to the holy shrine of the Imam Reza, a row of ancient plane trees was miraculously saved, but otherwise no American road builder could have made a cleaner sweep of obstructive trees in laying out these modern *Champs Elysées à la persane*. The shrine is a mosque of the fine style of the seventeenth century, resplendent in golden dome and minarets and said to contain many art treasures that during its existence have been donated by the pious rich. It is one of the holy places of the Shia Moslems and attracts thousands of pilgrims and of course money. A visitor to the shrine henceforth is entitled to affix the title of "Meshedi" to his name, just as a pilgrimage to holiest Mecca confers the title of "Haji." At the Reformer King's suggestion, the shrine's bank account was taken out of purely sacred hands and entrusted to a commission, a procedure which of course was resented by the more righteous element of the population. This account was tapped to build and maintain a fine hospital, and its grounds and the public park are the most attractive we have seen in the country. The hotel is also a creditable institution and has an entertaining cabaret of dancers and singers. One of the performers is a huge girl who executes Russian-looking dances very well, and one is a mute girl who does clever dances in pantomine.

The people in the streets and shops are nice looking. They say half the shopkeepers are Tabrizis or Turks from the Caucasus. The fruit and melons are the best we have seen so far in the country. The muskmelons are the incomparably luscious things we first knew in Afghan Turkestan, and they are now in season. We got about 50 sorts and gave the hotel staff a feast, since we needed only the seeds. The *hulu* from here is renowned—a 3 inch white-fleshed peach, very juicy and well flavored with an edible kernel. There are large bright crimson nectarines, large ivory-colored sour apples and sweet red ones, a large Golden Egg plum, nice golden apricots, three kinds of pears of good flavor, a half-dozen varieties of good grapes, some figs, crabapples, and even sour cherries.

---

1. Meshed (36°18′N, 59°36′E, 3300 feet). The major town of Khorasan in northeastern Iran, it became a center of pilgrimage in the tenth century A.D., but emerged as an urban center only during the sixteenth century. In addition to the shrine of Imam Reza, its mud walls, many mosques, religious schools, and caravanserais survive. In 1940 there were about 176,000 inhabitants within its garden-girded limits. Their water supply was primarily from *qanats* and wells. A traditional center of cloth manufacture and stonework, Meshed also had some more modern textile mills and food processing plants. There were four foreign consulates, banks, and several hospitals. Motor roads passed southeast toward Afghanistan and Baluchistan, west toward Tehran and northward toward the Soviet Union. There was also an airfield.

Off and on someone rapped at our door in the hotel, and every time we found no one. At last a lad of seven or eight with a dazed little thing of three was standing there. "Excuse it," said the older one with a grimace, pointing down to the other, "he doesn't know any better." In the hotel's kitchen a man has a contract to boil their rice, and Rup Chand says he does it over a fire made from an amazingly small quantity of pulverized horse manure. I had always heard how skillfully frugal the Chinese were in the use of fuel but I never saw anything remarkable in that line myself.

The nights here are chilly now. Summer is mild and passes soon on the Persian plateau. Except in the region of the Great Desert, the summer climate is not more trying than that of Detroit, and in most places is much pleasanter.

Chapter XI

KHORASAN, LAND OF LOST CITIES AND GREAT POETS

August 21. We took the bus that runs toward the Afghan frontier and came on through the king's model village of Fariman[1] to the village of Abdullabad and then on through Karizan to the Bizak mountains. At Fariman there is a good-sized village that looks much like one of our modern suburban developments, with the same bright-colored stuccos, but if some Rosedale or Fernwood of ours was the model, what the imitator failed to grasp fell out to the advantage of the result. An Agriculture Office at which our companion was the director was there. He had laid out in the grounds several formal gardens that were the most ingeniously and effectively designed of any I had seen.

We are camped on a little plain grown up to barberry bushes with pretty red fruits, and rose bushes with crimson hips and small white flowers. From two directions through the rocky bed come foaming streams of clear, cold water. The mountains rise around us dry and barren, except that here and there are green-black blotches where scrawny cedar trees are glued against the steep cliff faces. Farther back in the shelter of deep valleys there are groves of wellgrown trees, and often in the lap of the slope where springs come out, there is a meadow of tall herbage. Over the slopes are sprinkled the tantalizing dry stalks of spring flowers: tulips, irises, and onions. A lavender *Colchicum* is in bloom.

The mountain is called the Kuh-i Bizak and rises to about 9300 feet. The forest of junipers is named after the village of Bardu nearby. The junipers grow slowly, about 2 millimeters in diameter a year or 4 inches in 50 years, and those that are 6 feet through must then be ancient indeed. Two camps of charcoal burners are busy eradicating the remaining vestiges of what was once a pleasant forest.

All the birds of the high places are about us. Along the streams pairs of dippers splash and dive in the spray and now and then sing a sparkling little

---

1. Fariman (35°43′N, 59°53′E).

trill. Grosbeaks and mistletoe thrushes frequent the forest and feed on the juniper berries. The warblers *Cettia* and *Phylloscopus neglectus* hunt in the shrubby bushes of the streams and slopes. Bands of rock swallows and house martins hawk over our little plain in evening. Flocks of redbilled choughs gather something on the hillsides. Kestrels, shrikes, blackbirds, magpies, and wheatears wander at large. Vultures and golden eagles often soar overhead, and in the night the little owl and the great horned owl give a call or two.

We see a flock of ibex every day and tracks of the leopards that follow them. An old Turkoman and his son with muzzle-loaders were hunting on the mountain today and asked me not to go into the valley whither the animals had fled. The boy had a nosebleed and his father said there was too much blood in his brain. Our escort has been stuffed with the tales country people will tell their unsophisticated city brethren and is too afraid of leopards to sleep at night. He had them tie one donkey away from the rest so that the leopard in the night would find him first, and thus we'd be spared. Brigands are another bugaboo. At each out-of-the-way place we come to, the people have just been raided, somebody has been killed, and lots of others wounded by these robbers. The wounded never are visible, but neither that fact nor our assurance that we are well armed soothes our escort. The natives persuade him that for the very reason we are armed the danger is greater: the thieves will be tempted to take our guns away from us! The natives of course can't be blamed for having their little fun. The visit of government agents is hardly a pleasure to them. Even though it may not cost more than a good meal or two, you can't tell what they may get into their heads, and it is certain no good will come of it.

Our donkeys are as happy here as we are. Each of them has a colt. One of the colts spends the night near me because his mother is tied nearby. He drinks out of my water basin and steps on me as he walks back and forth. His mother is very careful not to. One donkey has a saddle cloth of a piece of rag carpet exactly like those we used to make at home. Rinchen Gialtsen always loads donkeys as we do in the Himalayas, with 80 pounds, a much lighter load than is given in most parts of Iran. In fact, one of the most unpleasant things one sees in the country is the hard treatment these poor beasts often receive. After their vacation with us in the mountains, our animals felt so fine that one threw his load and galloped off. The donkey driver said that's what comes of our foolishness. We could have got along with half the number of donkeys, saved our money, and it would have been better for everybody. Our friend said the air in the forest is much purer than elsewhere because of the evergreens, an opinion I have often heard expressed at home.

August 22. The donkeys brought us down to the Meshed highway, and we got aboard a truck going toward Afghanistan that let us down at Turbat-i Shaikh Jam.[1] We are still on the Persian side of the border, but the little town has all the earmarks of adjacent Afghanistan. Not that one can see a change in the style of architecture or city planning (though it may be the Afghanis are even more ambitious and forward-looking than their Persian neighbors for the overbuilt string of empty shops tails farther out into the desert), but definite similarities to Afghan towns meet the observant traveller's eye. Muskmelons are abundant and good; the people are now no longer Shia but Sunni Moslems; the little dove (*Streptopelia senegalensis*) is seen in the streets.

The tomb (*turbat* means tomb) of Shaikh Jam, who has been dead these 800 years, dates from the time of Tamerlane, and inside the building are good examples of plaster work of Mogul times. The decorations of the facade are of a century or two later. The design executed in tiles of blues and green is extraordinarily effective. An ancient-looking *pista* tree grows on the Shaikh's grave.

"Baluch" rugs are commonly seen here and they say are made roundabout. That explains why the Afghans call them "Herati." Those I saw are still dyed with the original vegetable dyes, and except possibly for the Kashgais and the Kurds, these are the few people left who have not given up the old dyes and adopted the more convenient coal-tar preparations. —The melons, they say, come from the nearby villages of Taiabad and Ahmedabad. We got seed of one sort that is said to mature in 40 days, a remarkably short period.

A boy of sixteen came to the *serai* in the evening and asked for help. He was penniless and sick. He had left home to find work and had worked 20 days on a bridge, when he came down with malaria. The contractor refused to give him the 4 tumans ($1.50) due for his 20 days work, and he was now destitute. Our friend gave him money to buy quinine, but when he came back to sleep in the garage they said it wasn't allowed, so Rinchen Gialtsen took him in for the night. He came here from Gunabad, 150 miles to the south of Meshed and has a mother and three little brothers there. His father had been a policeman but this year had been killed on duty, and the boy was taking his place as breadwinner of the family. He had taken on his father's hat and cut-off pants, and all too soon, his troubles. Rinchen Gialtsen

---

1. Turbat-i Shaikh Jam (35°14′N, 60°36′E, 2300 feet). A town near arid border of Khorasan and Afghanistan on a plain given mostly to grazing, it had only a few thousand inhabitants predominantly Persian speakers, when Koelz made his visit. The town is on the modern road connecting Meshed to Herat in Afghanistan.

PART OF A GOAT FLOCK ON THE MARCH NEAR THE AFGHAN BORDER. The goats are tied in pairs to a lead rope to prevent their straying. These beasts yield the famed cashmere. This grows in winter under the guard hairs and in spring it loosens into flocks and wads which are then plucked and combed off for use in weaving fine fabrics. The long hairs are often sheared then for making rope, saddle bags, and other heavy weavings. The driver of the caravan is bundled up to keep cool. He wears a quilted cloak over his coat and is about as well insulated as the goats.

promised to see that he got back safely to Gunabad. The poor thing said he'd work to pay him back.

Many people in these parts have the nasty hair disease that is so common in the country. It may leave the victim completely bald or with hairless patches. Another common skin affection is *salak*, an obstinate sore that usually attacks the cheek and requires months to run its course. Many Persians bear its burn-like scar. Trichoma is common and there are many blind. Venereal diseases are said to be prevalent. One sees pock-marked people occasionally, but the commonest diseases seem to be malaria, dysentery, and typhoid fever. Colds are not frequent and epidemics are few and light. We have been healthier here probably than anywhere.

On the way in the truck today, a half dozen soldiers played a child's game well known in Iran, called *kelagh par* ("The Crow Flies"). They put their fingers on the knee of one of their number who sings out "sparrows fly," "frogs fly," etc., and at each phrase raises his finger or not, as he pleases. The others must raise their fingers only when he mentions things that actually can fly. The one who doesn't raise his finger appropriately is beaten by the others, to a rhyme I didn't catch.

A woman passenger had the healthiest, fattest, dirtiest baby I ever saw in the country. She must be a careless sort of a mother else she would have had it bled—so much blood isn't good. I have heard that in some parts of the country they make a large number of light cuts on a two-day-old baby to let out the surplus blood, and at any rate, once a year the old blood should be drained off, especially in children. I have often seen a mass of scars on the backs of the boys where slashes had been made between the shoulder blades for this purpose, but they say veins are tapped too. I remember one mother who took her nice brown apple-cheeked baby to the bazaar and cheerfully brought it back sallow and withered, but rid of its "dirty" blood. Tibetans too like bloodshed of this sort but prefer vein cutting on forearm or leg, though the nose-tip, forehead, and behind the ears are favorable localities. Rup Chand has only a few marks and those he got when, recovering from a nearly fatal attack of malaria, they bled his living skeleton.

The Tibetan regards vaccination with disapproval, and vaccinators sent among them by the Indian Government for compulsory smallpox vaccinations earn a pretty penny by passing up unwilling patients. Injections they don't know about. The Persian seems not to mind vaccines and has a real mania for injections. They seem to treat all diseases with the hypodermic needle. Most of the patients survive, but some die before they get home, and not infrequently the victim nurses a nasty infection as a souvenir of the treatment. An old woman of our acquaintance was complaining that in all her life her son had never given her an injection and her new daughter-in-law in a few months had three, and that in the little town the last doctor had killed four patients with his needle before he moved on, probably to try his skill among less sensitive subjects.

There is a medical school in Tehran and in time there may be some capable physicians turned out, but for my part, I can't see how anyone with the sort of training that is given the Persian youth can grasp the scientific viewpoint. I have, however, seen foreigners who praised the skill of Persian physicians, but I should as soon think of consulting a Central African medicine man as any native physician between here and the Himalayas, nor for that matter have I boundless confidence in the generality of healers of my own country.

In the bearing of illness and pain, the Persian shows considerable fortitude. Disease-stricken people often walk about till the heart collapses, and in their religious festivals of mourning the ritual is one of self-immolation, which I understand may result in instantaneous death and certainly may eventually end fatally, as a result of shock and exposure. Among the Tibetans also one sees remarkable self-control. Medical workers among them and my Tibetan companions have told me many anecdotes of their stoicism in undergoing painful operations without anaesthetic, and Rup Chand tells the story of a neighbor of his who, in sewing a patch on his new daughter-in-law's shirt, stitched it to the skin of her back. The girl out of modesty didn't even squirm!

August 27. We returned to Meshed from Turbat-i Shaikh Jam and then took another conveyance that carried us on the road to the south. Since we shall have to return by this road, we arranged our stopovers so that the length of the journeys may be as suited as is possible to the capacities of endurance of the human frame.

Ferdos is a large village enclosed in an apparently ancient and tumbledown wall. There are few trees and these having been planted in recent times are small, so the town disturbs in no way the dreariness of the steppe in which it lies. Large patches of millet (*kavars*) and chini (*arzan*) are grown here (as in other parts we have lately passed through) as substitutes for or to supplement the other cereals. The northern and the western parts of Iran have more rainfall than the eastern half of the country, and there the natives can usually supply their bread wants with wheat. In other parts where the rain is less or more capricious, supplementary crops, such as corn and millets, are sown after the grain harvest. Cotton here is also a common crop.

From the melon fields we got some small watermelons with huge seeds. A boy was much distressed that one he sold us was green and started slashing up his crop to make it good. Another urged us to come out of the sun and eat the melons in his house where we could also have tea and a lunch. The boys were watching their fields from small domed huts scattered about the cultivation. Their villages are an agglomeration of such huts—each room having a domed roof, a common arrangement in the desert, where wood to make a flat roof is not available.

There is a large spring on the plain, full of fish, that boils and bubbles and throws gravel to the surface. The water is rather bitter but people say its taste varies from day to day. There are flocks of green-winged teal flying about and family parties of sandgrouse, and curiously, flocks of chukors. At first I thought we had found a new partridge, because in all my wanderings I never found chukors far from the mountain slopes, but here they were out on the plain with the sandgrouse and even inside the town, where probably the ruined old walls reminded them of their ancestral hills. Numerous ravens have also taken up their abode in the town.

The donkeys are handsome, short-necked little beasts that don't have to wear blankets made of the usual old rugs and *ghilims* patched together. They have neat black and white rugs woven especially for them, and their loads are lighter too. These must be nice people. On the way from Meshed we have met numerous caravans of donkeys that seemed to be family groups of nomads or pilgrims going to holy Meshed. A crowd of women came to the garage today to see some friends off for the holy pilgrimage and made a great hullabaloo. They wept and wailed, probably out of ancient habit. In the old days it might have been a bit risky to travel even to Meshed. Certainly a trip to Mecca used to involve considerable risk. The Yarkandis we used to meet in the Himalayas on the way to the Indian coast to embark for the sacred cities had wound up their affairs at home and were ready for the end. Nowadays they say the government here discourages trips to Arabia for economic reasons, and the flow of pilgrims toward Meshed is probably the greater. Whether because of propinquity or greater poverty in these parts of the country, the attraction of the holy place is stronger. Much of the population in the arid East is desperately poor and hence can only look with hope to the Hereafter.

Chickens here are of the form and size of White Leghorns and have a feathered topknot that conceals the comb. The dogs are nice big fat things that don't rush out to eat you. In fact, if they decently can, they ignore you. At Gunabad, where we left our protégé (the poor fellow spent the afternoon with us instead of going straight home), there was a breed I never saw, gray in color, of almost mastiff size with an Airedale-like bearded muzzle. It is a curious circumstance that I never heard of a dog in Iran, or anywhere else I have been in Asia, with the habit of killing sheep that ours so commonly acquire. And Persian dogs don't chase cats, nor do their horses shy. In Iran, hydrophobia also seems as rare as it is common in India.

August 31. Tabas[1] is one of the larger oases in the great eastern desert, on the route that connects Yezd with Meshed. The road between Tabas and Yezd is still rough, but autos traverse it. The town is a pleasant little place at this season, with lots of date gardens that have an undergrowth of citrus, pomegranate, and other shrubby things, not so dense as at Shahdad. We drove through an avenue half a mile long lined with orange trees, willows, date palms, Judas trees, and mulberry trees, and camped in the Bagh Gulshan, an attractive garden laid out in flowerbeds and the usual fruit trees, with three playing fountains under the great date palms and trees of apples, apricots, and quince and pomegranate bushes. The dates are beginning to ripen. They seem, however, to be of inferior quality, whether because they are unimproved sorts or whether the climate is not suited. We

---

1. Tabas (33°36′N, 56°54′E, 2330 feet).

THE BAGH GULSHAN AT TABAS. Few of the fine old gardens are left in Persia and little attention is paid to beautifying the remnants. In a climate that permits the culture of woody plants as far apart in their requirements as apples and dates, where roses grow like weeds, and weeds like roses, little talent is needed to make a pleasant display. Persians still know what a garden should be, and now and then effectively designed beds or sections of grounds are seen around some public building.

are near the limit of date culture in Iran, and dates are grown farther north only at a few localities about 50 miles northward. A woman came running promptly on seeing our guns and said we mustn't shoot because there was a pregnant woman in the garden. It seems pregnant women in this country can't stand gunfire. A prominent foreigner once told me that he had to pay some $25 damages for allegedly having caused two women to miscarry by firing a gun.

In the market are a few kinds of indifferent muskmelons. Watermelons are varied—the flesh is pink, apricot, or bright yellow—and some are good enough. There are some yellow-green peaches, pomegranates, and a medium-sized pear. Tomatoes and onions are the only vegetables.

Our friend has read an article on Persian cats written by a foreign connoisseur who praised the cats of Tabas, and he has made strenuous efforts to get one. It seems cats aren't common, and with difficulty he finally has got his desire. This specimen seems hardly to justify any kind of praise and is not even a good example of an alley-cat. In some of the other towns I have seen very attractively marked short-haired cats in red-browns, but he has been so impressed by the cat specialist's opinion that I can't persuade him that he can get a better cat in his back yard at home and to let this one go. The added argument that a caged cat will be a cumbersome item of luggage on our tour of the desert has also failed to impress him as it should. —In Afghanistan when people wanted to keep us from going some particular place, they always told us we couldn't go on account of the dog, or that there were women, or there wasn't a road. Here we are told there are bandits or wild pigs. —The weather is not disagreeable. A hot wind blows from the east to northeast in the afternoon, but the evenings are pleasant.

September 2. We have come some 75 miles on the rough road that leads from Yezd to the plain, where *taq* or *Haliodendron* grows. The plain has sand-drifts here and there. There are some half-dozen kinds of woody plants; two of them, the black *taq* and the white *taq*, grow to little trees. The ground around the trees seems clean and bare, but looking sharp you see there are a few desert succulents, some clumps of a sedge and a grass, and an occasional dry onion stalk. The *taq* trees are leafless but green, grow 10 feet or more high, and attain here a diameter of up to a foot. Round the edge of the plain rise tiers of sand dunes on which are better and thicker growths of trees so that the landscape in this waterless waste is green enough. Beyond the dunes are high, bare mountains. Against this grim bleak background, the green trees on the billows of sand are like a painted landscape, with somewhat of the weirdness and fantasy of a submarine forest of coral. Few living things disturb the phantom scene. Now and then a lark flies up or runs out of sight behind the green screen; an occasional hare jumps from under the bushes; there are sometimes tracks of gazelle. Burrows, probably of a desert rat, are the commonest signs of life. Two handsome little lizards, one with a purplish back that gets brighter when he is frightened, the other larger, with an orange head and blackish tail, two kinds of wasp, and a beetle complete the census of living things. Everything that moves, or the tracks in the occasional piles of shifting sand that mark even the passage of an insect, excite the hungry attention. At night there isn't a sound. A wind arose at noon and drifted the sand toward the dunes.

September 4. Our donkeys are fine strong beasts, white and sturdy, of a sort seen from time to time throughout the country. We followed the stream that brings water down from the mountain to irrigate the fields and gardens

CAMP AT DEH BALA NEAR YEZD IN A FIELD BESIDE A MULBERRY TREE. Poplar whips have been planted on the edge of the irrigation ditch next to the wall, and these as trees will be one of the crops the field will produce. The stones of the wall when properly laid require no mortar and are surprisingly durable.

of Tabas—a sharp green line across the desert, broken here and there where the water has gone underground to cross a torrent bed or to overcome some elevation. One mulberry and a fine plane tree have grown up along the way. Some 7 miles away, the green thread and the water disappear against the foothills through which the road climbs into the valley of Khaur. We meet the water that disappeared at the border of the plain as it comes down from its sources in the mountain springs and enters the long tunnel that carries it a couple of miles through hills a hundred feet high out onto the plain. The lovely gardens of Khaur lie in the lap of the mountain, dense with trees of walnut, apricot, and other deciduous trees and bushes of fig and pomegranate, with grapevines clambering over them all.

The figs are in season and the natives brought us five kinds: (1) *maibut*—green-yellow, 2 inches, said to be the best; (2) *zard*—yellow, early, and nearly gone; (3) *surkhak* or *sharbati*—rose-purple, 2 inches; (4) *sabzak*—yellow, 1 ½ inches, fine; (5) *siya*—black, 1 ½ inches. On the mountain walls fastened into the limestone rocks are bushes or trees of wild figs, with yellow or blackish fruits from ¼ to 1 inch in diameter. Some of these are edible and some have no pulp at all and are so varied that I was reminded of our hickory nuts, where no two trees have fruits alike.

The pomegranates are beginning to ripen but are still too tannic to be pleasant, though they are already being taken to the market. They showed us eight varieties: (1) *agda*—3 ½ inches, outside deep rose with port-colored acid juice; (2) *may sharafi*—like *agda*, but husk deeper in color and juice sweeter and paler; (3) *malas*—brown-red, juice cherry color, acid; (4) *shahwar*—4 inches, green-tinged pink, juice sweet pale rose; (5) *palangi*—similar but larger cells (12 mm); (6) *malaskuhi*—like *shahwar* but darker and more acid juice; (7) *mirzai*—similar to *malaskuhi*, but ripens earlier; (8) *kuhi*—much like *malaskuhi*. —Of walnuts there were five kinds, one of them a fine paper-shell, 1 ¾ inches in diameter.

At the edge of cultivation next to the mountain is the old feudal palace, now in ruins, but the pond with walls of stone and ancient cypresses on guard beside it holds water. A hundred feet above on the hill, the citadel, strongly made and beautifully designed, stands defiant still.

The goats here are mostly black and the rest are red. There are some dwarfed horseflies that are very annoying. In spite of the chilly nights they are up at the first streak of dawn and make for us human radiators. The feeble glow of our bodies hardly dispels their grogginess, and our swattings and switchings are met with a sullen persistence. But when the sun comes out they are electrified into a *joie de vivre* against which there is no resource but resignation. The Persian yellow jackets, which superficially look quite like ours, are also a wonderful insect. They come out late in the summer but are about the last insect to disappear, and they buzz about their business into the dark and, burning the candle at both ends, begin again in the chilly dusk of early morning. About the virtues of Persian ants, fleas, crickets, and sandflies, I have already discoursed. Their mosquitoes are poor-spirited creatures, disheartened at the slightest obstacles and with little ambition, not even enough to multiply themselves as they could. You seldom see one, but in proportion to their rarity and bashfulness, they seem to be deadly in bearing malaria. Few humans escape it.

Another famous insect of Iran is the locust, which, while it is said to clean some people out of their year's provision, provides a livelihood to others who dispense the appropriations the government grants for fighting them. The locusts even diverted attention from the Germans during the War and engaged airplanes to halt their invasion; they stimulated communiques and prophecies, which were, however, quite the opposite of those made about the real war: the enemy was daily getting stronger. On several occasions an international gathering of anti-locust specialists was fed under our plane trees at Karaj where they said champagne at $50 a pint was served, and from which it is said the starving menials were able to steal enough in the way of food, drink, and utensils, so that not even the most socialistic-minded had a word of censure for the extravagant expenditure.

A straight, green old man of 6 feet who is said to have been a famous hunter is tending a nice field of blooming beans. He watched Rup Chand shooting at the swallows with great interest. "Shoot higher," he said, "between the shoulders. They're tough things."

In the mountains of the southern half of the country there are numerous wild almonds and *pista* trees. (The real *pista*, *Pistaccio vera*, I have not seen wild in Iran, but it is common enough in parts of Afghanistan, even near Herat, so it may occur in some of the mountains along the Afghan border.) The fruits of both these wild trees are gathered by the natives for food, and the trees (besides their value as fuel) provide a picturesque element for the otherwise barren landscape. In some regions both these wild species are grafted with scions of cultivated varieties, but the practice never attains commercial importance. The trees are scattered; by far the majority are too large to graft, and their remoteness from habitation makes their care and preservation difficult. It seems some enterprising people in the capital saw the possibility of helping the country by a large-scale grafting program, which they say the Finance Department undertook. In this section some fabulous number of such trees were grafted, we were told. Before this I had searched for the scenes of this interesting activity but this time asked the agriculture office for a guide who could show me. The guide was a big, dignified fellow out of a Dicken's novel who called everyone "my dear sir" and who in his speech never descended from the lofty histrionic tones which so moved us adolescents in the declamation of the opening lines of Ingersoll's sermon at his brother's grave. The guide led us up the valley and across the ridge into another valley and on into the next without finding any evidence that the wild trees had been treated as described. When he saw we'd be the last to get tired, he gave up and came home. He didn't mention his grafting experiences again. This morning he was seized with diarrhea which he said he contracted from eating a slice of muskmelon. He took some native medicine that put him to bed for the day. Tonight a little old man came and tied a bundle of herbs around his belly.

September 11. Yesterday we started back from Tabas on the Meshed road and didn't stop over until we got to Turbat Haidari. On the way we passed clumps of a tall iris growing in the salt desert. The tender-hearted driver picked up an old man and woman who hadn't money to pay their fare and had no room for the man but on the roof—the helper then had to call up every few minutes to be sure he wouldn't go to sleep and fall off. We got some muskmelons at Maina which are rightly famed for their excellence.

We arrived at Turbat Haidari in the night and got off in an apricot orchard at the edge of town, the favorable location we had marked on our downward journey. The driver and his helper shook hands with us all around, and the passengers who had been our companions in the twenty-four hour journey from Tabas took a friendly farewell. The people here are nice looking and well mannered. For that matter, most Persians are pleasant mannered. Rude or rough Persians are so rare that I can't remember any except in the upper classes, where, in every country, one finds the worst as well as the best of the population. Our companion wanted Rup Chand, and the gardener sent his son to locate him. "Shall I tell him to come back?" "No," said his father, "don't say anything. Only come back and tell us where he is."

The gardens are fertile and well kept, and as usual, no one minds my trespass over the walls. The gun in my hand explains my purpose and removes the first resentment one feels at an intrusion. In one orchard I found two yellow-fleshed peaches, one nearly 3 inches in diameter. In all my travels in Asia I have found few peaches with yellow flesh. In most places they don't occur at all, but here I found a dozen varieties, all freestone. The local peach tree bears very early; a graft on a strong root may fruit the following year. Here were fruiting trees 3 feet high, and in places I have seen blooms on trees less than half that height. The trees bear well, many were even broken from the weight of their load and seem to be short-lived. A stump that had been cut showed ten annual rings. Most Persian peaches seem to be of this quick-growing sort, and nowhere have I seen anything like the trees in Himalayan Chamba that were 3 feet or more in diameter. In Chamba the mulberry trees also grew to exceptional size: over 8 feet through. In Iran, however, I saw the largest willow of my experience, a patriarch 7 ½ feet through in Luristan and near it a juniper 93 inches, and a walnut 5 feet in diameter. Plants in Luristan do many interesting things. The 4 foot rhubarb leaf and the giant-flowered dwarf iris I mentioned before are examples, and once I found a tulip bulb, presumably *Tulipa montana*, 31 inches below the surface of the ground. They have a sour mulberry there that ripens in September.

We never had a livelier seed market than here. All manner of things pour in. The gardener acts as broker and often brings the goods of those who can't clamber over the wall. There have been some fine muskmelons and good watermelons, both picked too soon; a variety of squashes, marrow, and pumpkins, and even gourds: one turtle-headed dipper and a 4 inch dwarf dipper, a very warty round yellow and a smooth flattened bright orange one. Green eggplants that are common enough in India we saw here for the first time. Whenever we buy something the broker exclaims: "Why didn't you say you wanted that! I have a lot at home." One woman who came to sell figs tarried to watch a moment after she had got her pay. When our guardian tried to hustle her along, she said something to him, and he called her shameless. "I don't see it's anything to you if I am," she answered. One man seeing me packing up herbarium specimens told me not one of them would ever grow. Usually it is assumed I am gathering plants for medicine, and my understanding is much admired, since my collection includes things no one ever uses for medicine here. "See, he knows. It's only we who are stupid."

Lots of pilgrims go up and down with their donkeys, often in flocks of 25 or 30, sometimes led by an old woman. Full buses pass too, and in them are often mullahs who lead the pilgrims in prayer at prayertime. The pedestrians frequently are singing the *chavushi*, or pilgrim's song, the burden now carried by one, now by another. On this route some are dismally poor, and their meals are often nothing but the miserable bread they have brought with them from home.

Cotton, as in most parts of the country is of two sorts: *bumi*, or native, and the longer-staple *filistini*, or foreign. They use the former for themselves because their gins won't clean the coarser seeds of the latter. Silk is also cultivated and silk cloth woven. —People are busy now spading for fall grain and mending the garden walls. There is a spring of cool but slightly salty water in a gully nearby. The Turbat (tomb) of Haidari here has nothing of interest to the sightseer, though it dates from the Moghul period. —Our men picked out half a dozen of our neighbors here who resemble folks back home. The Turkomans of Gurgan and the Hazaras we saw in Afghanistan couldn't be distinguished from Tibetans. —Lahulis often drink kerosene for digestive troubles. A drunkard once drank it by mistake for water and felt fine afterwards and spread the news.

There are numerous colonies of the big colonial sowbug that digs burrows. They and also the more common little sowbug are called *gav khuda* (God's cow). Not many things seem to be thus honored with the Deity's name. The milky corm of a sort of wild salisify (*Scorzonera*) is sometimes called *khuda jozeh* (God's walnut), and the little owl (*Otus scops*) *murgh haq* (God's bird). A tiny sedge in Lahul is called God's buckwheat (*konchok-barapo*), and of course there is God's Acre in English, and especially German, for cemetery. The devil's name has been fastened to more interesting things: besides devil's food and devil fish, Lahulis call the mullein the devil's walking stick, a long thin grasshopper his riding horse, a *Cotoneaster* his wood, the will-o'-the-wisp that is said to be quite spectacular in part of the Himalayas his fire.

A dervish at Turbat-i Shaikh Jam had his clothes made of carefully sewn-together patches. In the early days of Islam such patched clothes were the prescribed garb of certain sects of dervishes. The common dervish seen in most parts of Iran wears white and carries a special bowl called *kashkul* and a sort of two-edged axe called *tabarzin*. They are consecrated to Ali and are always singing in his praise. Pious people put money for their support into the bowls. Sometimes they give you a sprig of mint, but they don't beg directly and unlike other beggars, they take nothing but money.

September 18, Meshed. Apples are common now, in some half-dozen kinds, all sweet, in shades of yellow and red, some handsomely colored, mostly of medium size (2 ½ inches) and one with attractive salmon-colored flesh. There is a fine big green pear 4 inches high, and another similar but with a shorter neck; the nice *hulus* are still to be had as are some white peaches and a huge globose green grape, with berries 1⅛ inches in diameter called *maliki*. Cherries that we last got here on August 23 were no longer found. The Persian cherry ripens early and hangs on the tree till the end of summer. In northern Afghanistan near the Pamirs we found them nearly as late. In a Borujird garden where they ripen about mid-June, we got them until August 12. The tree is much like our undeveloped sour cherry in form and foliage and character of its fruit. A dozen sorts of winter-keeping watermelons about 12 pounds in weight, of very good quality, have come to the market. One shopkeeper was unwilling to sell me any; he said it was no time to be buying these now.

They brought a letter addressed to one Smart, and when I wouldn't take it they gave it to Wangyel. In one of the Afghan hotels they once tried to force on me an accumulation of letters of assorted addressees, all of which were already opened. Most Asiatics, and foreigners often get the habit, don't share our ideas about the sacredness of a seal, and no one in his full senses would confide to the mails what he wasn't ready to tell his own or his neighbor's wife. In Iran watchers are posted beside most mail boxes, who take the letter from your hand to see where it is going. They always throw mine into the box, and of course may only have wanted to see whether they were properly stamped.

The shops around the big mosque had a few Parthian coins in silver among their stock of religious medals, pieces of turquoise, glass beads and the like, and around each a cluster of peasants was gathered. One sees in Iran more commonly than anywhere else clear pieces of turquoise, not turquoise matrix. Indians and Tibetans seem to value fine specimens more than the Persians do, and the stone brings a much higher price among them than here. There are said to be turquoise mines near Meshed with produce of high quality. One rug shop had a nice old Bokhara, one of the few rugs of 100 years of age I have seen in the whole country. The last old one was a silk Kashan in Tehran, of the sort they say rich Americans like.

There was some trouble in getting off today because, being a religious holiday, the offices were closed and we had to rely on our own ingenuity to get transportation. Otherwise the agriculture department representatives were always able by their official or personal influence to make satisfactory arrangements. After several attempts in which we employed various ruses learned in our wanderings, we at last got into a car that left at seven and landed us in Nishapur[1] at one in the morning. In the courtyard of the garage, uncurbed, was a bottomless well, and one speculates automatically

---

1. Nishapur (36°12′N, 58°50′E, 3865 feet).

on the number of people that have probably fallen into it. Children commonly fall—sometimes two at a time—into the pools around houses where the mosquitoes hatch and drinking and wash water is stored, but what falls into the thousands of *qanat* holes throughout the country no one ever knows. In Asia one lives at his own risk, and no one forsees the day when you will be able to sue the government for damages incurred by slipping on a banana peel on the sidewalk.

I suppose the general fatalism that pervades the whole of Asia arises from the general wretchedness of humanity there, since the population is of many races and many creeds. Fate clouds the sky so thickly that the golden sun of Opportunity never shines, and not even a ray of Hope ever pierces the leaden blanket. All wealth is catalogued and assigned, and the individual must, as the proverb says, stretch according to his *ghilim* and make ready to share that *ghilim* with unnumbered posterity. For offspring that at the upper end of the social scale are a luxury are here a stark necessity, and however heavy the burden of the family be, only in the family is there to be found shelter and soul refreshment, as indispensable as bread in the bitter battle with the hostile environment, and when at last strength fails, hope of sustenance for the body. And so among the millions of Asiatics who don't know where their next meal is coming from, there is never the thought that it would be better to bear that misery alone. There is nothing in this world then but resignation and hope for better things in the next. Religion offers a promise of happier things in the Hereafter as well as the balm of resignation to endure what must be endured till then. In Iran the priest-ridden piety of the population is irksome to the youth to whom the memory of their own new-shed chains makes more impatient the bondage of others. They are influenced too by the modern political philosophy, which is also opposed to religion. Political philosophers have come to the realization that emotion is generated in an individual in a fixed quantity and like the electric current, can be diverted. What heretofore was led to flow in the channel of devotion to God, they seek to divert into the channel of devotion to the Idea Politic. The current war is splendidly demonstrating the results of this.

September 20. We went on a pilgrimage to Omar Khayyām's grave in a little garden outside the city. There is only a tombstone beside an old mosque, the Masjid Imamzada Mahruq, and it doesn't matter whether Omar lies under it. At least a pleasant place in the war-smitten remnants of a once glorious city has been set aside to honor his memory. For their other great poets—Ferdosi, Saadi, Hafez,—more elaborate, but perhaps not more fitting, monuments have been set up, and in the Occident we have often speculated why the Persian apparently doesn't value Khayyām as we do. It has even been suggested that Fitzgerald has improved on the master in his translation, but such a suggestion would hardly have been made by anyone who has read the Persian. I should say rather, that Khayyām is held by his countrymen in as high esteem as Shakespeare is by his, with this difference—that those who show appreciation of the former are sincere, since it isn't the thing to praise Khayyām as it is to laud Shakespeare. I should be certain of a wager that a far greater percentage of the literate Persian population can quote Khayyām than of the English-speaking that can quote Shakespeare.

Literary taste and criticism in Iran is of course fettered and undeveloped, but what can be expected from a society whose literature was mostly written before Columbus discovered America? The half-baked opinions of contemporary critics derive from a background of literary appreciation that does not call the Koran a book and to which the mystic poets of the Middle Ages represent the nebulous climax of poetic endeavor. The Persian then must feed his hungry soul with musty hay, with a bit of browsing on the sickly shoots of imitations of the ancient classics and the half-comprehended foreigner and the few socialistic-tinged thistles that have sprung up around the fallen dictatorship. His spring has not yet greened.

A little farther on in the desert is the site of the old city that was destroyed in the Mongol Invasion. The imperceptibly moving dust in half a millennium has covered the ruins so completely that one comprehends how it is that many of the cities of antiquity have disappeared from the earth's face, leaving not a trace of their location. After doing my own sweeping and dusting in my house in Karaj, I marvel how the existing cities keep their heads above ground. The Metropolitan Museum of Art has lately completed an excavation program and has recovered some magnificent examples of early Islamic pottery. The walls of the now subterranean rooms show frescoes which the weather will soon obliterate.

The town of Nishabur is near a high dry massif that rises abruptly from the plain. Gardens of trees are scattered among the fallow fields. Trucks are carrying cotton toward Meshed, probably to transship it to Russia. In the bazaar there are a few sorts of grapes, seemingly exceptionally sweet, one of them a remarkable *askari* with berries an inch long. There are a few yellow-fleshed peaches still, though the peach season is past, and large compressed (1 x ½ inch) thornapples called *zalzalak*, yellow in color, dotted pink and as edible as the best *Crataegus* fruits at home. The watermelons are good, and the muskmelons very good. We gave a man some money to buy muskmelons for us and when he brought them, we gave him a tip. He took it unwillingly and then seeing a donkey passing with some more, he bought three with his money. A broken one he kept for himself and the other two he offered us. They were better than ours, he said, because they were dry-grown.

A bookshop keeper was being shaved in the barbershop when I went to have a binding put on a pamphlet. They sent for him and he hurried over and did the work. The price was the oftheard "whatever you please." Of the proffered money he returned two-thirds with a "Merci." Almost everyone in Iran knows "Merci" and "Monsieur," and also "antique." The latter means "high class" or "lovely" and may be applied to comestibles, clothing, or even live things. A peasant once described one of the handsome kangaroo rats as "antique."

Many foreign words have been incorporated in modern Persian, though recently there has been a move to expurgate the language. Even Arabic words that have been in use a thousand years and have changed in meaning and in pronunciation—so that they wouldn't be received back in their original home—have had successors from the old Pahlevi, the pre-Islamic language of the country, proposed for their place. The percentage of Arabic words in use in the ordinary journalistic Persian is high, as it also is in Urdu, and it was and still is considered a finishing touch of erudition and elegance to insert a line or two of Arabic in a poem. On account of this heavy debt to Arabic and because the sacred Koran was sent from heaven in that tongue, Arabic is taught along with the mother tongue in the schools. Other foreign words are derived mostly from the French and many such are still commonly used, often in competition with perfectly adequate words of native origin. The French pronunciation is fairly well retained. One such, however, had to undergo an amusing amputation. For "cosmetic," not even the nimble-witted Arabs who have often a score of words for such important concepts as friendship, hate, envy, and trust had a suitable equivalent. Since the French form has decidedly indelicate insinuations, it was docked

Sobhanah Rabii al'Alah va bahumdah! "Glory to the great God and praise be to him!"

of the offending first syllable, which in Persian suggests fornication. The Persian for cosmetic thus has become "metic." It is not often so much thought is expended in creating words, except of course in scientific parlance, and then the results are taken for granted and, if possible, ignored.

For the last few days there have been a few clouds, harbingers of fall in the desert parts of Iran. In Mazenderan, along the Caspian Sea, the sky is seldom cloudless and I am told there often is fog for days on end. In most other parts of the country, and the same applies to most of Afghanistan; from November to March, inclusive, are months in which precipitation may be expected. There may be showers in April and perhaps a sprinkle till July, but then nothing till winter. The Indian monsoon—already enfeebled by its encounter with the Great Indian Desert—is rebuffed completely at the Afghan border, and the clouds that roll in from the Caspian are hurled back at the crest of the Elburz mountains that rim the Caspian plain. From the west and south there are no summer storms. The fall rains soften the ground for plowing the grain fields, and they start the germination of the seed. The winter snows determine the abundance of the drainage flow and the strength of the springs on which the bulk of crop growing depends; the spring rains decide the fate of the dry-sown fields and influence enormously the yield of even the irrigated fields. As I have said, and as is self-evident, the irrigation waters carry in this desert country a heavy mineral load, and at every soaking of the soil, important plant foods are rendered inert by the chemical reactions that follow, and in the end the land is made barren (*abmurdeh*—killed by water). The peasant therefore hails the rain and knows well that death lurks in his life-bringing irrigation stream.

There are two mosques in the town, unbelievably sorry concoctions of mud, tins, wire, poles and stones, as misshapen as if made of dough and then smitten by an earthquake. Iran has excelled in all the forms of art— architecture, weaving, rug making, metal work, pottery making, painting—and creditable work is still being done in some of these arts. But here truly the pendulum has swung to the other end of its arc, or has been dislocated altogether, and one would have censured as slipshod even Australian bushmen if they had been architects of such a structure.

They have *cherok* here (the article and its name apparently are Turkish and are used also by the Yarkandis of Chinese Turkestan), made much better than those we used to buy from the Yarkandis in Ladak. A *cherok* is a leather mocassin without a sole, cheap and comfortable—the best we found in northeastern Afghanistan. The Afghan *chapali*, a sort of leather sandal common in northern India, I have seen only in the Tehran market among the collection of foot gear calculated to tempt the sophisticated. The Persian *giveh* is better than all these and has the important advantage that it is in the power of everyone to make his own. Given a piece of leather for a sole, you loop-stitch your upper on it with cotton thread.

September 22. We got a ride on a truck carrying marble blocks to Tehran. The chauffeur and his apprentice were Turks. A "Turk" in Iran is a person of Turkish blood or one who speaks the Turkish language. There are large areas of the country inhabited by such people, many of whom can't speak Persian. These Turks are often of lighter complexion than the average "Persian," sometimes distinctly handsome and are considered to have different psychological traits from their Aryan neighbors. These latter frequently use the epithet *khar* (donkey) in speaking of them, and they are accused of having some of the traits we often ascribe not to donkeys but to their bastard offspring, the mule. They say the Turk element is more conservative, more obstinate, and less fickle, which shows itself in religious bigotry, and it is easy to see how this trait which makes for mental slowness has earned the contempt of the more sprightly-minded and easy-going "Persian."

The Persians, for that matter, like to classify everybody. They have not only assigned traits to all the foreigners but to themselves as well. One of the less hackneyed of the classifications of strangers, which sprang out of the war, referred to the accuracy of the war communiqués. The Turks were accused of complete fabrication; the British came a close second, with the

THE ZURKHANA. Every town of any size has such a physical culture club where members meet regularly for weight lifting, wrestling, and such exercises. This seems to be a special occasion to judge by the decorations and by the elaborate tights of the sportsmen.

Russians not far behind. The Americans and Japanese came next, and then with considerable interval, the Germans near the halfway mark. Of the Persians, the inhabitants of the various towns are spoken of as having special characteristics: Isfahanis are considered hard and stingy. A Kirmani said if you buy fire from an Isfahani, be careful he hasn't diluted it with water, and a Shirazi on the same subject, said that if you buy a sackneedle from an Isfahani, the chances are he'll have hollowed it out and filled it with

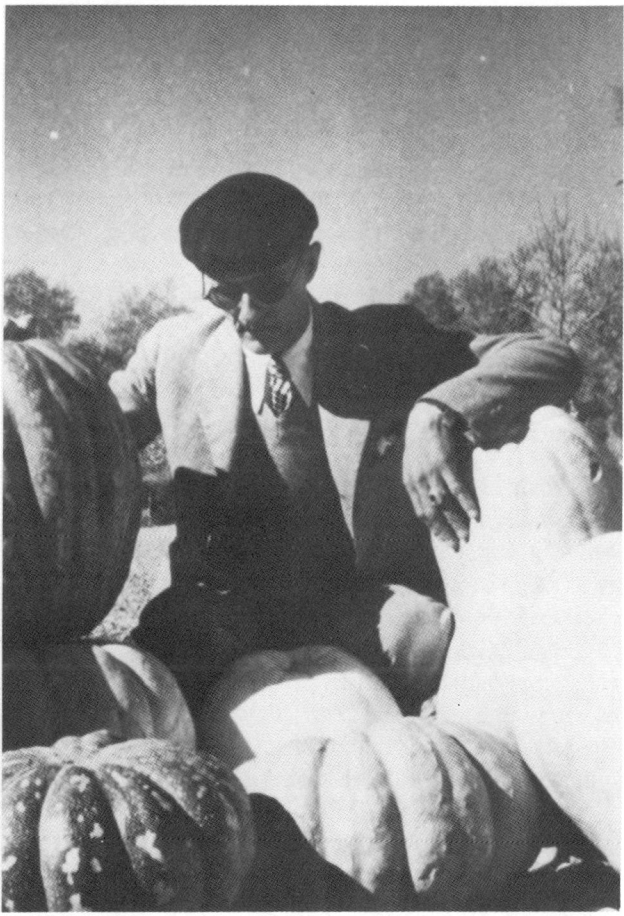

A COLLECTION OF SQUASH FROM QUETTA. Squashes are of many sorts in the Near East and may grow to exceptional size, but they are rarely edible; at least they cannot be served as we are accustomed to serve them, without the addition of stock and flavoring. The seeds, however, are an important element of the *ajeel*. Squash and pumpkin leaves and fresh shoots are an esteemed potherb, and the small fruits are a table delicacy, as we have lately learned here.

sawdust. The Kashanis are famed for timidity, and a popular story is of the sentinel who was armed with a gun in one hand and a knife in the other. Next morning when the thief had carried off the stores and the sentinel was hauled to account, he asked how he was expected to fight with both hands full. Qazvinis are supposed to be dull-witted. They once brought a frog to a Qazvin savant and asked him to identify it. The sage said from its voice it obviously was a nightingale, and since it had no feathers it was either an unfledged one, or one that had become bald with age.

The chauffeur's apprentice was a nice husky lad who once had an attack of malaria that put the fear of the Lord into him. He had never been ill before, and this blow brought him so near the pearly gates that he was always ready to tell us about his experiences with "that malaria."

We stopped for lunch at Sultanabad, a small oasis, with beautiful growths of cotton and squash. The squashes in Iran are usually inedible and are grown for seeds which are an important element of the *ajeel*. They grow to good size, often even 18 inches through, bigger than any I have ever seen, except at Quetta, but they lack sugar and flavor, and even cattle don't seem to want them. I grew American squashes at Karaj, and Banana, Delicious, and Buttercup were of first class quality. The Hubbards grew big enough but sometimes had no special taste. The pumpkin group provides the popular Japanese Pumpkin which is sweet and takes the place then of our squash. There are two or three types of marrow; the best and commonest are elongated cream-colored things when ripe. Another looks much like an unripe pie pumpkin. They had some good muskmelons at Sultanabad, and the truck took them all aboard to sell in Tehran where such good things seldom come. The apprentice tried to feed us with them during the rest of the journey. If we had accepted his invitation, his chances of profit would have been seriously diminished.

There is every indication that the Persian gets real pleasure out of feeding you, even when he can ill afford it. Even during the worst war years, when I didn't know where to turn for such essentials as flour, sugar, and butter, my neighbors with less resources than mine cheerfully entertained their visitors, and when Persians come to visit, it is from our point of view a visitation: the whole household, including the servants, and a few friends thrown in. Only in Lahul have I seen anything comparable, but it may be only because I know these two peoples best. There, where every house is on the main highway and everyone in the course of providing his necessities has long journeys to make, hospitality is as much a matter of course as—as, well, any indispensable human exercise. At all hours some weary traveller may be cared for, or more likely, some weary band of travellers. At one village at the foot of the pass that leads across into the Indian plain, most travellers are obliged to stop for the night; often the villagers are driven by the multitude of their guests to sleep with their sheep, and much of their time is spent in providing fuel for the visitors. And besides their own people, there are the droves of strangers that pour every fall out of the cold highlands beyond to spend the winter in pleasant India, and these—one and all—beg as they go. More wonderful even than their liberality is their ability to provide even for themselves, in a country where snow is apt to fall every month of the year but August, where fields have to be chiseled out of the mountain slope, and water for irrigation brought for miles, often over rough and broken ground.

Sabzavar[1] is a nice little place. The Jaghatai Mountains run east and west to bound the northern horizon, while to the south are two separate masses, one higher than the Jaghatai, called Kuh-i Mis, the Copper Mountain, said to have copper mines. In the north there are pockets of cultivation all over in the low foothills and up on the lap of the mountain. Deeply worn paths running toward the mountains bespeak their populousness.

We stopped at a mill that was packed with sacks of wheat. The harvest is freshly garnered and people are crowding the mills with their grain. We looked over the sacks and selected samples of the various kinds. The miller refused pay—the wheat wasn't his and besides the samples had no value. From a garden we wanted a few pomegranates for refreshment, and for the money we offered, the gardener insisted we take the money's worth of fruit, though we protested we had no use for the surplus. In another place the gardener was a bit suspicious and hesitated about showing us the grapes. Just then his wife came back from town and took the situation in hand. The inspection of the vineyard went as smoothly and thoroughly as a conducted tour through a cathedral, with the same, but friendlier, cascade of language. When we couldn't stay for tea, we were led over and introduced to the neighbor who had other things worth our seeing. The garden of about two and a half acres was only rented. It was a bit trying when the fruit ripened, because of thievery—not just ordinary children's plundering, but robbery by thieves who sold the booty—and a watchman had to be posted at night. And last week, an enormous cloud of starlings had descended to eat the grapes. I remember in one village in Afghanistan one year the pink starlings (*Pastor roseus*) carried off all the fruit, and when we commiserated the people, they said it was of no consequence; this year, thank God, there were no grasshoppers, on which the birds ordinarily fed, so they had to eat the fruit, didn't they? They had nine varieties of grapes in their garden: (1) *shast arus* (Bride's Finger)—a tapered berry 1¼ inch, crisp, fresh flavor; (2) *gulabi*—subelongate, ¾ inch, very sweet; (3) *nishaburi*—subglobose, ¾

---

1. Sabzavar (36°13′N, 57°42′E, 3800 feet). A market town on the arid inner margin of Khorasan, only beginning a return to the prosperity it had before the fourteenth century. It is watered by *qanats*, with whose water the Persian-speaking inhabitants grow castor beans and silk. The town is on the southern motor road from Tehran via Shahrud and toward Meshed via Nishapur.

inch, crisp, heavy bloom; (4) *bargamadi*—globose, to ¾ inch, firm flesh, tough skin; (5) *alini*—somewhat flattened, tough skin, they say keeps into the winter; (6) *divaneh* (crazy)—subelongate, 1 inch, crisp, fresh flavor, bunches to 4 pounds; (7) the usual seedless green *askari*; (8) the pink *sahibi*—here smaller than usual; (9) *siya*—a subglobose black sort with firm puckery skin. If we had come earlier they would have had three other kinds: *maskati*, *lal*, and *saraghi*. They probably forgot to mention the very early *yaquti* that is ripe in early July at this latitude.

The pomegranates here are the best we have found in Khorasan, probably because the fruits are now riper. They say they won't really be well ripened for another three weeks. They keep then until spring. Well preserved fruits can be had into March and even later. (The winter grapes till then will often be only half dried, if the bunches are hung up in an airy place.) They had five names for some eight varieties of pomegranates *maikhush*, *shirin*, *binigaji*, *leyli*, *turshizi*. (*Turshiz* is a town to the west of Turbat Haidari on the edge of the Great Desert, and everyone praises its fruit, especially the pomegranates and the grapes.) The first three are predominantly cream to greenish in color, the last two crimson, size 3 to 4 inches, juice from nearly colorless to port, flavor sweet to sub-acid.

Alfalfa is called *yurunji* here, at Nishabur, *orunje;* at Turbat Haidari, *sevisk;* at most other places we have been, including Kurdistan, *yonje*, sometimes *espes* or *aspi*, which is near the old Pahlevi name; *yonje* is said to be a Turkish name; in Afghanistan *rishka*; in Punjab *shaftal*. A widely cultivated fodder plant in most places of the country, it has been mentioned in the most ancient records dealing with Iran. It is commonly also found wild, and its cultivation may well have originated here. Throughout the mountains of the country there are important wild fodder plants, and most important are Umbellifers (parsley family) that grow on the barest mountains and are gathered for winter fodder. In Luristan there are some dozen species that are thus used as hay. The plants are mostly sturdy, generally from 3 to 5 feet tall, with finely dissected leaves, often 2 feet and more long, and all are strongly scented like all members of their tribe. Certain ones are said to be preferred by the domestic animals. The Lur names and a few remarks follow: (1) *razuna* is said to be good sheep and cow feed; (2) a species apparently like *razuna* but shorter for which I heard no name; (3) *kema* (Shirazis call it *koma*) is good donkey feed; (4) *chevil*, for sheep and cows, said to blind equines; (5) a similar species unnamed; (6) *lam* or *zool* for sheep and cows; (7) *shablile*, for sheep; (8) *bij;* (9) *koiva;* (10) *bike*, a *Heracleum* of which the scented young stalks are eaten fresh; (11) *kolpar* or *karso*, another *Heracleum* of which the seeds are sold for spices; (12) *belahar*, which is boiled for greens when tender and has a strong asafoetida scent, but neither this nor any of the others, so far as I know, yield asafoetida—that substance is not gathered by the Lurs I know. Members of

ON THE ROAD. Domestic animals of all sorts serve as beasts of burden, though not all of them may be so employed in any one place. Horses and camels are generally used to carry loads, though in places horses are only for riding. Sheep and goats are the main burden carriers where the going is rough and fodder is scarce, their place taken by the camel where the road is smooth. Cattle are the least satisfactory for such purposes, since they can't stand hard or long journeys. These are carrying straw in a rope net. Usually the carriers have a basket over their muzzle to keep them from eating one another's load along the way.

this group of plants are collected for fodder in places from Luristan to Baltistan beyond the Himalayas, and it might be worthwhile to look into their qualities. In the market there are a few handsome pink-cheeked yellow-fleshed peaches.

Our Sikh driver who brought us from Tabas to Turbat Haidari passed through on his way to Meshed from Tehran. Sikhs are a Hindu sect, more progressive than most of their brethren and are found from here to Hong Kong. Though they are probably as fine a class of people as one can find anywhere, the Persians seem not to like them, possibly because they aren't used to seeing men with uncut hair and beards. He advised us always to go on the buses carrying mail or in cars that had Sikh chauffeurs. The former had a schedule and the latter, being Indians and non-Moslems, had no friends on the way to visit with and hence got along faster. He didn't give us any advice the first time, but we're friends of several weeks' standing now. I have often noticed among my Asiatic acquaintances that after a separation, instead of being farther from them, as usually happens in absence with us, their Asiatic reserve has melted and an intimacy has been established that constant association during that time could hardly have improved. —In Iran a toss of the head upward means "No." A rapid shake of the head means "What?" Tibetans move the head as we do for assent and dissent. —We are usually taken for Russians or Germans, rarely English, probably for a reason something like that which led a man in Genoa to decide I wasn't English: I was eating an apple in the park.

September 25. A truck loaded with chick-peas came along yesterday afternoon from Bujnurd, and at half-past nine we started off in it. We rolled up on the load and slept till we got to Abbasabad at midnight when we got out and continued our sleeping in the desert. At half-past five this morning a policeman came and told us to get up, and a little later another came and shook me. I vociferated and he left. He had wanted to see the gun licenses, the driver said.

To the south of us lies that Great Desert, the Kavir Lut, the dead heart of

PLOWING AT SHAHRUD. The plow throughout Asia is a simple affair with a short point that only scratches the earth. Though the tool is simple, there are distinctions in the types used in various places. Traction is most commonly effected by cattle, rarely donkeys or camels, and never—that I recall—by horses. The plowman doesn't usually wear his foreign felt hat on such occasions, but it is more or less compulsory for appearance at the market, where the police would probably find fault with native headgear.

Persia. The village of Turun, an oasis at its northern edge, can be reached from here by caravan, they said, because there are wells on the way. There are wild asses along these shores too, we were told. They have been recorded from the desert between Tehran at the west end and Turshiz at the east, and I have heard they occur also in the Niriz desert. They seem to be found only on the edge of great desert expanses, and it is said they are shy and difficult to approach, often even keeping entirely out of sight.

When we got ready to leave, we found a truck had stopped in the middle of the road and blocked our way, a usual practice in these parts. Our driver asked mildly, "If you had got a bit to one side, would it have been a sin?"

Asiatics in general let future troubles take care of themselves, and the pound of cure is thus too far removed from reality to make even a grain of prevention worth the consideration. Their troubles then are always regrets, and seldom worries. The Persian has developed his philosophy even farther—he sees no reason on earth for ever doing more than he has to. None comprehend the fact that there is pleasure in work, and two concepts are ever in the mind: *zahamat*—trouble (in the sense of exertion) and *istefada*—benefit (in the sense of profit or advantage). The one must be avoided at all costs and at least must be followed by the other. It seems to be considered the right thing to tell folks that you are sorry you haven't been able to take advantage of them, or perhaps the Persian *az shuma istefada*

TINNING COPPER DISHES. Cooking pots are usually of copper or brass in these parts. Copper ones must be kept coated with tin to guard against food poisoning, and every town has a place where the protective wash can be applied.

burdan can be rendered into more euphemistic English.

A handsome, well preserved old fort and caravanserai at Miyan Dasht, with designs in the wall effected by varying the presented face of the bricks, stands as a reminder of the artistic skill and country-building enterprise of the seventeenth century.

September 26. Shahrud[1] lies near the Elburz Mountains that rise bare and lofty to the north, but still for all their sterile aspect, give forth abundant springs that permit extensive cultivation round their base. To the south the plain extends downward and onward into the endless Lut.

We found the largest watermelon yet seen in the country: 18 inches by 10 inches, with a weight of 30 pounds. Between here and India we have always heard of localities where large watermelons grow, and the size mentioned was always impressive, even to half a camel-load when the narrator was exceptionally enthusiastic. But we never got to the place where they grow, or if we did, the season was bad that year and the watermelons we saw, though sometimes of extraordinary quality, were never extraordinary in size. We saw in the course of the search hundreds of varieties of watermelons: round, elongate and pearshaped; blotched, striped, spotted, reticulated and plain-colored, with green or gold *cutis*, with flesh color from rose and pink to yellow and cream; with white, red, brown or black seeds, from ¼ to 1 inch long, smooth or wrinkled; dry-grown and irrigated. Some with firm flesh and little air space keep long, and one of the very best, with all desirable qualities, has almost no seeds in the stem half and only a tablespoon or so in the rest. Indian watermelons were almost never better than mediocre in taste; Afghan watermelons were often good and sometimes superlative. We usually found that the melons of good sugar content and good flavor also had other desirable characteristics: good flesh color, good size, thin rind, etc. Except for grapes, most of the other fruits are out of season. A wine-colored grape, called *dishabi*, ½ inch long, sweet, and usually seedless is the best of the several new sorts of grapes we found here.

There are huge flocks of pigeons in the fields and in a few plane trees I counted 97 ravens. While in bed I counted 350 going south. Donkeys are busy hauling gravel from the torrent beds for the railroad embankment being built toward Meshed. The stretch toward Tehran is finished, they say. This morning there was a sprinkle of rain.

---

1. Shahrud (36°25′N, 55°01′E, 4600 feet). On the arid southeastern edge of the Elburz this oasis market town of perhaps 10,000 inhabitants, largely Persian-speaking, was a center of chrome and copper mining. It was in the early 1940s the terminus of the railroad from Tehran, with oil and water facilities, as well as the point at which the all-weather road from Tehran divides into roads and toward Gurgan to the northwest and Meshed to the east.

Chapter XII

AGAIN IN THE GREAT FOREST

September 28. We found a truck going to Gurgan and at ten started off. For 6 miles the road runs through extensive cultivation and then across a 20 mile strip of foothill waste into a deep gorge, thrust far into the mountainside to divide the desert from the forest that begins at the mountain crest. Rock masses in deep red, marbled with lichen blotches of yellow and orange, dense patches of black-green cedars, and clumps of dove-gray and lavender sagebrush, paint sharp patterns on the purple slopes of the great gulf and draw a parti-colored band between the desert and the forest—bright relief in the monotonous and sombre sweep on either side, like sunset colors, between the monotony of night and day.

Thickets of oak, maple, juniper, and barberry begin on the pass, and heavy woody growth covers the steep slope to the plain below. Small settlements have been cleared in the floor of the high-walled gulch that runs up the mountain, and the harvest of the thrifty rice is under way.

At the first settlement on the plain, Shahpasand, our driver was at home and from then on he stopped at every chance. He drank tea wherever it was sold, he talked with every vehicle he met that would stop, and the night was well along when we reached our old place in the agriculture garden. We had left July 30 for our tour of Khorasan. The chauffeur thought he ought to take us over and register us with the police at the other end of town, but I protested effectively and I suppose they never found out we arrived. Only two members of the splendid frog-chorus were left in the pool, and their singing was feeble.

September 29. The horses came at five in the afternoon. The nice big-nosed official who had started us on our way to Bujnurd came to see us off. I always like to see large noses and large ears on people, perhaps from my long association with Tibetans who always represent Buddha with long ears and arms. Big chests that we so much admire, they seem not to notice. Our friend wanted some medicine for his child who has the painful eye disease that is epidemic, but he couldn't find a bottle and said he'd wait till we came back. One might think the man had no regard for his family, but there must be some other reason for this nonchalance. In the first place, life hasn't many refinements for these people, and the senses are pretty well blunted to suffering, whether their own or someone else's. I have several times found people with painful eye affections neglect to come for medicine, though they knew that I had cured their neighbors. One constantly sees people scorched by fever or choked by pneumonia dragging themselves about by the help of the last remaining drops of life force.

We set off toward the mountain and by dusk reached the last village of the foothills and turned onto the road leading through the scrub jungle that invades the plain. The blackberries are as laden with fruit as when we were here two months ago, and they still are blooming. The quantity of this fruit that could be gathered from the wild bushes that entangle the Caspian landscape is inestimable. One would think someone would have developed such an everbearing blackberry for the United States or that even this one would be cultivated there. The fruits are not of the largest but the flavor is good, and they lend themselves to wine- and jam-making as well as our cultivated product.

The air was quiet and the evening was pleasant. Numerous nighthawks that rest in the day in the shade of the bushes and nightingales that avoid the sun were now active in the road, and on all sides the roosting pheasants were croaking. The rice is being cut, and the owners are sleeping in little thatched coops on stilts, out of reach of the bears and the pigs, just like the watch huts of the peasants in the Himalayas. Some travellers were cooking supper by the roadside. Their donkey came so close to the fire that someone pushed him away. Donkeys have leopards to fear and try to find a safe place at night. In the Himalayas we used to be particularly watchful of our donkeys toward evening lest they find hiding places and disappear. The horsemen wanted us to camp with these people, but we never are so sociable as that and went on till at 7:30 we found a nice place in a clearing among the bushes. The horsemen and the animals as usual slept near us. They said they knew by certain signs that there was a leopard about—the donkeys quickly spot anything strange in the environment and point it, all the same, whether it be a jay, a fox or a leopard—and now and then the men yelled out into the darkness. The evening was cool and very damp, and there were no mosquitoes. I have often noticed that the rice fields, even in the mild climate of Kashmir, do not breed mosquitoes in any degree comparable with a marsh at home, and I never in Asia have seen these insects so troublesome as on a summer evening in Michigan. It might be found that there is some factor in the rice marshes that might be applied to control our mosquito plague. A nocturnal squirrel chirped about in the trees, and robins (*Erithaca rubecula*) sang in the bushes, as though spring and not winter were at the door.

Chapter XIII

AGAIN IN THE CAPITAL

October 3, Tehran. There were some letters from home waiting for me, plus one from Japan and one from Germany—the accumulation of the several months that we had been away. The Department of Agriculture had written that my appropriation had been approved till the end of the year and to come home accordingly, but the Legation said it would cost $700 and take two months to get home, so we decided to use up the money in exploration here. The letters from the Axis countries had obviously been opened.

In the Legation's garden, the rooks, crows, magpies, chickadees, and woodpeckers were still as common as in the early summer. These, with the house sparrows, are the principal year-round garden birds of these parts. With the exception of the rook (which doesn't go far south except in winter), they are also the principal birds of most Persian orchards and gardens. In the winter, flocks of a few kinds of northern sparrows seek the shelter of the trees, and in the summer a stray oriole, nightingale, owlet or warbler is added to the census list. Even with this paucity of flying things, I seldom have heard a name for the chickadee and never for the warbler. The woodpecker always has a name and while the appellation of the others is pretty much the same all over the country, the woodpecker's varies. I have heard 14 names for him in the Persian only. The children know that woodpeckers are the philanthropists among birds—they make homes for others, and I never knew anyone to blame them for drilling holes in the trees. While the woodpecker is thus respected, the little owl that lives in the desert and is especially at home among ruins, generally is regarded in Iran with distrust. Its presence on a house is not a good sign—it must have had a finger in making the ruins it is so fond of frequenting.

Rinchen Gialtsen came back. He had got off the train at Garmsar yesterday to buy some melons and missed the train. The melon sellers had dallied in giving him his change, about a dime, in the expectation of course that he'd go on without it, but they didn't know him. The train whistled the warning that summons the passengers who disperse in search of refreshment at every station, but Rinchen Gialtsen stayed behind and recovered his dime. The restaurant keeper at Garmsar said, whether he had money or

MUHAMED REZA PALEVI. The picture was taken while he was Crown Prince, during a visit to the Government Agriculture School at Karaj.

not, to stay with him. "After all, what can you eat, only a couple of eggs." The police loaned him a bed.

We bought two old *ghilims*, and the transaction so excited the shopkeeper and whetted his business acumen that he thought of an ancient ruse to get some more of our money. He put on a mysterious look and shut the door which made the place so dark he had to turn on the light. Then from under a pile of odds and ends he pulled out a new and badly dyed Turkoman rug and waved and wiggled it as our rug dealers do when they display their shiny flat-ironed wares to inexperienced buyers. This rug, however, didn't have any sheen.

Several little girls came to visit the Legation and of course came to see us live Tibetans. Their parents are workers in the British oil fields, and they are in boarding school in the capital. They said their school has endless rules, new ones every day. Probably the administration is composed of women. In Indian hotels run by European females we always found a formidable list of thou-shalt-nots posted on the wall of our room. I used to feel as though I were in the house of correction, but I may be supersensitive. The grim uniformed brass-ticketed conductor that demands your fare on the train always puts me in mind of the turnkey and prison-bars.

I needed some books in German and as a last resort thought of the possibility that the German Legation might have them in its library. I inquired from our Legation if I might apply to the Germans and was told the Legations weren't on good terms, but that if it were a matter of great importance, to ask.

THE SHAH OF IRAN WITH THE CROWN PRINCE. Ca. 1939, in Andimeshk, near Dizful.

The Swiss dentist today said it was a pleasure to see American dental work, that our dentists did the best work he had ever seen and Italians probably the worst. I had had a filling put in by a native dentist in Kirman, and though his equipment was primitive and old, the work seems to have been done well enough. They like here to block the cavity with disinfectant a day or two before putting in the filling. Persians in general have far better teeth than we; the teeth of youths of twenty are often sound. Whole wheat constitutes a large percentage of the diet of all Persians and may be an element in the maintenance of healthy teeth. It would be interesting to examine the dental condition of that part of the population that uses dates in place of sugar. We found when using the crystallized date juice as a spread or in cooking, our consumption of fresh fruit fell from 2 pounds per day per person to almost nothing.

October 17. We managed to get our seeds sent off to Washington a week ago. They had only perfunctorily examined the boxes to see what we were shipping, and since they had finally found instructions in their files allowing me to export seed samples and plant parts, the sealing up of the tins and turning them over to the shipping agent was done in a day. Our Minister, in order to be helpful, had signed the export papers as shipper, but Customs would not recognize his right to ship such things, so to save time and a possible jangle from which I'd suffer in the end, I submitted. It only meant I'd have to pay some fees.

The recovery of our supplies sent us from India hasn't been such a simple matter. The boxes arrived duly in the southern seaport, but there began a hopeless correspondence with brokers who required impossible papers, or if such were furnished, they needed others. There was a way to have the goods sent up here to be cleared locally where it was hoped, with the Legation's assistance, the matter would be a simple one. It didn't turn out that way, however. The papers wanted by the Customs at the southern port weren't wanted here, but others were, and today at the end of two weeks of wandering in the official wilderness, fortified by the Legation's blessing and shielded by members of the agriculture department, the end seemed near.

I was invited to visit the agricultural school at Karaj today, but there was a chance the custom's papers might be ready, so I went to the Station office to look for my man of yesterday. He had gone back to the main office, but the officer in his place said the letter I needed hadn't come, and that I should come back in a couple of days. I insisted on staying. He then started fumbling in his files and found not that letter, but one issued five months previously that authorized the delivery of my goods. I had spent two weeks traipsing about with bundles of papers and sitting for hours in offices to be told to come back tomorrow, only because it gave pleasure to the Persian officials to make me do it.

It is not an exclusively Persian trait to take advantage of any opportunity, however humble, to display authority. It is a trait exhibited by anyone the world over who dares exercise it. Our officials have been taught better than to make it an open practise, but in Asia where government machinery operates casually and crudely, the smallest officer likes to keep you waiting, and your wait is in proportion to the fear you can inspire in him. Even the

A Water Seller in the Capital. Water comes down from the mountains in canals that run through the towns, and it is regularly used for various purposes en route. The water seller, however, has ice in his glass, which is a tempting article for the thirsty. Ice is supplied from structures like our ice houses of the pre-refrigerator days. Lingering snow brought down from the mountains on donkeyback may also serve as a coolant.

servants may make the peasants who deliver food wait for their money, though they are a nuisance and may possibly carry off something, but it still is pleasant to make someone do something he'd rather not.

The official made some silly excuses and took refuge in French which he didn't know and from which I easily drove him back into the English in which our negotiations had been conducted. The officials are always obligingly ready to converse with the foreigner in any foreign language they may know and will even accept letters written in such languages. This official set to making out the orders I needed, but before he finished a friend came for a visit and held me up an hour. Then the letter went to another office for typing, which the boy said would take some time, and that I should come back in half an hour. Expressions of time in Persian are highly figurative. If you are told, "He is expected now," it means he is long overdue. If the "now" is replaced by "in half an hour," the speaker expresses his expectation of an eventual arrival. "In two hours" means "God only knows when." In this case I sat and waited, there was no place else to go—the office is at the remote end of the city—and besides, I knew if I stayed I'd be a reminder of the letter. The letter was of half a page, and the girl finished it duly and surrendered it to the boy after 15 minutes. He let it lie for 10 minutes while he sat with folded arms waiting no doubt for the foretold half hour to elapse. Then he took it, got it signed, and took me over to another office where I gave a receipt for it. My droshke that I had kept waiting (droshkes don't often show up in this part of the city) hurried me off to the other office where we arrived at 11:55. "We close at 1," said the Director, "come back day after tomorrow." Then followed a conversation that ended in his ordering the laborers to begin of releasing my three little boxes. The boxes were opened and were discovered to be exactly as declared by the American Consul in Karachi. The officials thereupon disappeared and in 15 minutes returned to say the work couldn't be finished today, did I have my seal to seal up the packages? One box had been smashed in the opening and sealing was out of the question, so I walked off.

One of the gardener's cats has a blue eye and eats grass. Fresh meat is often refused, but fried bacon never. The bacon, being *haram*, is handled only by Armenians and is usually poorly prepared. The salt doesn't penetrate properly, and the meat becomes red and semi-putrid. The bacon sellers also have several sorts of mediocre sausages, hams, some simple cheeses, caviar, pickled herrings, and sometimes sauerkraut. Wangyel bought the largest pomegranate we have seen in Iran, 5 ½ inches in diameter. In Kandahar, Afghanistan, we found plenty of fruits this large, and their quality was as good as any I ever saw anywhere. Pomegranates are generally good in Iran, but those from Saveh near here enjoy a particular renown, though I have seen nothing that justifies it.

Rup Chand tried to make a lemon pie according to a recipe he had got in the United States and made a mess of it. Rinchen Gialtsen who does the cooking was delighted. Someone sent a note for me. Rup Chand saw it and asked Wangyel if I'd read it. I had looked at it, he said, but I hadn't read it. He could tell because my lips hadn't moved.

The Agriculture Department approves my plan to visit the western part of the country but can't spare any of the young men I asked for to accompany me. Instead they are giving me the chief of the division of foreign relations, and the poor fellow is horrified. It is common knowledge that I go on foot with donkeys through leopard- and robber-infested wildernesses, and he says he can't be ready for a considerable time. I said it didn't matter, I'd go on and he could follow. His colleagues can't hide their delight at his misfortune and have arranged for my speedy departure.

I visited a merchant at his house and was shown a clock that seems to be the sort of thing the present generation of Persian likes. A gilded elephant had a clock face in its ribs and at the hour wagged its tail, curled its trunk, and wiggled its ears. A phenomenon I have not yet been able to explain to myself is the general lack of what we call good taste in most parts of Asia. In India, excepting the Moghul period, there has been no manifestation of a high-class artistic sense for a thousand years, but in Iran there is an age-old artistic tradition, and it is striking that at the present day there should be so little trace of it left. The composition of the society of today may offer an explanation. Art has taken its encouragement from the upper classes. Its sources lie in the people, and there are abundant signs that these sources are still fresh. The upper class that once was composed of those foremost in war—the bravest and best—has been recruited (since the decay of the military) from those foremost in petty trade and political machination. The same is of course true of us, but with this difference—the complexity of our economic conditions has called for a higher degree of intelligence in the same class, and while our artistic achievements have not been remarkable, the number of people with good taste is probably as high as it ever was in any period of history. They said during the war with Italy, the Abyssinian King gave guns to volunteers expecting they'd want to go fighting Italians, but instead they went out robbing, and besieged the American Legation.

October 23, Qazvin.[1] We stopped at Sharifabad on our way here yester-

---

1. Qazvin (36°16′N, 50°00′E, 4220 feet). This town of 55,000 was founded in Sasanian times and was a capital of the Safavid Dynasty before their establishment at Isfahan. A few mosques and part of the palace are the major evidences of the town's former importance. At the time of Koelz's visit, the walls were still visible. The agricultural regions around the town are watered by *qanats*; the town is both a major crossroads with all-weather roads leading east to Tehran, southward to Hamadan, westward to Mianeh and Tabriz, and northward to Rasht, and a meeting place between the major language groups with strong representations of both Persian and Turkish speakers. It has long been famous for its dried fruit and also had textile factories and flour mills. There were a major rail station, a garage, and several banks in 1940.

day and bought watermelons. The place is justly famous for the quality of its watermelons, and so far as we have seen till now, they are the best in the country. They are grown without irrigation, measure about 9 inches through, and as in most places, there are numerous varieties, all grown together. We are camping at the edge of town in an orchard, and while we prepared the watermelon seeds we had numerous visitors. It is a fast day today, and even some of the children wouldn't eat the melon we offered them.

The night was cold and for the first time this year there was a frost. A shepherd lad warned us last night it would be chilly and urged us to come home and sleep with him. The grape leaves began drying by noon and gave off a sharp autumn fragrance. There are numerous vineyards about with fruit trees scattered among the vines. All the fields are small, about 10 rods square, and have banks 3 to 5 feet high. The water is led in through deep channels with stony beds. Just now no water is evident anywhere near, so we get ours from a well in town. Long before fall the snow has melted in most places and all water comes from springs. These too grow progressively weaker and many go dry as the underground store is exhausted. In years of drought, whole villages are left without even drinking water, and cattle have to be moved. They fill the vineyard beds in the spring when the melting snows provide water to give them a soaking or two that has to last through the summer. The culture of grapes varies from one locality to another and depends no doubt on the character of the soil and the location of the groundwater. In some places, summer water stimulates the spread of mildew, and the crop may be ruined. The vines are 10 feet apart, already trimmed short, and boys are at work hauling home the leafy branches of the pruning. Grapes from Qazvin are famous for their quality. Some kinds that they say grow here are: *shafta, eloghi, yazandai, surkhak, bidaneh, tukhmi, bastokh, mushpistan*, and five others that are widely known in the country: *yaquti, askari, shahani, fakhri*, and *rishbaba (pashmak)*. —The almonds we saw are sweet and tender. Pistachios are said to be good also, but for the last two years the spring frosts destroyed the crop. —There are plenty of barn swallows, chickadees, house sparrows, grey crows, and rooks about, and woodpeckers, garden redstarts, and willow warblers are not rare. The rooks are in clouds sometimes, a thousand or so in a flock.

Our car has a talisman, a square made of straw, 6 inches on a side, bordered with red cloth. From it dangle colored cords on which are strung seed pods of *isfand* or *sipand (Peganum)*, a common desert plant whose seeds are widely used as ceremonial incense. Each day the driver crushes one of the pods after circling it around his head and around the wheel.

A little white dog came to see us on our arrival last night, and pleased with his reception, came this morning to wake us up. —The children here got into a fight. I don't remember seeing children in Iran fight before. Like

Indian children, they always look clean, well behaved, and old, and the young men tell me their parents go to considerable trouble to keep them like that. —There are turkeys about and on occasion water buffalo. The buffalo have developed a sort of hairy coat in this chilly country. In India they are virtually naked.

October 25. We left Mianeh[1] at eight without seeing any of the bedbugs for which the town is famous. There is said to be some disease-carrying human pest in this vicinity, probably a woodtick. Bedbugs we have not met anywhere in Iran, but it must be said we don't go halfway to meet them. Wherever possible, we sleep out-of-doors on the ground, or at least on the roof. Often we rent a garden instead of staying in hotels. Lice we have with us almost constantly, especially in cool weather, but luckily it isn't difficult to get rid of them, and mercifully none have been disease carriers. Lice seem not to thrive in hot weather, so there are times when we are relatively free of them.

The road was up and down over smooth earth hills, till at eleven we got to the little settlement of Gharibdast where they had wanted to take us before stopping last night. It would have been more pleasant than the dirty garage at Mianeh, but I suspected that the extra hour the driver said it would take to get here last night—plus the two hours the car owner had said might be the three hours it did take, not even counting possible flat tires. When the big Kuh Savand came into view, its top was white and a storm was gathered around it, filling its deep valleys with mist and blotting out the smooth forehills with a gray sheet of rain. The storm came on, black and furious, and rushed across our way, scattering the sky with tatters of smoking clouds.

All along the way, yokes of oxen were plowing, and the plowers' donkeys were parked at the side of the field, waiting to be ridden home in the evening. American workers have their autos waiting for them and here we have our donkeys. The foolish donkeys still switched their tails savagely as they grazed though there haven't been any flies these weeks to bother them. When the storm came, the donkeys turned their tails to it. Cattle face the tempest, and in swimming I have noticed the same tendency: cattle strike against the current while horses go with it.

There have been rains, and everywhere the landscape is sprouting. Even the roofs that have had a fresh waterproofing of earth for winter, have a shimmer of green—grain growing from the straw that is mixed with the

---

1. Mianeh (37°26′N, 47°26′E, 3510 feet). This large village in a poor Turkish-speaking district is a crossroads and river-crossing halfway between Qazvin and Tabriz on a more or less all-weather road. At the time of Koelz's visit the railway was under construction, but service from Tehran up to Mianeh was not opened until 1942.

THRESHING. The flail of colonial America is unknown in Iran. Threshing is effected by making cattle trample out the grain. The harvest is piled on a smooth clean bed, preferably a natural one, and the animals are driven around over it. A child or a woman keeps the animals in motion. Usually they are muzzled to keep them from nibbling as they work.

mud to bind it. The stubble-fields look almost as fresh as those that have been plowed and sown. So much grain was lost in the harvesting, and that takes no account of what the sand-grouse and pigeons found in their gleaning through the summer. The Persian government has harvesting machines and probably uses them, but all the harvesting I have seen has been done with hand sickles. Machinery can hardly be used except in large flat areas where watering isn't necessary, since the irrigation canals interfere with the course of the knife. Most of the wheats grown are toughhusked and stand well after ripening, and yet great quantities of grain are lost in the cutting. In the threshing also there is much waste, and here it would seem feasible to do the work with threshing machines, since these can easily be moved from one locality to another. The peasants' method of threshing, almost universally followed in Iran, is to pile their straw on the threshing floor—a circular place which has been smoothed and the ground watered and beatened down. The soil is usually such that a hard smooth floor results. Then oxen or other large animals are driven round and round over it to pulverize it with their hoofs, or more often they drag something after them, even a modified disk harrow made of wood. When the heads are thoroughly broken up, the grain is separated from the chaff by winnowing and then swept up. The winnowing is dependent on a good breeze, and it often happens that the wind doesn't blow for weeks on end while the grain lies out. What isn't threshed out of the straw by the crude manipulation of the peasant is of course eaten later by the cattle, but a lot of grain is trodden into the earth in the process or is lost in the winnowing. In spite of all the searching of the poultry flocks, the *kharmanja* (threshing place) is turned into a lawn with the first good rain of Fall.

Near Yusufabad (Josephville): The story of Joseph, which the Koran gives in a somewhat different version from that of the Old Testament, is frequently referred to in Persian literature. The various colorful episodes of his career are woven into metaphor but especially his beauty, which was probably inferred from the story of his difficulties with the governor's wife, is the subject of many similes. In fact, he and the moon are the most common standards by which Persian poets measure human beauty. He is of course reckoned among the 125,000 more or less prophets of Islam, of which Mohammed was the greatest and with whom the divine stock of prophets gave out, and countless towns in Islamic countries are named after him.

Near Yusufabad the road to Ardebil turns off, and there is a little lake on the plain in which ducks and coots are swimming. The road then climbs a steep ridge and promptly descends again in nasty echelons chiseled out of the steep mountain slope to the Tabriz Plain. At Basminj the road police took our papers, put them in an envelope, and told the driver to deliver them to the city authorities at Tabriz. They took us to the Hotel Ferdosi, as pleasant a place as one could expect to find. The rooms were large, new and clean, with running water and pleasant attendants, but no apparent heating apparatus. That is no surprise in a country where fuel is so scarce.

In their homes, the Persians have an ingenious and effective warming device called the *garmkursi* (warm chair). In a basin of ashes is buried a small quantity of live coals. This is put under a short-legged table and the whole covered with an insulation of blankets and quilts. The family sits on the floor on cushions and bolsters, with legs under the *kursi* and manages to keep very comfortable. If the fire is too hot, it makes one sleepy. A very small quantity of charcoal or charcoal dust will last all day. The *kursi* provides also a comfortable bed, and the young people of the family commonly spend the night under it. When it is necessary to heat the whole room, as in offices and at public gatherings, stoves that usually burn coal dug in the Elburz mountains or simple devices that burn oil are used.

Chapter XIV

AZERBAIJAN AND THE TURKS

October 26. Tabriz[1] was once a famous city, and there are a few remains of its glory. Some, like the Masjid Kabud, the Blue Mosque of the era of Timur, in the fourteenth century, are worth anyone's looking at. For the rest, the town is a dreary hit-and-miss collection of narrow bumpy cobblestone-paved alleys running through high, unsteady mud walls, joining on one side the large roofed-in bazaar and on the other, the long torn-up main street that runs out to the railroad station. Now and then death-traps in the way of uncurbed wells and pits are sunk into the streets.

There is a railroad line that connects the town with the Caucasus but it seems it doesn't carry much of importance this way. The shops have the same cheap trash one would find probably on the Baluchistan border, except that in one shop amid cards of false teeth, fishhooks, cheap flashlights, and saws, I found a fine assortment of German newspapers and magazines, some not over two weeks old.

The natives on the average are taller than those we have seen in most parts of the country, seldom good looking and for the most part uninteresting to look at. They also lack the pleasant manners of the rest of the Persians and are gruff and explosive, but probably have a heart of gold underneath. Most of them can't understand Persian and we don't know Turkish, so we offer a handful of coins to pay for a purchase and are always satisfied with the amount the shopkeeper leaves us. They seldom let us handle things in the

---

1. Tabriz (38°05′N, 46°18′E, 4460 feet). This city of 213,500 is the second largest in Iran and the center of Turkish-speaking Azerbaijan. Its early history is obscure, but it was a major center during early Islamic times and has since many times been a capital and many times been sacked and occupied, most recently by Turkish and Russian troops during World War I. Little remains to attest to its past importance. The surrounding gardens and agricultural regions around Lake Urmia produce grain and fruit, but the water supplied to the city by streams and canals is often insufficient. The city has much commerce and has various minority communities, particularly Armenian. There are factories for leather, soap, and matches and many smaller establishments. A railway to Russia via Julfa existed since 1916. Relatively passable roads lead northwest to Julfa and Erzerum in Turkey, southeast toward Qazvin and Tehran, and southwest to Marageh and eventually Kermanshah. In 1941 there were five consulates, a hospital, five banks, a wireless station, and an airfield.

shop because we are, of course, unclean. The campaign of enlightenment that has made such progress in other parts of the country in eliminating the more foolish customs that Islam has fostered, here has made little headway.

The Persians claim these folks are of Persian race and that the Turkish language has been imposed on them by the conquering Moghuls. Whatever the facts may be, there is in the country as sharp a distinction between these "Turks" and the Persians, especially in the Persian mind, as there is between Protestant and Catholic or Jew and Gentile in the United States. One of these differences that the Persians point out is the more conservative nature of the "Turks"—at least that is how I interpret the appelation of "donkey," which is the common synonym for "Turk."

The Persian in general is easygoing and open-minded. Nothing goes too deep, and he likes to avoid trouble. He isn't fanatical and has no interest in dying for principles or bothering you on account of yours. He is accordingly probably the poorest Moslem in all Islam—his religion is only skin-deep—and accordingly the best. Religion hasn't warped his sense of humanity as a formalized religion like Islam or Christianity is likely to do, if taken too literally and seriously. In all the country, this is the first time I noticed that anyone was really concerned with my religion.

There are special shops here, as in all Persian towns, for turning out donkey *pallan*—the padded saddle that is put on donkeys' backs to cushion them against the load. The coverings of the *pallan* are often of specially woven cloth, but frequently old *ghilims* and carpets are used, and many a time I have stopped to admire a fragment of some lovely thing of a bygone time. The donkey owners usually thought I wanted to buy the donkey. Similar old pieces are to be seen on the pads that porters use to ease their loads and that are used as upholstery in carriages.

Sitting on the streets are numerous people, often with a small glass case, displaying everything you can think of in the way of secondhand odds and ends, just like the night street-vendors of Paris and Tokyo. The difference is that the quality of the merchandise is hardly superior to what one would find on an American ash pile. There are odd pants buttons, empty medicine bottles, used corks, rusty screws, bent nails, frayed detachable collars, odd copper or brass coins of foreign countries, but occasionally too, something of value. I once bought a good hand lens among such debris, which of course to most of the customers had hardly the value of any one of the other items it was found with.

A similar institution of great benefit to the poor is the porcelain mender who plies his trade from here to the Indian border. His business is to put together your broken dishes. By his drilling and cementing and binding with metal bands, the shattered teapot is restored to its pristine usefulness. If one of the pieces should be lost he can grind down another to fit it. After Piggy reduced our teapot to fragments in a place where it couldn't be

THE TIBETAN COUNTERPART OF THE MOUNTAINTOP CAIRN. This is a *burje* on Taklung Pass, over 17,000 feet above the sea, in Ladakh. The stones have been added by travellers. Quartz fragments are popular additions both here and in Iran, and in both places rags and tatters of paper are commonly added to the pile.

replaced, one of these magicians laid hands on it, and it has done service ever since.

Similar skill is displayed in the restoration of ancient pottery and porcelains. Most of them are recovered from excavations as fragments and are joined together again, and what is missing is reconstructed either with clay, which is then appropriately painted over, or often by cleverly grinding down other fragments similarly designed and fitting them into the gap. If the piece is a rare and valuable one, much time is expended in this way.

There is a distinctive bread here called *kiuke*. On round slabs of well raised dough, a foot across, a design is put on with a mold, or even by hand, and the whole smeared with eggwhite and saffron so that it has a glazed golden surface. Its attractiveness is further increased by a crimping of the border. There are several types of bread baked in Iran, and each varies in shape and size locally, so there are a dozen or more names in use. Unlike India, where most bread is made of unleavened dough, the dough here is usually raised with a sourdough leaven, often with soda added. An unleavened bread called *fatir* is sometimes seen. But as in India, all the bread is baked in thin slabs on a griddle or against superheated oven walls. The thinnest types are *tiri* and *lavash*, usually made into circular sheets 15 inches across. Such bread dries readily but is commonly freshened with heat and water. The thickest sort, like a thick pancake, is *taptapi*, and in Tehran, *barbari*. Other types intermediate in thickness are *taftan* and *sangak*, the latter baked on gravel in slabs a yard or more long. These are the most common types seen in cities. During the war, a loaf in form and size like the American one appeared and was sold to the starving population. It had the advantage of permitting the use of any kind of flour and adulteration and was surely one of the most repulsive concoctions that ever appeared in the bread line in any country. The Persian usually likes a thin, white bread and often displays with pride its whiteness. To make it thus, his wheat must have a good gluten content.

The bread here is good in taste but gritty, and our companion, who has been educated several years in France, said the grit is due to the millstones being made of gypsum. I think more likely they grind gravel with the wheat. When the winnowed grain is finally swept up from the ground, many other things beside grain get swept up with it, and unless these extraneous items are cleaned out, their influence is felt in the bread. Weed seeds and gravel are the most common adulterants. The former are often so numerous and of such a sort that the bread tastes bitter or brings on a giddiness, and the latter so abundant that the bread is gritty. Wheat is commonly rough-cleaned by the peasants before grinding. It may even be washed, but after such cleaning plenty of foreign ingredients remain, which can only be removed by hand, and I don't suppose hands are often employed in that way. If the seeds were cleaned before sowing and the worst weeds pulled in the fields, the one obnoxious element would be eliminated. In parts of the high Himalayas grain is regularly weeded and even hoed.

There are the usual late fruits and vegetables on the market. The carrots are about a foot long and smooth, and of three colors—yellow, orange, and black-purple, round or elongate. The beets are long and bloodred. Eggplants are black-purple. Peppers are noteworthy, large red bull-noses, usually with just a bit of hot flavor so that they can be used for something besides stuffing. Persians for the most part don't like pepper, either red or black. They plant peppers to have something to stuff in season. The stuffing is a mixture of boiled rice, ground meat, horsebeans, onion, raisins, fat, and seasoning—the dish is called *dolma*. In the spring when the grape leaves are tender, the *dolma* are wrapped in them, and later cabbage leaves are also used. The grape leaves give a pleasant acid taste. *Khoresh* and *pilo* are two other standard dishes of the Persian cuisine. The former is prepared like the Indian curry, to be eaten with bread and rice and is made of combinations of meat, vegetables, and pulses with flavoring of herbs and acids. *Pilo* is steamed buttered rice, with additions of meats, vegetables, dried fruits, nuts, often colored with saffron. A sort of soup called *ahsh* is prepared with pulses and vegetables, with cheese instead of meat furnishing the stock. *Khoresh*, *pilo* and *ahsh* are of many kinds, and the *pièce de résistance* of a Moslem cook is the *pilo*.

The meal ordinarily consists of one of the above *pièces de résistance*, with bread and perhaps an entree of sour milk and a dessert of fruit. Beverages are not drunk with the meal, and only tea is likely to be served as a follower. A very elaborate meal would find the *sufreh* (a cloth usually on the floor) provided with a variety of *hazari*: sour milk, green herbs, bread, cheese, pickles, *halua* (a spiced confection of flour, sugar, and fat), jams and the like, and in season, muskmelons and grapes. The meal would consist of a *pilo* and three sorts of *khoresh*, (at least one of vegetables and one of meat), followed by fruit in season, and then tea. The character of the feast is determined by the abundance and variety of food, so to do things well you put on the table everything you have. The Persian cuisine pleases the palate of most foreigners. It has two economic drawbacks: its repertoire is limited—many food substances are not exploited—and it takes hours to prepare most Persian dishes—a serious objection in a fuelless country.

The muskmelons on the market are varied, with seeds broader than usual, but the quality is not particularly good, perhaps because the season is so far advanced. Watermelons are diversified as is usual. Here there is an exceptionally good yellow-fleshed one. Ordinarily we have found that the best watermelons are those with clear bright pink flesh while rose-fleshed or yellow-fleshed kinds are mediocre. Some 15 sorts of grapes are still on sale, and everyone assures me there are 50 or 60 sorts to be had during the year. I do not doubt that there are even more. In the matter of differentiation of kinds, the Persian is conservative. Grains he recognizes, and he names the kinds fairly sharply but of fruits the classification is loose. The grapes in Iran are all the *Vitis vinifera* that we grow in the warm places, such as California. Our strains, they told me at the Quetta Agriculture Gardens, were tender there and the quality so much inferior to local sorts—they had supposed Californians had everything so much better than the rest of the world. Certainly in Afghanistan and Iran there can be found strains that will approach *Vitis rupestris* in hardiness, and out of the great wealth of varieties, valuable new sorts may be added to our catalogs.

A few kinds of white-fleshed peaches are still on the market, one 3 inches through and another with very sweet yellow flesh, clingstone. Clingstone peaches are rare in my experience in Iran. Three kinds of plums are interesting because of their lateness. Comb honey is common. There is a village near Ardebil where they say the best honey is produced. By that they probably mean the most. Naturally most Persians have an inexperienced palate and accordingly dislike everything they aren't used to, but they also show no great discernment in the criticism of things they are accustomed to. The deplorable state of the markets bears witness to this bluntness of sense. They have bees in many parts of Iran, mostly in the colder mountain regions, where flowers are to be found during the active season of the bees. But in most places, bees have nothing to work on for too long a period, and unless honey-producing crops are planted, beekeeping can never become general. The kind of bees they have here seems to be like ours and not the migratory sort we have in India that builds its comb in the open and flies off when the food supply of the region gives out. There, a large hawk preys on the swarms and seems to subsist on the comb. One swarm that hung under a railroad bridge near Bombay supported a flock of bee-eaters (*Merops*). They sat on the telegraph wires that ran conveniently past and picked off the helpless bees as they went to and fro at their work. Honey here seems to be milder in taste than ours.

There is an orchestra in the hotel that has a limited repertoire of European music, mainly Strauss waltzes, which it plays with creditable appreciation of tempo. The rhythm of Asiatic music is so different from ours that it must be rare for a musician to play both even passably well. One of the players has a good tenor voice that would be appreciated in the United States as much as here. Persians seem to like music and are often singing as they walk along the roads. While not so incomprehensible to my ear as the music of countries farther east, it is nevertheless simple and monotonous, and the song is sung mainly for the words.

October 30. We went out to Basminj some 8 miles on the road toward Tehran. We took along an interpreter since the natives probably wouldn't know Persian and might wonder who we were, but it turned out to be unnecessary. The walls around the gardens are low and enclose orchards of the usual deciduous fruits. Willows are common, pollarded as is customary, but these seem to send up straighter longer branches from the decapitated trunk. Water is abundant and the soil in places is a good loam. Some pink-cheeked youths were digging potatoes, of which they had a good crop. There were two kinds, white and red, and each hill yielded from 25 to 45 tubers of walnut size up. This year, they said, hail damaged the plants, or the crop would have been better. The village swarms with children, all of one size, like a brood of chickens, livelier and therefore dirtier than those ordinarily seen.

The fields are filled with rooks and for the first time we saw Hungarian partridges. In a flock of 15, I got 3 and all had a cancerous growth on the bill.

Another bird we haven't seen since we left the oak forests in the south is the jay. There are small parties of them in the orchards, and here their plumage is much darker than below. Wrens, hedge sparrows, robins, and warblers seem to have come from the nearby forests of the Elburz to spend the winter or are enroute to winter quarters. —On the road big flocks of turkeys, small herds of sheep, and now and then a beef are being driven to the city. Winter is coming and they have to die. —The yellow jackets are still flying happily about though the weather isn't at all summery. Otherwise insect life, even the housefly, has retired, except that on the desert an occasional black beetle lumbers about when the sun is at its warmest.

November 2. Ardebil[1] was once a famous city, and the mosque that yielded the renowned carpet of that name still stands as a reminder of bygone splendor. The mosque, however, is so completely buried in the jumble of mud walls that comprises the present town that it hardly even contrasts with the uniform squalor of the place.

We took a pair of nice horses and drove out across the plain toward the Savalan peak, a great earthy pile that rises some 20 miles from the town by a series of steps to a height of over 10,000 feet. Half the plain was sown with grain, and teams of oxen were still plowing. The grain is sown thick. They say they cut it for fodder at an early stage and then take a crop of stunted kernels. The cattle hereabouts are larger than in most places, and those today were like middle-sized breeds of ours. There were water buffalo, too, but they seem not to have to work. In India they work very hard pulling carts, plowing, turning mills, etc., but I don't remember seeing one in yoke in Iran. Quantities of birds are feeding on the plain: rooks, crows, pigeons, sparrows, goldfinches, linnets, larks, starlings, lapwings, all in large flocks, and with them a flock of 15 kites. In the trees of cultivation we saw goldencrowned kinglets for the first time. Several large droves of turkeys are grazing on the plain, too, and geese are not rare. There is the ruin of a decagonal tower, probably of the period of the one at Gunbad Qabus, built of baked brick on a base of stone blocks.

Cultivation ascends the mountain, and the nearby slopes have all been plowed. In places there are ugly gullies. The peasants try to guard against erosion by crossing the plowed land with deep trenches. These slopes are not irrigable and can be planted only with *daimi* crops. We ascended the slope to Kalazukh, a small village on the first step, and stopped for lunch in an old orchard.

---

1. Ardebil (38°15′N, 48°18′E, 4100 feet). A town of 64,000 ca. 1940. Founded in Sasanid times, it was the home of the Safavid Dynasty and contains impressive shrines. The town was often sacked and occupied, most recently by Russians in 1916-17. It is a local market center of Turkish-speaking farmers and is known for cloth, carpets, and dried fruit. There are roads northeast to Astara in the Soviet Union and southwards toward Tabriz. The town had an airfield but few other amenities.

TREES GROWING IN A PERSIAN GARDEN. In the background are growths of young poplars, the common tree in such plantations. The poplar grows quickly and needs little space. Other trees of slower growth and of longer usefulness, like the mulberry, are sometimes interspersed in the plantations and left when the harvest is gathered. Birds collect in such places, and the nightingale is a common denizen.

The orchard was of the sort one often sees in the country: trees of all kinds, planted without order and left to grow by themselves. The unpruned apple trees, the great pear trees 2 feet and a half through, the tangled quince bushes, with purple *Colchicums* studding the carpet of fresh-fallen leaves had shaken off the hand of man. The woodcock that flushed from the cherry thicket that has encroached beyond the forest borders was as much at home as in his primeval woodlands across the northern mountains.

Time notoriously soon effaces the traces of man's activity, and in Asia where mankind was born and has now grown old, there is no longer zest or power to flaunt Eternity with Luxors or Persepolises. Mankind here has settled down to the calm, quiet course of age in the historyless society of the philosophers, where, to quote Spengler, "man becomes plant again, adhering to the soil, dumb, and enduring." The charm of Asia is this charm of the mellow age of the human race. Man no longer harrows and tears the earth, nor eradicates his fellow creatures, nor seeks to impose on Creation his physical and moral order, as in the younger lands to the west. Rather he has found his place in the scheme of things. He struggles only to maintain himself and tolerates other men and other things that live along with him, reconciled to the fact that their presence may be now and then annoying. So it is, in the Asia that I know, there are still pleasant wildernesses, and wild fowl and beasts hold forth in virgin abundance at the gates of cities. Neighbors perforce are pleasant where humanity has outgrown the maxims of its childhood, and one wonders that it ever was necessary to enjoin against bearing false witness and to do unto others as you would be done by.

Our lunch was a piece of bread a yard long and a foot wide, some eggs, comb honey and apples that some pleasant youths found for us in the village. A troop of nomads was coming down from the mountains with their animals, where they said they had spent the summer. They were heading now for the Moghan Steppe along the Russian border. In one place a sheep was lying with her fresh lamb, and to one side the shepherd's dog lay guarding them. I remember once in the Himalayas a shepherd came back along the road looking for a dog that had stayed behind on similar duty. We were able to tell him where the laggards tarried.

Wangyel moved my bed today from under a huge mirror hanging on the wall. He said he had seen a little girl narrowly escape being crushed under a sheep carcass. The mice chewed off the rope that held it and it crashed down beside her head. That evening the poor fellow met with a nasty accident himself. He slipped and thrust his arm through the skylight of the bathhouse below. Luckily the wound looked worse than it was and the bleeding was easily staunched. The hotel employees were distressed at the gory sight, and one of them brought us her best silk scarf to stop the blood.

November 6. We took a horse carriage and drove out on the road that leads to Astara on the Caspian and Russian border and stopped at the village of Namin.[1] There is a Persian frontier guard here, and we put up in their yard. If the sun shines, it is always warmer outside than in the dark thick-walled rooms of a Persian house. The houses are mostly built of sun-baked mud bricks that provide a cheap and effective insulation. There were a few chickens and a very friendly turkey already in the yard when we got there, and subsequently all the inhabitants of the house came out to sit with us. At night a flock of ducks waddled in and went into a little mud coop with

---

1. Namin (38°25′N, 48°30′E, ca. 5000 feet).

the chickens. The turkey wanted to roost on top but a soldier came out and shoved it in too.

The night was bright and mild. Magpies croaked off and on from their roosts in the orchard, a few ducks whistled on their way to some feeding place in the fields, and shooting stars flamed across the sky. I slept lightly in the tonic fall air and was awake with the first rift of light in the east before the village mullah sang out his call to prayer. Gray masses of crows flapped silently off in the half dark. Lapwings fluttered past like great moths except for their plaintive cry. The familiar farmyard sounds that proclaim the day were strangely silent. It may be the poor roosters in their dark coops have no way of knowing dawn is near.

A moth-eaten leopard skin is hanging in a tree in the garden, of the smaller spotted kind that inhabits the forests of the north. The desert sort that occurs throughout the country is larger. This particular beast is said to have eaten several people, but such performances are probably not common, since I had never heard of leopards eating folks in Iran.

We are near the Russian border to the north, and the Russian outpost can be seen on the hill. To the east the distance is not great to the cliff edge below where lies the Caspian Sea. The forest that clothes the steep slope to the sea is heralded by thickets of hazelbrush in that direction. We should like to explore the country, but everyone is nervous about our being here at all, so we take our walks down the valley and away from the Russians. The officer in charge is a hunter and told me a lot about game in Iran. He sent a hunter out to get some Hungarian partridges (*kabk chil*), but he didn't get any and returned all my cartridges. Cartridges are not to be had except at Tehran, and the man might easily have claimed he missed a shot or two.

They raise nice cabbage here—heads are flat, 15 inches across, but though solid enough, the leaves at the heart are widely spaced, leaving large air spaces there. The potatoes are among the best I ever saw: white, smooth, with eyes at the surface, solid at the core, to 9 inches long; they cook dry and floury. The most common type of potato seen in Iran (and the kind best liked, if potatoes can be said to be popular at all) is a deep-eyed yellow-fleshed sort, pasty when cooked, not mealy. The vine is weaker and the leaves smaller than the above and it is slow to ripen. Most people plant a handful of the smallest potatoes as seed and then at blossom time, pile earth a foot or more high around the vines. They claim they get a larger yield with such culture, but so far as I could see, they got only a lot of marble-or walnut-sized tubers. Of such I have seen over a hundred from one plant. They have an early potato, called *stambuli*, that I never saw in the United States, though I hear it is grown in Europe. The tubers are long and thin. There are few enemies of the plant in Iran, so far as I have seen: I saw a mild blight one year, but never insect enemies. Most of the soil is too heavy for good potato culture.

A WILD PEACH TREE IN THE HIMALAYAN STATE OF CHAMBA. The peach occurs sparingly in the wild state in the Himalayas, and such large trees can be found in its range. There are no wild peaches in Persia even though the peach is named *Amygdalus persica*. Quinces, pears, apples, grapes, figs, cherries, almonds, walnuts, and the like do grow wild there.

November 8, Sarab. We camped in a nice orchard jungle of giant pear trees undergrown with cherry trees in autumn colors—orange and red. The police captain helped us get located and said we could stay here peaceably if we preferred; he'd give a man to watch over us. Later when our escort who arrived long after us protested at such dangerous exposure, it did him no good.

The plain here is perhaps 25 miles across with the now white-capped Savalan[1] to the north. There are hot springs on the slopes of the low range

---

1. Savalan (38°15′N, 47°49′E, 15,800 feet).

on the opposite side, and the steam rises conspicuously from them. Toward sundown it rests as a mist band over the valley but fades before dark. There is an abundance of water, as is often seen in the vicinity of high mountains, and about the plain are patches of boggy meadows. As at Ardebil, villages can be seen in all directions, but here their position is marked more clearly—they have more trees.

Some boys went out in the desert with three *tazis*—a small native greyhound that is used in Iran and Afghanistan for running down game. Two were of a breed I hadn't seen before, large white things, but one was small like those of Afghanistan, and grey-black. In Afghanistan I remember seeing only brown *tazis*. In half an hour they came back with a large hare, which they said was dog food. Hares, together with donkeys from which they derive their Persian name *khargush* (donkey ear)— Tibetans call them *ribung* (wild donkeys)—belong to the *makru* class of foods, things not forbidden but that had better be left alone.

There is a woodcock in the garden. This evening he flew out to a pond in a field, and we couldn't get him up again. At sundown a hare came racing through camp pursued by three longeared owls. The owls must have been having their fun with it. I have never known them to eat anything larger than field rats.

The soldier who came to watch over us had a dog that disliked our looks, and all the master could do didn't quiet him. Rinchen Gialtsen, however, bribed him with a piece of meat. The soldier was a nice big fellow who liked his dog and in the morning refused the substantial tip we tried to give him. "Taking money from friends is bad," he said. An Afghan peasant once told me money is easy to come by but not friends.

November 10. We arrived in Tabriz at half-past three this morning. On the Tabriz Plain in the early morning we passed endless strings of camels and droves of donkeys bringing loads to the city. The donkey drivers fluttered around their beasts at the car's approach, shooing and shoving the nonchalant donkeys out of the road, but the camel drivers were of different mettle. They sauntered on as unconcerned as their handsome animals that pitched along, unmindful of the chauffeur's honking and yelling, nose high in the air and lower lip hanging in disdain. The chauffeur and his helper then would get out and chatter and gesticulate, and the camel drivers would do the same. By that time the camels were to one side and we went cheerfully on. Once there was a polite fray with a little shoving and dragging with the camel driver's stick as the point of contact and separation, but even after that our people promptly returned to their usual good nature.

We heard from our companion that Roosevelt had been reelected, that Molotov had gone to Berlin, and that Churchill said the British must look to

A Fleet of Camels Like This One May Be Seen Anywhere in Desert Persia. The beasts are usually tied one to the other and then require little attention in the march. Horse caravans usually have an attendant for every 3 or 4 beasts, depending on the character of the route. Even in competition with the truck, the camel caravan can maintain itself in many places.

1943 and 1944 for victory. I went over to see the American Mission—Presbyterians, I think—that run a hospital, but the doctor was going out to supper and I didn't stay long. One of the nurses walked back to the bazaar with me to show me where I might find something to read. I found a copy of *Window in Thrums* and a selection of Spanish stories, and the nurse found a lot of Christian books that had belonged to a missionary who had gone home. She wondered how they had got there because the owner had told her he never wanted his books to be kicked about in the bazaar. —There are two good fall pears: one 4 inches, yellow, with handsome pink cheek and the other 3 inches, greenish, also cheeked; both fine grained and of excellent flavor. A few yellow-fleshed clingstone peaches are still left in one shop. A pomegranate I have not seen heretofore is black-purple, 2 ½ inches through, with sweet purplish juice. —In a secondhand shop, I found four blue Spode plates. —A ragged boy was buying half a boiled potato. A passerby gave him a coin and with the same move that received it, he thrust it at the seller for more potato.

November 13. We engaged a Ford pickup to take us to Livan. Our companion with his assistant and a soldier went along. From Basminj a homemade road full of stones and boulders that have rolled down from the slope winds up the edge of the valley to Livan, about 12 miles above. The valley is deep and narrow, and the village of Livan—some 250 houses—sits far above it on the bare shoulder of the mountain. There are fields in the valley along the stream and on the slopes below the village, and wherever there is water, poplars and willows have been planted. The willows, if not pollarded, grow tall. The people are busy cutting off the second growth limbs, converting some into charcoal and splitting others to sell as wood in Tabriz. For themselves they keep the twigs and the leaves. Leaves here, as in the high Himalayas, are gathered for fodder and perhaps the cattle eat the bark off the twigs before they are burned, as they do in the Indian mountains. Women and children are sweeping up the leaves with brush brooms. In the gardens the apple limbs are as salmon and red as March's blasts burnish ours, and the cherries still hold their brightly colored leaves.

We put up in a large house that they say is occupied by the owner of the land hereabouts, when he comes up in the summer. Fanciful rams and lions larger than life-size, carved out of stone in the crude manner of the grave decorations of Jahrum in Fars stand guard at the doors. Even though the openings do not seem to need such guarding, the architect is so far from being of that opinion that he has painted the eyes and teeth of the beasts white to increase their ferocity. If the eye wanders away from the house, it finds a pleasant pasture in the valley straight below with its boulder-bedded stream banked by green fields and sturdy willows. An arched bridge built of small stones in the picturesque style of past centuries spans the stream, and against it shaded in willows crouches the low stonewalled mill buried in the spray of its foaming race. Up the valley are the snow-shrouded peaks in which the stream takes its source.

The men here wear loose, western style coats and trousers stuffed into high moccasins, and a sheepskin cap, the cloth homespun of light brown wool. They are all fair-skinned, red-cheeked, dark-haired, well featured, and friendly. Only a few speak Persian. Two 14-year-old boys stay with Rinchen Gialtsen to help with the household. They come early and stay late. They speak to each other only in whispers. How they take orders from their master who doesn't know a word of Turkish, I can't imagine, but I have no doubt they have a clear medium of intercourse. Both Wangyel and Rinchen Gialtsen manage to make themselves understood and to understand very quickly wherever they go. They seem to memorize phrases

A Collection of Water Mills in the Himalayas. Mills driven by water grind the grain in all mountain villages of the Middle East. Where there is no water power, hand mills may be used.

readily and construct their conversation out of a patchwork of such fragments. Their discourse is far from grammatical, but it is much clearer than my more reasonable attempts. Wangyel has learned correctly several French expressions from overhearing my conversations with our Persian companion and in one summer learned well the language of one of the Himalayan villages where he went to gather plants. He is genuinely puzzled at my method of learning Persian with books and justly points out the relatively feeble results.

November 16. The car came and took back our Persian friends. We are to come later on foot. It drizzled off and on, and snow has dusted the nearby peaks, but still it hasn't been cold enough to freeze the petunias in front of the veranda.

The sheep here are the usual fat-tailed sorts. The various sheep breeds of the country seem to be distinguished by the size of the head and of the fat tail and by the length of ears and horns. All of them are coarse wooled. Some are large bodied, notably those from Kurdistan, but nowhere have I seen anything that approaches the breed of Afghanistan for size of tail or probably quantity of flesh. There were especially large examples at Balkh, and one often sees them in the cities of northern Punjab where the lambs are sold by the Afghan nomads who winter in India. There are races of *karakulis* here (the "Persian lamb" of our fur trade), as in Afghanistan, mostly among the Turkish tribes. The fat of the tail of sheep is used in cooking and is one of the common adulterants of butter. All local sheep are much more easily kept than ours; our sheep introduced here and in the Himalayas require special care. The desert herds are used to roaming far, for grazing is often scant.

They have plenty of goats here, but none are cashmere-bearing. The

AN EXTREME DEVELOPMENT IN THE FAT-TAILED SHEEP. Such beasts are found chiefly in Afghanistan, from whence they are imported into north India. The meat is superior to ordinary mutton and the tail rates high as cooking fat. Such animals with their cumbersome tails cannot wander with the herd and are commonly kept at home.

cattle are large, like those we have seen in other parts of Azerbaijan. Sometimes two yokes of oxen are hooked to one plow, with a child sitting on the front yoke to keep the animals moving since they are out of range of the plowman's stick. The dogs are nice, big, long-haired things, often whitish, inclined to mind their own business as long as possible. So many of the dogs in the country yap and howl at every passerby and as a consequence get constantly stoned. Today I ran on to one sleeping on the hill near his resting sheep. I turned off so as not to disturb him, but when I looked back he was watching me. A white cat comes to see us every evening. It doesn't like meat and often spends the night on someone's bed. Horses are rare. I saw my first mule colt.

Both wild goats and wild sheep are common on the mountains. There are two skulls of wild rams in the house with horns larger than any we have seen between here and Tibet. In fact, old males of the species have rarely crossed our path, even in places where females and young animals were commonly seen. There are hares, and foxes are not scarce. I saw one run out of a stone pile just as a golden eagle swooped down at a cackling chukor, but neither fox nor eagle seemed interested in the other. I saw a weasel, always a rare animal in these parts.

Birdlife is diversified. There are horned larks, bloodbreasted finches, bullfinches, pied thrushes, linnets, snowfinches, and dippers about. For the first time since the Tibetan plateau have I seen pinkrumped linnets. Golden eagles are common. Two attacked a lammergeier and one of them struck him. Another with a roar of wings shot down a cliff a few yards behind a chukor that swerved easily into the shelter of a rock pile. A fresh carcass of an eagle that they say got clubbed to death when it attacked a native's hunting-hawk is lying along the river. We recalled an episode of a similar sort when a wild thing attacked a man in the Himalayas. One of our guides was lying in the grass waiting for pheasants and got seriously chewed on his head and arms by a jackal who mistook him for game. The affair might have ended still worse if his gun hadn't gone off in the struggle and scared the jackal.

Rinchen Gialtsen's boys are well enough acquainted now to talk out loud. They don't seem to mind what he feeds them, though a good Moslem ought to be careful not to eat pig derivatives, etc., but it probably doesn't occur to them in their simplicity that everybody on earth isn't Moslem. They like cake especially, and Rinchen Gialtsen's cakes are indeed nourishing food. He cooks on the principle that you can't get too much of a good thing and uses a dozen eggs to a cake and so much butter that the grease drips from the baked article. I have tried to get him to use a more conservative recipe, but he thinks I am trying to be economical and pays no attention.

There are some nice trout in our stream—red-spotted like our brook trout. One of the villagers caught some in a cast net, and we traded partridges for them. —Donkeys are carrying the bees to Tabriz for the winter. The bees are carried in their hives, long cylindrical baskets a foot or so through, plastered outside with mud. Probably spring comes sooner there.

November 27, Maragheh.[1] Some of the staff of the agriculture office wanted to go along with me today, but after half an hour tramping in the mud, they got tired and told me we'd have to go back now. We also were approaching a forbidden zone—the horse-raising farm of the army.

The town lies near the east shore of the great salt lake and probably is not more wretched than everything else in Azerbaijan seems to be. Perhaps too, things look drearier under an autumn sky. Certainly spring will transfigure the large stretches that are planted to fruit trees and vineyards and mayhap not mock the seeming misery. On the hills outside the gardens are unirrigated fields for grain. The orchards are being given the usual annual spading, at least in those where the weeds have been cut and the leaves raked. Vineyards are always tended better, and peach trees that require better care are planted in them. The plum and apricot trees seem badly damaged by borers, and apple trees and all saplings have another enemy—the hares that swarm down from the surrounding mountains at the approach of winter. In a day's walk about the town we count 40 to 60 big jackrabbits. There is also plenty of other game. Flocks of Hungarian partridges and chukors live in the vineyards, and woodcock are common. There are three very tame storks that fish along the stream that flows through the town. Two nests have been built on the roofs. One across the street from our hotel has a substantiality that indicates long tenancy. A cat this morning was sitting in it trying to catch the sparrows that have lodged themselves in the lower part, but because the storks made the nest progressively wider till it looks like a great inverted pyramid of sticks, she can't even reach over the edge.

A little dog that belongs to a shoemaker comes out and sits on its haunches all day at a certain spot in the street. It shivers a bit but pays no attention to anything, whether dog or man, and only gazes across the street. A blind man wrapped in a cloak and smoking a pipe likewise sits all day in a doorway on the other side of the street, barely leaving room for those who want to enter.

Maragheh is noted for its fruit. There are still half a dozen kinds of grapes left in the bazaar, fine and sweet, and especially nice large quinces, 4 inches

---

1. Maragheh (37°23′N, 46°13′E, 4702 feet). A town of at least 40,000 people, largely Turkish-speaking though close to Kurdish-speaking areas, Maragheh is surrounded by luxurious orchards watered by the Sufi Chai stream. Railway construction had not reached this town by 1940.

through, both sweet and acid sorts. The Persian quinces stew better than most of their apples and melt smoothly, while in the United States, they stay in obstinate lumps no matter how much you boil them. The hazelnuts and pistachios are also of good quality. Sumac has been a common bush at the fringe of cultivation since Qazvin. Its acidic fruits are widely used in cooking and can usually be found in the bazaar. The Persian, Turkish, and Kurdish name is like ours—sumac! The comb honey here is very good.

A policeman today spied me near the hotel and dashed out after me. We have been here for several days and the officials have been notified of our presence, but I didn't know Turkish to tell him all that and walked away. The police captain is an agreeable young man who has been in the American school at Tehran.

Our companion is wretched from dread of what's ahead of him. So far it hasn't been so bad because he has had with him the agriculture director of the district, a kindred soul, and there were always automobiles and hotels. But he knows that I propose to go into the Kurdish mountains outside the confines of civilized amenities, and for days he has tried to dissuade me from my fearful purpose. Most of the objections he has advanced reflect desperation rather than intelligence. In vain I have told him he could sit beside the stove at the last comfortable place we came to till my return. His immediate job is to keep me from going to Saujbulagh, the last point to the south that the auto can reach, except on the direct road to Kurdistan itself. He knows he is sentenced to stay with me till the end of the year, and my best weapon is to threaten to go to even a worse place than that. —Dogs in these parts usually have their ears uncut. —There are several interesting ruins from the time of the Moghuls, from as early as the twelfth century. — A few tortoises are still walking about and yellow jackets and some butterflies appear when the sun shines.

December 4. Saujbulagh[1] lies in a narrow valley in the low smooth hills that reach out from the Kurdish mountains toward the great salt lake. The hills are already turning green, though fall has not yet shaken the leaves from the orchards that fill the little bowl beside the town. There are many new buildings, and we are said to be the first guests in the new hotel. Certainly the windows never have been opened since they were glued shut by the paint. The people seem to be mostly Kurds, many of them as miserable wretches as I ever saw anywhere. The women often wear their elaborate old style dress, and the men sometimes have the native headgear. In general, outlandish attire in male or female is pounced on by the police, and in several places we found that folks have their own sort of hat for wear

---

1. Saujbulagh, or Mehabad (36°45′N, 45°43′E, 4800 feet).

KURDISH MEN. The Kurds are one of the four great Persian-speaking tribes of the country and live on the western border. Their territory extends into Iraq and Turkey. They are handsome, independent, often nomadic, and wear the most colorful costumes in Iran.

at home, but a European style felt hat for wear when they go to town. Once or twice the police have eyed Rinchen Gialtsen's stocking cap suspiciously. He looks less like a Tibetan than the rest of us; in fact, in India I am often more readily accepted by the Indians as genuine Tibetan than any of them.

The rugs here have better art value than others so far seen in the province. At Tabriz they are atrociously colored. We bought a nice blanket woven in two colors of undyed wool, well designed, and made with hard twisted thread.

A green woodpecker is very noisy in the orchards but I can't find him. In the forests of Mazenderan and Luristan its crazy laugh could be heard often enough, but the bird itself was most difficult to see. There are plenty of thickets too for woodcock, and in our walk today we flushed a dozen. There are dippers along the stream, still singing, and also little grebes and gallinules. We found what was left of a great horned owl. We more often find such remains than we catch sight of living ones and can't even conjecture what accident can befall so ferocious and mighty a bird. A female here weighs more than 4 pounds. Not rarely we found where little owls (*Otus scops*) have been killed and likewise the shorteared, but these presumably can easily be captured by the numerous more powerful predators.

In the bazaar were a couple of sorts of pears much like our Kieffer in size and character but of better texture and livelier taste. They say they come from the Kurdish forests around Sar Dasht. I have since had similar fruits from Kurdistan, said to have come from gardens in the region southwest of Senandaj, that are justly an esteemed winter fruit there. There are several species of drought-tolerant wild pears here and in Afghanistan. If these pears today are from the oak forests, then they are used to getting along without summer rain. One species that I have seen in the region of Ardebil has fruits smaller than these, yet the quality induces natives to collect them. In the Afghanistan steppes, there is a sort with leaves irregularly compound like misshapen rose leaves. In Luristan wild trees of pear and apple are occasionally found on the mountains but usually where groundwater is apparently near. In the lower Himalayas wild pears are very common and, besides being attractive decorations of the landscape, provide a good quantity of food to the wild things, notably the jackals, in the shape of their small late-ripening persimmon-flavored fruits. I have been told by fruit growers there that they are the most satisfactory stock for pear grafting, and it may be that something of value could be found by testing these others. —The bazaar had also a large globose grape we hadn't seen before, crisp and sweet, probably a good keeping kind, since it was still fresh at this late season. —For some reason they throw away the heads of the sheep and goats here. In other places there is a special seller of cooked heads in the bazaar.

December 6, Rezaieh.[1] The road from Saujbulagh to Rezaieh runs for a long way along Lake Urmieh, or as it has been rebaptized, Lake Rezaieh. The water is sapphire blue like the Mediterranean but the shores are often muddy, even marshy in places, and a strong salt stench rises from the mud. Sometimes feeble, dead, shingly beaches mark a former higher water level. They say the water is too salty to support fish life, but something must live in it if flamingoes frequent the shores, as we have been told. For our part, we saw no water birds of any kind.

The town lies against the foothills in a huge plain on the lip of the great bowl that holds the salt lake, the great sea that runs for a hundred miles from north to south. In the background are high, black mountains where the Turkish border lies. There is apparently plenty of water but villages are fewer than in the more barren districts of the east, and I am told workers of any kind are hard to find. Snow is said to lie on the ground for two months, and the temperature regularly to fall to 5° F. and even to 4° below zero F.

---

1. Rezaieh (37°33′N, 45°04′E, 4630 feet). Traditionally called "Urmia," it is a town of unknown origin, of at least 40,000 inhabitants, with gardens well watered by a mountain stream. In Kurdish territory, it has a Christian community and Persian- and Turkish-speaking minorities. A difficult route leads west into Turkey toward Van. Roads go north toward Khoi and around Lake Urmia to Tabriz and south and east to Mehabad and on to Kermanshah.

THE BAZAAR IN A KURDISH TOWN. The bazaar in the old days was roofed in and thus protected from the extremes of climate. Goods are exposed on the ground or in stalls. Most of these colorful structures in Persian towns were pulled down during Reza Shah's regime as unsuited to the modern trend.

Fruit orchards are not common but vineyards are, and the region is noted for its grapes.

The method of grape culture differs from place to place, even where the climate does not. Around the lake, for example, there are several modes of treatment. At Maragheh the vines are planted in the bottom of deep trenches and trained against their sides. At Sardarud near Tabriz, they grow against the high walls of the gardens. Here the vines crawl over the tops of flat ridges. In some places they cover these with earth in winter—others, leave them exposed. It is plain that among the grapes of this province are the hardiest of the varieties of *Vitis vinifera*.

We are staying in the agriculture office, located on premises that used to belong to the American missionaries. The buildings are attractive, with pleasant rooms, and the grounds are nicely laid out. There are rows of huge plane trees along the drives, as is usual in modern Persian gardens. As is also usual, all the limbs are chopped off, leaving only a tall straight trunk standing there, bristling with clusters of the year's growth of twigs that have sprung up to compensate the amputation. Men are now engaged in cutting these. In the garden there are red-twigged willows, perhaps like those I saw first in Kirman, though these seem not so brilliant and more inclined to be orange and Chinese red. The director is a nice sort and has a charming wife. Both have been in France. He showed me his museum of local seeds, among which was a good assortment of dent corn and beans. The corn of course was foreign. The only native corn is a flint that has no special qualities other than that it matures in about 90 days and often pops passably well. They frequently sell such popcorn in Tabriz and Tehran and perhaps other places. The variety is extremely susceptible to smut, which all American corns—sweet, pop or field—completely resisted in my trials at Karaj. In Afghanistan, they grew kinds with similar ear and grain, one of them remarkable in its habit of producing an ear or more at every node. Most of the beans in the collection were probably also foreign, since one commonly sees on the market not over half a dozen kinds. One of them is in appearance like a Lima bean, but of the climbing *vulgaris* group. The museum had also a collection of some dozen kinds of oaks, with leaves and acorns, which the director said he had got from the southern part of the province. In the forests along the Caspian, he said, there were plenty of wild cyclamens in winter, and violets grew everywhere.

There are large flocks of jackdaws about. Hitherto we have seen only a few and those only since we came to Tabriz. In one orchard there was a flock of the little long-tailed tits (*Aegithalos caudatus*), probably migrants from some nearby oak forest. There are clouds of starlings and the usual crows, magpies, woodcocks, finches, and other winter birds.

The market still has a few kinds of grapes and several varieties of good winter watermelons, with seeds ¼ inch long in red, white, and brown. Such small seeded watermelons were last seen in southern Afghanistan, and those were probably the finest examples of that fruit I know. A magnificent bull-nosed red pepper 6 inches long and 3 inches across is of the mild, not sweet, sort I mentioned from Tabriz. A curious netted green squash, 2 feet across, is a novelty.

December 10, Khoi.[1] We arrived at six last night and put up in the agriculture office in two rooms, each of which was furnished with a table and chair, a wastepaper basket, and a bottle of ink. In another room lived a nice old man and his wife, apparently the caretakers. Several other rooms without occupants finish the two wings, built against a torn-up court, bare except for a dead plum tree and a mutilated apple tree. A disagreeable little stream flows in under one of the courtyard walls and disappears under the house. The whole town is as cheerless as our surroundings, and the cheerful, friendly people stand out in bright relief. The agriculture officer tried his best to move us into his own house where he would of course have insisted on feeding us besides.

---

1. Khoi (38°33′N, 44°58′E, 3800 feet) is a town of Turkish-speakers in a fertile well-watered basin with easy road access to Russia to the north, Erzerum in Turkey to the west, and Tabriz to the southeast.

There is to the west a lofty mountain, which must be an alluring place in spring. There are snowcock there they say, and sometimes in the winter they bring them down to market. The snowcock here I have found to be the wariest of game, not worth the trouble of anyone's hunting. They live often in mountains so rough that even if chance grants a shot, the game falls out of reach, or a fox or eagle retrieves it ahead of you. In the Himalayas and Afghanistan the natives often trapped kindred species in a pit-trap dug around their drinking places, but I never saw such used in Iran. They tell also of strange people who live back in sheltered valleys of these mountains: of villages peopled by remnants of the ancient kingdoms of Assyria, Chaldea, and Armenia, and of people who worship the devil, who is after all only a fallen angel and someday may return to favor. They may also have the point of view of the Tibetan who believes it advisable to keep on good terms with dangerous deities and demons and consequently addresses his offerings and petitions to them. It is inconceivable that a benevolent god should do harm in any case, and most assuredly he won't take it amiss if you fail to flatter him and make him presents. Hence flattery and bribery are reserved by the heathen Tibetan for the type of divine being that is most likely to appreciate them.

Willow and poplar groves are common, likewise vineyards, but fruit orchards seem scarce. In the market there are still several sorts of good watermelons, two of them with cream-colored flesh. We hadn't seen such things heretofore. There are also several kinds of grapes, three of them new in our experience, one crisp, black-purple, with roundish berries an inch in diameter.

Two great bustards (*doidak* in Turkish, *mish murgh*, "sheep bird," in Persian), flew out today, and a golden eagle perched on a crag took after them but was easily outdistanced. These bustards occur in several parts of the country, sometimes in flocks of up to a hundred. I have seen 300 in a day's walk. The female's weight is from 8 to 10 pounds and the male's thrice as much, increasing in weight apparently with age. Our biggest one recorded weighed 28 ½ pounds, but once we saw one with more completely developed plumage that probably was heavier. In the breeding season the males inflate their throats and strut like a turkeygobbler and can then be seen for long distances on the plain. They like fields of young wheat and feed on wheat leaves or on the leaves of wild chicory. When the wheat is ready to cut, they leave these haunts, and I don't know where they stay then. They return when the fields green in the fall. The natives say they nest in the wheat. —A big prairie falcon easily struck down a sandgrouse from a flock we flushed today. Two pairs of ruddy sheldrakes or *anqut* were feeding in the wheat. We have seen these big ducks rather rarely in this country. On the lakes of the Tibetan plateau they are common in summer, and they are not rare in their winter quarters in northern India.

WANGYEL AND RINCHEN GIALTSEN AT WORK AT CAMP, SKINNING A COLLECTION OF FLAMINGOS. We were mostly on the march in Asia, and our workplace was most often a casual camp like this. In Iran it doesn't rain in summer, in India not in winter, so no other shelter than shade, and a mosquito net perhaps, is needed. Nowadays one would hardly dare such exposure.

In the bus yesterday our friend found a louse crawling up his nice overcoat and made a fearful fuss. All the passengers wondered what the noise was about, and it would have been as comprehensible to them if he had made a to-do over a fly or an ant—lice are the badge of Islam.

Today our friend found a relative of his, a colonel, and made tea for him, according to Persian custom. The number of colonels in Iran, as in Afghanistan, must be considerable. I am always meeting them, but it may be that the title is used loosely, like Professor with us. It is always pronounced as it is spelled, in French fashion no doubt. Doctor is also an appellation freely used. For such as qualify for horse doctors, the honor is accorded as a matter of course *causa meritis*, and there seems to be no objection to the simple assumption of the degree. I am told some of the prominent scientific and educational positions in the country are filled by enterprising individuals who have unblushingly assumed the title.

On the way yesterday on the low pass that opens onto the Khoi plain, there was a police post. Our car brought a tin of water there, as is apparently the custom, since there is no water near. Our chauffeur carefully cleaned and rinsed his tin before he filled it. —On this side of the lake people often push the donkeys instead of beating or goading them.

December 12. We started out from Khoi at 11:15 in the mail bus. Two turkeys sewn up in sacks with their heads sticking out rode on top inside a tire, and over them was tied a table that cracked in two on the way and fell off. In all the countries from here to the Himalayas little consideration is shown to animals. Here perhaps people are kinder than elsewhere but one constantly sees fowls transported in cramped containers and broiling heat, succumbing to the torture; overloaded donkeys; stoned and wounded, but not starved dogs. Yet they have a notion of kindness too; they would hesitate to deliberately kill. I couldn't bribe even the street urchins of Tehran to kill a crippled kitten. In India the treatment of animals reflects no human feelings whatever, and it seems the environment dries up the milk of human kindness because the rulers are both white and black. Among Tibetans and here too for that matter, a woman killing even a chicken is a scandal, and one would not so much as cut a switch to drive on the oxen.

The road leads over a low dry ridge onto a great plain with a stream, on which a large herd of camels was grazing. A little farther on across a low earth band stretches a reedy marsh from which some mallards rose. The road then runs to the right against some black hills half covered with snow and near Marand enters cultivation. At the edge of the first town, nine blackish wolves crossed the road directly in front of us. They were watching a herd of sheep grazing nearby, and we could easily have shot one from the car.

At Marand we waited for lunch and since we carry our own food, there is always time to look around while the rest are finding theirs. In the market were some small pepper-red plums, sweet and pleasant; a quince-shaped green pear of medium size and of good quality. The raisins were particularly fine, of six sorts: (a) *askari*—shade dried, therefore translucent green-yellow, seedless, 19 mm; (b) *kishmishi*—seedless, red-brown, 14-17 mm; (c) *sabza*—seedless, plump, firm, light red, 10-12 mm; (d) *dizmareh*—dark, plump, one seed, 20-23 mm; (e) *tabazi*—dark, weak flesh, one seed, 16 mm; (f) *mevij*—dark, seedy, weak flesh, 20 mm. Near the bazaar I found a well cultivated orchard of apricot trees with well formed and properly spaced trees, something I hadn't yet seen in all the land. The town is the home of an attractive breed of chickens; the birds are of good size, black, with erect tail and heavily feathered legs and feet.

AZERBAIJAN AND THE TURKS

From Marand the road follows the railroad track that runs to Russia, through a narrow valley flanked by low smooth hills. At the police outpost of Tabriz for some reason the inspector searched the floor of the car as thoroughly as if he expected to find something, even making the passengers lift up their feet, but he concerned himself not at all with the baggage on the roof. Arrived at the hotel we of course wanted to get out, but the police wouldn't allow the unloading of our luggage there, so we rode on to the garage.

The sun sank tonight in colors that, tangled in the meshes of the cloud net overhanging the west, painted the west in reds and purples of a softness and richness that is as rare as foreign to the desert scene. More often in the clear and cloudless sky the sun departs in a glare of incandescent brassy light that is thrown back from the burnished barren landscape scorched and scoured by the rays of the day.

Tomorrow is Juma, the weekly holiday, so I hurried to get some newspapers. There were some soldiers in the shop who spoke Persian, and the proprietor took advantage of them to satisfy his curiosity about my nationality. He had supposed I was Chinese.

The yellow Bartlett-like pears are rather common now and another sort, called *natanzi*, has appeared, a green quince-shaped fruit, 5 inches across. Natanz is a town near Kashan, but such winter pears are widely distributed over the country. There is also a new winter grape, a firm pale yellow-bloomed berry with a tiny beak.

They are selling popcorn in the bazaar. It is popped in the coarse sand in which they roast their *ajeel*—pumpkin and melon seeds, pistachios, hazelnuts, and chickpeas (*nakhud*)—and is apt to retain a little of the grit. By way of game there is an occasional wild duck, some partridges and hares, and even a few jays. The game is always old because it comes from long distances and/or because the demand is dull.

Rup Chand bought a sackful of goose down to make himself a bed. He had thought of making a rabbit robe after the fashion of the one he got from the Minnesota Indians—a light net of strips of rabbit skin, a few pounds in weight, but perfect insulation against even arctic cold. Hares are common enough and so are their skins, but the incomprehensible call for the quantity he needed rocketed the market price, and he resorted to the down.

Chapter XV

THE LAND OF THE MEDES

December 17. They told us we'd leave Tabriz at eleven and the truck would come for us at ten; everything happened as foretold. The hotel staff blessed and godspeeded us and urged us to come back in spring when it was really pleasant here. We had been here off and on for two months and they had carried us in their thoughts, so that the seed of a friendship had grown. The agriculture officer came to the outskirts of the city to see us off. The departure ceremony is an important one among the Persians. When a member of the family or pleasant guest departs, a tray is brought out of the house; on it the Koran, a mirror, a dish of water with a sprig of green floating in it, some flour, and a dish with *noql* (a small confection that looks like popcorn). The traveller passes under the tray, returns then and kisses the Koran, gazes into the mirror, eats the candy and touches the flour. The water is then sprinkled on his departing footsteps to insure his safe return. After unwelcome guests, two black stones are thrown instead, but the execution of this ritual is obviously difficult, so it remains rather as a metaphorical expression. Tibetans have a similar ceremony. A bowl of home-brewed beer with one or three, never two or four, dabs of butter on the rim is brought. A prayer is recited, and someone dips a branch of cedar in the liquor and sprinkles it to the winds. The party tastes the beverage and the guest departs, perhaps preceded by a burning censer. The equivalent of the two black stones for some unwanted guest is ashes. A present of money or something else called *sarrahi* ("head of the way") is given also to the traveller, and he may even be accompanied on his journey for a stage or two. Tibetans call such a present *lamzhuk* ("tail of the way").

Our travel papers for some reason are in our hands now. Ordinarily our companion's servant kept them in his inside coat pocket which he used to tap proudly when his master, who first assured us we had them, asked if they were safe. There were two other passengers with us, Assurian boys who wrapped themselves in their bedding and spent the time eating sunflower seeds which they shelled as dexterously as a parrot.

A restaurant keeper on the way had a dog with one front leg hobbled. They said it chases children and the hobbling is to reduce its speed. While we were talking, two schoolboys fled over the hill ahead of it, and its master and two others disappeared in pursuit. At one of the old caravanserais, a donkey was having lunch from his nosebag, his leg tied to something on the roof, just as donkeys have been doing there for the last 300 years. When our car came snorting and puffing along he acted as though he wanted to run away, and his master, mouth crammed with bread, rushed out and threw his arms around his neck. The donkeys of 300 years ago at least could lunch in peace. At three we had left Bustanabad, 58 kilometers on our way, but an hour later an axle broke and left us sitting in the desert.

Rinchen Gialtsen has learned to sign his name, because in our travels there are always numerous documents to be signed. He has admired the flourishes that characterize the signatures of distinguished people and has added a sweep to his *r*. But Tibetan letters don't lend themselves well to ornamentation, and his swirl converts it to an *h* and thereby changes his name from "the one of great price" to "the great fool." —Tibetans, like Indians and Afghans, have no surnames. Persians do, since the new dynasty came into power. While most of them use Christian names of the old Muslim style, among the upper classes one finds the names selected more frequently from historical than from religious characters. —The weather so far has been unusually warm, they say. Today was dark and raw but not freezing.

December 19. We spent the night at Siah Dehan, the junction of the roads to Tehran, Tabriz, and Hamadan, in the office of the king's winemaker, a friendly person who had learned his business in France. Rinchen Gialtsen fried the bacon with his usual blowtorch fire and spattered grease all over the cement floor. It took some time to clean it up.

A wind that started in the night was blowing fresh in the morning. At eleven, we climbed on a truck loaded with boxes for Hamadan, along with ten other passengers who had got aboard earlier and had settled into corners as shelter against the half-gale. We perched on top, fortified against the stinging wind with the heaviest of our bedding.

For some miles the road runs across the desert plain with nothing in sight except now and then a big hawk (*Buteo ferox*) or a kestrel on a telephone pole or a ground owl sunning himself on a clod. The hawks and kestrels paid no attention to the noisy car but the owls, if it came too close, gave a couple of jerky bows and then, with happy hop skip flight, flew off to a safer perch. A thick band of earthy hills succeeds the plain, and in the valleys lie pleasant villages with groves and orchards. At Avej there are numerous thrifty walnut trees with trunks 2 feet through, so densely branched as not to be recognizable from afar. A little beyond Avej is the pass, now snowy, beyond which the bleak Hamadan Plateau begins. Toward sundown we met two buses that had started from Hamadan at dusk on their trip to Tehran, and one of our passengers commented that the buses like the bats seem to like the night. A soldier was apologizing for the inconvenience his gun was giving us, but before we could disclaim any discomfort the driver's helper answered, "They'll remember to their grave the way you have poked it into their ribs." The sight of Hamadan awakened in Astolla, our companion's servant, memories of a more glorious entry, not on a load of boxes and not with associates indistinguishable from the common run of humanity except to their disadvantage. He had once accompanied a distinguished American specialist on a trip in the latter's own automobile, and it had been such a pleasant experience that he had been eager to go along with us—a trip which turned out to be nothing like the one he had conjectured. His specialist had had the tent put up and chairs brought and they had drunk tea. The expert had then written in his notebook and they had driven on. He had also been, Astolla assured us, extremely clean.

The hotel had a clean room with a stove, carpeted with overlapping rugs of good quality. Though there seemed to be no other guests, they were able to give us the usual requisites of comfort, even wine. One bottle was recommended as being eight years old, but it seemed to have no commendable traits than those of senility. They brought us some excellent apples, much like a Baldwin in size and color, sweet like most apples in Iran but outstanding because of their tender juicy flesh. We were told they came from Meshed. The greater part of the apples I have seen in the country are summer or fall sorts, sweet, often insipid, and woody. There are European and American varieties grown in the gardens of amateurs, especially in Tehran, but not in quantities to affect the market. The Indian likes sweet fruits, and it may be the Persian has a similar preference.

Hamadan is the site of the ancient Ecbatana, the capitol of the Medes, established some six centuries before the Christian Era. The splendors of the city of the Medes are fabulous, but what remains of them still lies under the sands of the millennia that have rolled on since in the march of empire hegemony passed to its neighbors. The present town lies at the foot of Alwand Peak,[1] which rises grand from the plain and loses its head in the clouds. It is such a town as others in arid Asia, made up of huddled masses of despondent houses facing each other across dingy streets that in a pleasant setting would stand as an emblem of dejection and despair. But in the awful immensity of the desert, which like the ocean transcends the power of man, human misery too shows trifling.

---

1. Alwand (34°40′N, 48°30′E, 11,960 feet) Peak rises high above Hamadan (34°48′N, 48°32′E, 5850 feet), founded in the seventh century, B.C. as Ecbatana, chief city of the Median Kingdom, and thereafter was a provincial capital often sacked. A city of 104,000 at the time Koelz passed through, it had major Persian and Turkish-speaking Shia communities and Jewish and Armenian Christian minorities. Traditional carpet weaving and leather work were supplemented by a modern leather factory and several flour mills. All-weather roads led north to the Tehran-Tabriz road and south to Borujird and through the mountains to Khuzestan. Several consulates and a number of banks are tributes to Hamadan's key position in the road network.

December 21. It snowed in the night, and morning found the world transformed into such a scene as furnishes the theme for the decoration of Christmas cards. All the sombre landscape had been blotted out. Town, mountain, and desert were gone, and under the burden of white were distinguished only sparkling glistening masses and expanses of different size and shape. The hotel boy awakened us early to hurry to see the lovely sight. Before the sun drove away the last of the clouds that brought the storm, it made a brilliant rainbow that for ten minutes painted the western sky.

Tonight they celebrate the Shab Cheleh, the winter solstice, by eating fruits, melons, etc., and people are buying watermelons. We bought some too. Most were too old to eat, but one was fresh and of unusually good quality. These ancient watermelons that have decomposed to brownish water are considered medicinal here, as in Afghanistan. Astolla said they improved the looks and hinted that the superior beauty of his people lay in the use they made of these fruits. There are still two kinds of grapes on the market, some half-dried blue plums, Isfahan muskmelons such as keep on into the spring with crisp sugar-watery flesh, mediocre citrus from Mazanderan, and pomegranates. The turnips are of an attractive purple, and there are some watery red-purple radishes a foot long like Indian *muli*. Some hares, a woodcock, a great blue heron, and four rooks were hanging up in a shop. The heron (*havasil*) is a famed medicinal article in these parts and the shopkeeper wouldn't sell it to us, because he said we hadn't proper use for it. The fat is used in massaging rheumatic joints. Porcupine grease is also said to be good for the purpose. Astolla said the rooks were "warm" and he couldn't eat them. And indeed they aren't exactly edible, though I have heard they are an esteemed gamebird in parts of England. Here, all members of the black crow tribe are eaten, including ravens and choughs. Only the grey crow and magpie, so far as I know aren't on the approved list. Often I think the flesh is wanted for its healing qualities, not for its good taste, though an old woman for whom I once provided a medicinal raven willingly overlooked the plumage differences of an eagle and added its meat to her cure.

I got off a Christmas cable to Mother. The telegraph office handled it with breathtaking expedition. The operator quickly found which one of the Grass Lakes in the huge directory of world telegraph offices it was going to, counted and multiplied and finished the transaction in five minutes. —The chambermaid feels sorry for us, rattling about as we do in the wastes, far from home and fireside. She says she knows what it is. Like us, she too is a foreigner. Her home is 30 miles away.

Lahulis don't marry within their clan, which follows the main line. Some of the clans are named Dog, Wood, Sugar Cane. Persians, especially in the upper classes, seem to prefer to marry in their own family, and cousin

A GLEANER. After the fields are cut, they may be searched for the fallen ears. This gleaner's reward has been a basketful of grain, no small prize in an economy that provides too often only from hand to mouth.

marriage is common. It would be interesting to see how far inbreeding is responsible for certain traits that seem to mark the members of this class.— Lahuli women consider it disgraceful to be idle and are often seen knitting or spinning, even as they walk. Persian women have relatively an easy time of it, though their duties vary from place to place. The women of the tribes have of course more responsibilities than their sisters in the cities, and correspondingly more freedom. In Afghanistan, where women are still in *chaddur*, the nomad women walk unveiled and talk with the stranger on occasion as freely as the men.

December 22. It froze the ground an inch in the night, but the day was clear and it soon thawed. A big white pig in the hotel court (our landlord is apparently a Christian, an Assyrian or Armenian, or he wouldn't be keeping pigs) was busy rooting in the frozen ground. Wangyel watched the operation with great interest, first, because he had never seen a pig at close range before and then because of the effectiveness of its plowing. Tibetans know something about pigs, and these animals figure in one way or another in their social and religious arrangements, though most of them have never seen one. Wangyel brought the pig some melon rinds, and the friendly creature let him feel her nose and scratch her back, indicating her satisfaction with the meeting by an occasional grunt. He explained to us in amazement the snout was soft, and smooth, and even downy.

We took a droshke and drove out to Asadabad, 3 miles off toward the mountain where they have a powerplant for the town. The valley that opens here is full of orchards, with fine trees of sweet cherries, plums, and apples, also groves of poplar and willow. Woodcock are common in the thicket, and numerous dippers have come down from the snowy reaches of the high mountain above. We followed the stream through the cultivation and where the valley narrows found a lone house, built of the superfluity of rocks that have split off the cliff wall. Here a busy old man and a boy of thirteen kept a "coffee house." There is a village higher up, said the host, and when the villagers go back and forth from the town, he has plenty of customers. We ordered tea which threw the establishment into confusion. China cups were retrieved from a box and washed (tea is ordinarily served in such places in small glasses). The boy was sent flying about, and there was such a bustle as if a barbecue were in view. There should have been chukor in such a place, but they said they never stayed in winter.

A man at work in his garden hailed us as we passed and invited us over. We said we hadn't time. "Then have a little bread." When we said we'd had breakfast recently, he urged us at least to stop a bit by the fire; he had a nice fire. Then he happened to think of three lemondrops he had in his pocket. He fished them out and offered them to us. The only thing he had left to offer was an invitation to stop on our way back for tea and a suggestion as to where we might find something to shoot. A pig lived in a certain gulch, he said, and might be there now. Two villagers going up called and asked if we had a hare to sell.

The local agriculture officer came, and we had a pleasant chat. He had seen several parts of the country and knew of the splendid Kirman dates which he said extended to the Baluchistan border. There is a sort of desert tree called *kahur* in that area with an attractive wood used for making small objects like pipes. He said there are in the neighborhood of Hamadan 40 or 50 varieties of grapes and that the temperature falls to 18° below zero F. The British banker at Kermanshah subsequently told me a figure much lower.

A *Muscari*, like our bluebells, was blooming in a warm spot against the rock. It is one of the commonest and earliest of the wild bulbs that are so varied in Iran.

Chapter XVI

AT THE GATES OF MESOPOTAMIA

December 25, Kermanshah.[1] The doctor from the American Mission hospital took me down to an Assyrian friend's house to show me his Christmas-bearing grapevine. On a vine trellised 10 feet against a wall hung the still fresh bunches, enclosed in paper sacks. The doctor's visit pleased the family tremendously, and they brought out refreshments and the photograph of their sister and her family in Chicago.

The town is a sort of human zoological garden. The people seem to be of all the races and creeds known in these parts: Persian, Jew, Kurd, Arab, Assyrian, Armenian, Chaldean and maybe more, and plenty of each. A wine seller's guarantee of the quality of a bottle of his wares seemed a bit extravagant, but he reassured me that he didn't lie; he wasn't a Persian. It must be owned that the Persians, and for that matter, all the Moslems I have known, are rather free with the truth, as indeed who isn't, for a reason. With us truth has become a business tool, and with a certain simple and low class of people a social habit, and the rest of us are only more careful, not about lying, but about being found out, than the Moslem. In business the Asiatic of this sector of the world has no scruples; he doesn't value the good will of his customer, and the rule is plainly and bluntly *caveat emptor*. In his social dealings he thinks he has discovered that no one wants to hear the truth, (there is a proverb: *Khiyar harf rast zad, dumash talkh shud,* "the cucumber told the truth and its tail got bitter") and it follows then that one is doing his friend a favor by telling him something he wants to hear. The

---

1. Kermanshah (34°19'N, 47°04'E, 4600 feet). A town of 88,000, founded in Sasanid times and important in early Islamic times, it was restored as a goverment strong point by Safavid rulers. In spite of many military occupations, it has flourished as a result of its agriculturally rich hinterland watered by many streams and springs and its position on an important route. The town is predominantly Sunni Kurds, with small Christian and Jewish communities. There are small mills for agricultural products such as flour, oil, rice, and sugar beets, and a small refinery for the production of petroleum products to be distributed within Iran by motor vehicle. All-weather roads lead northeast through Hamadan and Qazvin to Tehran and through Qasr Shirin southwards to Baghdad in Iraq. Koelz apparently approached by the use of a difficult route from Tabriz to the north. The town had three consulates, a hospital, four banks, garages, a wireless station, and an airfield.

bulk of untruths one meets are of this sort, that give no advantage whatsoever to the purveyor. The Persian does not deny the facts and agrees that a truthful honest world would be nice. My friends seemed glad to hear that reliability and honesty were such matter-of-fact qualities as I assured them they were among us. As the war progressed and our propaganda became increasingly familiar, I heard expressions of astonishment that people so strict in their personal morality should be so careless of what they told each other and the world in military and political matters. When the American soldiery and officials became common they only shrugged their shoulders and said we apparently learned their habits with amazing readiness and thoroughness. (Of the British no one hoped anything good; of the Russians it couldn't be expected.) Our soldiery were not disreputable people; rather a selected group of well-grown and therefore decent men, but removed from their normal environment and released from its inhibiting influences, they showed a behavior not quite like what they were accustomed to exhibit at home. Even before the war and in a different stratum, I observed the same thing. At a benefit dinner given by the American colony of Bombay, grown men gave such an exhibition of roughneckism as no small town yokels could long have sustained without becoming ashamed of themselves. A Mongol prince from a distant and benighted region, who happened to get there, possibly to observe the manners of polite society, with all his racial sangfroid could not conceal his bewilderment at the way these superior beings of a rich and powerful civilization amused themselves.

We went out 9 kilometers to the Bisitun Mountain where the road divides to Hamadan and Kurdistan. On the marble cliff—from the foot of which powerful springs issue—are the Taq Bostan carvings. There is a series of them, dating from the Sasanid Period (or about the beginning of the Christian Era), surely to be reckoned among the world's finest stone reliefs. A huge equestrian figure and two hunting scenes are especially remarkable. The reliefs have suffered considerably during the course of time, and the deer hunt panel has been badly mutilated. In another place, one of the modern Persian kings had some figures carved to commemorate himself with an effect not very harmonious with the lofty conception of the Sasanid artist. It is believed the place was once the scene of royal gardens, and a pleasanter place could hardly be found in desert Iran. The Bisitun Peak[1] rises straight above, and in front stretches the broad cultivated valley. Traces of the walls that enclosed the military encampment of about a square mile area can still be seen along the modern road.

It is warmer here than in the city. Wild birds and domestic fowl are common in the fields along the stream. Great flocks of larks have gathered

---

1. Bisitun Peak (32°23′N, 47°35′E, 11,130 feet).

on the plain, and in one place a host of pigeons turned an acre of the desert blue. In a small, neglected patch of quince and cherry, woodcock in such numbers as I hadn't seen till now had taken shelter. Around the foot of the mountains, the rock nuthatches have gathered to make short sallies onto the richer slopes that join the plain. The rare and curious wall creeper too was busy searching out spiders from the shady chinks of the precipice. Now and then a great owl hooted, a muffled meditative hoot in the pleasant warmth that the feeble winter sun shed on the cliff.

One of the handsomest donkeys I ever saw went on up the Kurdistan road. The top of his back came a few inches short of my shoulder, and his forelegs were pillars like those of an elephant. I have seen but few such large donkeys before now and don't know why they should be so rare. The droshke driver gets paid by the hour for waiting, so when I got out I showed him the time on my watch. He pulled out his watch which read half past five, an indication that it ran with no regard for the position of the sun. When I returned five hours later and reported the period of his wait, he consulted his watch and said I was exactly right. Its hands now read 2:35. He is very pleased that there has been no cold weather yet. One expects cold weather in the two *chehlehs* that follow the winter solistice. *Chehleh buzurg* has 40 days beginning December 22, and the *chehleh kuchik* has 20. Every day of those periods that passes off warm is a special and unlooked-for blessing. The year is divided into four seasons of three months each, with spring and fall beginning at the solistices, and one gets approximately appropriate weather for each division. The Persian climate is relatively little affected by forces generated outside the country, so the progress of the seasons is regular, and there are no violent fluctuations of temperature from day to day.

Grapes here are often allowed to climb on trees or walls or are planted on the top edge of ridges and trained into bushes 3 to 4 feet high. A British bank official said the climate here is considerably warmer than that of Hamadan but that the thermometer falls to -12° F. With his help and that of the mission doctor, the shops at the British oil refinery repaired a gun for me that would otherwise have remained useless. —A local breed of chickens has no tail feathers and the "pope's nose" is undeveloped. Another has a bare red neck like a turkey's; yet another has an unusual development of the sacral region.

December 27. We planned to go down toward the Mesopotamian frontier, where spring is beginning. We left in a bus at ten. At one of the stops there was curious red bird among the flock of house sparrows—a sparrow had got into red paint. One of the passengers said with characteristic readiness that it had come from the south—the Persian never lacks an answer.

The side across the plateau is dreary enough till at Shahabad, a place the king owns and has therefore taken care of, birds enliven the landscape. There were great flocks of goldfinches, rooks and of wood pigeons on the fields and some ducks and great white egrets. At Karind they say grow the very nice, large, mild flavored figs we bought in Kermanshah, sold in sacks of goatskin. I have rarely seen figs of such fine quality in Iran, and nowhere have I seen better. From Kirman comes a superior fig, all but seedless, sweet, but small.

A little beyond Karind there is a stretch of rough ground with a fair growth of oak trees that miraculously hasn't been turned into charcoal or stovewood. Then the road drops several thousand feet to the valley of the river that joins the Tigris. Rain began on the way through the forest, and the passengers gave their nice rugs to use in covering the luggage on the roof of the car. I wondered if anyone but Persians would do such a thing. At seven we got to Qasr Shirin[1] and were shown to the modest hotel. The proprietor seemed not to be used to such demands on his hospitality but thought that he could arrange the accommodations we required. We were for bringing up the luggage. His 10-year-old assistant, however, told the porters to wait a bit until the guests were sure things were suitable. Our notions of fitness were somewhat startling but easily complied with. They carried out numerous beds and even the carpets, leaving the room bare. The distressed proprietor came every half hour to plead with us at least to have a rug on the floor, and look, it was a nice Bijari he'd give us.

Persians break bread and put the pieces in their mouth. Cutting it is *haram*. Our method of tearing it up with our teeth may look queer to them, as does the individuality of our eating habits. The Moslem finds it friendlier and warmer to eat out of the same platter and drink out of the same bowl.

December 28. Above us the plateau that is Iran awaits winter. Here spring has come and has given the magic touch that transforms the dreariest landscape. But Qasr Shirin has been endowed by Nature with gifts more substantial than those of fleeting freshness—such gifts as must have inspired romantic dreamers to lay the scene of Eden in these parts. In the rolling hills are ruins of ancient splendor—monuments to bygone appreciation of these blessings, of which the outward sign is all but lost. For what are Nature's greatest blessings but potentialities, possibilities to which man's creative genius gives the body and the form? On the little plain below the town is the proof of Nature's bounty in a rich and lovely garden, which combines in equal thrift and vigor the produce of the north and south. The little river from the great tableland above strikes the foot of the slope against which the town is nestled, and then thwarted in its work of further valley-making, turns abruptly and hurries down thru this little plain of its own creation. Handsome date palms with their undergrowth of orange- and

---

1. Qasr Shirin (34°31′N, 45°35′E, 1050 feet) the last Iranian town on the road to Baghdad.

lemon-trees and tall thickets of cane-like grasses crowd the scene with an air of tropical luxuriance and permanence, against which the fruits of colder climes have hesitated to shed their leaves and in half-naked branch stand not in winter sleep but dozing. Figs, grapes, pomegranates, plums, peaches, apricots, quinces, mulberries, almonds, even apples, pears, cherries, and walnuts, thriving and sturdy of limb are all here, as though nothing that grows in Persian gardens might fail the grand revue. Roses and half-wild narcissus in flaunting and fragrant bloom overshadow the small spring bulbs of *Muscari* and anemone that elsewhere are hailed as heralds of the spring. Gardeners are working in their gardens in which the cycle never rests. The last of the tomatoes and eggplants are being gathered and potatoes planted in their place, while other beds are green with the varied vegetables of the early year.

Birds in unwonted numbers have gathered in this pleasant place and heighten the atmosphere of cheer and plenty. Most of them are transient finches, sparrows, robins, redstarts, wrens and warblers, small gay things that, like the dewdrops and sunbeam splinters, make the thicket sparkle and are themselves scarcely noticed. But there are others that make clear strokes on the landscape canvas and give it form and color as the coming of leaves and flowers changes the character of the scene. Woodcock and jacksnipe catapult themselves from the undergrowth; big wood owls sit brooding in a dark retreat unnoticed till the flustered tits betray them; blue and brown and black and white kingfishers flash rattling above the impatient rivulet; troops of querulous babblers (*Turdoides altirostris*) creep mouse-like in the cane clumps that till lately hid them from the eyes of even ornithologists; francolins forage like barnyard fowl in the fields at twilight and scrape the air with their strident call. And quadrupeds—mongooses, wild pigs, foxes, wolves, and jackals—roam Eden-like in the gardens.

December 30. Wangyel prophesied the sky would clear today because the dogs were barking in the night. The dogs here are never quiet, but the rain did stop. It is a sign of clearing weather, too, when the choughs fly. And their flight is watched also for signs of a coming storm. Before bad weather they are often seen, like others of the crow tribe, soaring high, as the gulls do on our Great Lakes.

The hotel is full of cats, and there is no way of stopping them from roaming where they please. At night there is a rattling and scuffling and thumping as the troupe ransacks the premises and tries to open the boxes that shelter the things they want. Nothing is safe outside. A basket left hanging on the wall was somehow plundered, though it seemed to be out of the reach of everything that wasn't winged. In the morning, a cat or two is usually sleeping on someone's bed, and I suspect the fleas that infest mine come from these unasked bedfellows. A kitten made a cache of surplus meat in a pile of cotton and forgot about it. An old grandfather cat asked

Rinchen Gialtsen for a chicken head on the floor and with each request licked the head. Getting no answer the third time it took it.

Besides the dogs and cats, the jackals too disturb the peace. Several times during the night, beginning at dusk, bands of them at the edge of or even in the town commence their cachinnations, at first leisurely and deliberately derisive, then ascending hilariously to a finale of maniacal whoops. Then from the dogs of all quarters of the town bursts a frenzy of barking and howling as spontaneous as though the whole terrible performance hadn't been given an hour before. A fox too may bark now and then, but he barks alone. The Indian jackals are less likely to venture so brazenly into the towns. Come in they do, and so skillful and fearless are they in their thievery that I have heard natives complain of having their shoes stolen from their bedside and their sack of meal from under their pillow.

Leopards are similarly cunning and fearless in the Himalayas and come regularly into villages, even into houses, to look for their prey. Dogs are common victims of such raids, and most dogs are equipped with iron collars that provide them protection against strangulation by their foe. Two large dogs thus armored can keep a leopard off. The mere proximity of humans is in itself no protection, and one man told me his dog had been fished out from under his bed, with him stiff with fear in it. I have seldom seen a leopard, though I have wandered for years in their midst, but once in Luristan I spent a minute with a huge one within a paw's length of my back while I crouched to examine the marks he had left from his nap in the sand.

The Indian jackals, when they come to town, keep quiet, and their howling is most often heard at a distance where it sounds more appropriate and not unagreeable. On the Indian plains they sing in pairs and one pair takes its cue from the other, so that the Indians say those that begin to cry in the Himalayas start a relay of song that ends out in the Indian desert. Jackals seem to have a sensitive ear for music and at a proper pitch of the crescendo the partner joins the duet, or the second duo begins. One year near Delhi, every evening when the mullah sang out in the quiet dusk his high clear call to prayer, a jackal pair would listen till he reached a certain note in his exultant culmination. Then they struck up, drowned out the mullah and finished the call to the faithful on a not very religious key.

The river was so muddy today that the blue and brown kingfishers took to the fields to hunt the mole crickets that the downpour had flooded out of their burrows. They seem to have a catholic appetite, and there is no puddle so barren that won't yield something to their taste, if not fish, then crabs, frogs, or insects, and I have even known them to eat small birds. Their black and white brethren were gazing disconsolately into the muddy torrent and must surely have gone hungry.

The little boy who constitutes the hotel staff has been catching house sparrows for us and he has so far sold us three at about a nickel each. With this money he has been able to get an assistant, smaller than himself. Today when we asked to have the orange peels carried out, he went and got his understudy and gave him a cent to do the job. The helper solemnly salaamed him before executing the commission, and the salaam was probably alone worth the cent.

A sparrow comes in every night at dusk to roost in the thicket of the ceiling. The ceilings of Persian houses when they are flat, as they usually are where wood is available to use as beams for the roofing, are formed of brush piled across the beams. The roof is of mud mixed with straw, and the capacity to shed water depends on the nature of the earth used. At any rate, roofs must be repaired or renewed yearly and in spring often turn pleasantly green with the rains. The sparrow doesn't get up too early in the morning, and on his way out makes a loud buzz as he turns a sharp corner to leave.

The town is full of beggars who have fled from the cold weather of the cities on the plateau. They seem to be the chief customers of the cooked turnip seller who begins before sunrise to advertise his goods in the street. Our escort sits all day on the porch of the hotel gazing like our pet hawk, said Wangyel, into the street, where nothing ever happens except that from time to time there is a brawl between the beggars or a dog fight. Since we are near the Iraq frontier not much traffic passes, and the poor fellow has indeed a dreary time of it. I have begged him to go home and have paid $3.25 to send a telegram of his composition to Tehran asking for his release. Telegraphing isn't so expensive in Iran, but it seems one can't save words and preserve politeness in telegrams. This one started off with an Arabic preamble of several lines which boiled down to the correct "sir" of formal usage, and besides the kernel, contained a testimonial of thanks and satisfaction. Someone, however, seems to bear him or me malice. He stays on.

Astolla sold his suit and overcoat here, bought replacements, and looks grand. There was a louse under the collar of the new coat when he displayed it, and he dropped the creature into the lamp. Second-hand American clothing is a gift from heaven to the poor boys who are compelled to put on a front on nothing a month. At Hamadan when the heavy snow came, he spent a week's wages to buy a pair of rubbers. He didn't forget his wife either and bought a pair of silk stockings very weak in the heel and with two big runs, but nicely pressed. He cherishes the hope of taking her and the two children on a pilgrimage to Mecca. Head and footgear are very important in Iran. Everyone aims to have both of foreign make or at least of foreign style. My shoes are invariably the native *giveh*, if I have any at all, and my head-dress is seldom orthodoxly either native or foreign. The police are consequently drawn to me as a bull to a red cloth, and it is lucky that in view of the liberties they are allowed to take with headgear they don't like, nothing serious has happened to mine.

There is a sour pickle for sale in the market made of peaches, plums, and two kinds of whole cucumbers, and another of chopped peppers strongly flavored with herbs. The tomatoes are nearly gone because there has been a light frost, and besides, the shopkeeper says there is little demand now except to roast on the spit with the strips of meat. A small plum tomato with relatively more flesh than the others is used for this purpose. There are also some eggplants of good quality, the ubiquitous long black-purple kind but with no seeds in the stem two-thirds. The usual spring vegetables are displayed and a few citrus, among them two kinds of superior sweet limes. For the first time I have looked upon this fruit with approval. The one kind I never saw before, but the other is a common fruit in Iran, as well as in India, where in spite of their insipid character they are much esteemed. There are also two lemons, one a big sweet-sour thing, 5 inches high, and the other the widespread *limu khargi*. Carcasses of wild sheep are often seen hanging with the mutton in the meat shop.

Flocks of starlings were circling high about the fields this evening, apparently catching insects. I have seen them thus engaged before and since. Once I saw even rooks and kestrels turn flycatcher at the time of emergence of a kind of aquatic insect near Tehran. A wild pig and her six husky offspring were hidden in a clump of canes at the edge of town along a path where people were passing constantly, and in another place I came within 30 paces of four wolves that were sleeping on the open hillside.

The francolins come out in the fields to feed in the evening, and off and on, one hears the bang of some native's muzzleloader. Otherwise they stay as closely·hidden as the woodcock. Of these I flushed some thirty today, four from under a single bush. Everyone says they breed here, which seems unlikely, but they give the number of eggs correctly as four. No one, however, had a name for them and called them *"purr"* as they do the francolin. But a boy called a wood owl a *"purr"* too.

January 7. We went along the low, rocky ridge that runs away from the town, out into the desert. Perpendicular strata of alabaster and sandstone make a straight barren wall, broken here and there by drainage channels that outside the rock wall dig deep gulches on their way to the river. Nuthatches, linnets, wheatears, rock thrushes, and the little rock partridges are common, and there are numerous signs of mountain sheep. Once when I fired my gun, 27 of them ran out in front of me and filed along the mountain, followed at a hundred paces by two hunters who must have been about to fire when I spoiled their sport. They were un-Asiatically put out by the accident and vented their feelings in loud but incomprehensible language.

THRESHING. When the straw has been crushed to chaff, it will be tossed into the air with the wood-tined fork in the foreground and the grain thus separated. A windy day is needed for the winnowing, and often at the threshing season there'll be no wind for days. The winnowers whistle while at work. Whistling brings wind, as even our Great Lakes fishermen know.

They are plowing on the dry slopes for next fall's sowing of grain. This is common practice in Iran and Afghanistan. The soil "drinks sun." An innovation here is the use of a pair of donkeys to drag the plow. Oxen are generally employed thus, and I have seen camels, but horses never. The government in places has provided tractors for this purpose, and on broad level surfaces, they work to advantage. Fuel is cheap, and the great disadvantage in their operation seems to be the lack of competent operators.

Along the river a fresh old man whose energy the years seem not to have lessened, only to have shrunken its container, was busy working in his garden. From year to year he has been expanding his orchard, and a layer of

ON THE ROAD. The donkeys are carrying fodder done up in goathair sacks. This is a common landscape in desert Asia, and the road may run for days with no significant variation. There is usually some such scattered vegetation, at times annual, at times even shrubby, but there are vast stretches that are completely barren.

saplings at the rim marked this year's addition. He would like, he said, to have a few dates, but they are expensive. Dates bear in about eight years after setting out the sucker, and I thought of the story in our school reader about the king and the old man's fig tree. Rup Chand gave him money to plant four, one for each of us.

The day was beautifully fine, and shepherd boys shed their clothes and caught vermin in the caressing warmth. Peach trees have begun to bloom. Several shoots spring up from one root to form a thick bush 10 feet high that now blossom-laden is highly ornamental. On the mountain, their relatives, the thorny pink-flowered almonds, make a gayer show. In the river the fish came to bask in the shallows, huge things of the minnow family, and all the logs were covered with turtles. We found a magpie that apparently had succumbed to intestinal trouble. I have found corpses of magpies that seemed to have died of disease more frequently than any other birds, perhaps a dozen of them in Iran. On the great plains, there are often remains of many species, from the largest (geese, herons, and bustards) to the smallest (sparrows and warblers) that died by violence, and only their feathers attest to their erstwhile existence.

Women here, as in some other places in Iran, often have blue spots tattooed on their chins. The peasants of all ages and sexes have a curious song they commonly sing as they pass, a dreary, monotonous, falsetto staccato that I tried in vain to imitate when we were first in Luristan.

The crows here are mostly like those of the north, but the very different pale Mesopotamian race is also seen. The former may be a winter visitor, but at Dizful, the pale form was breeding about the villages and a few miles away in the mountains was the dark northern form with nowhere any evidence of intergradation. Biologists call these subspecies and like to have them connected by individuals that are intermediate in their characters. The two races here obviously differ in mental makeup and therefore don't mix. In the case of wheats—which are extraordinarily diversified in Iran—I have found 50 well marked varieties on one small plain. One observes an interesting biological phenomenon not often met with by the student of systematics or classification: two varieties may be virtually indistinguishable in morphological characters but may have marked physiological differences: one may be a fall wheat (slow-maturing) and another a spring (fast-maturing) sort, or one may require irrigation and the other may be cultivated on *daimi* (unirrigated) fields.

Chapter XVII

WHERE MY SOUL HAS LONGED TO GO

January 15. We left Kermanshah at noon in a mail bus with only two other passengers. One was a youth in military officer's dress which he obviously hadn't worn long. Wherever he could see himself, in the looking glass of the "coffeehouses" or in the windows of the bus, he practiced saluting. He seemed to find the trip interesting and made copious notes during the voyage. A few miles beyond Taq Bostan, on the other side of the Bisitun massif that rises a mile or more above the lovely plain, are the famous rock inscriptions of Darius the Great, dating from more than five centuries before Christ. A life-sized figure, supposed to be a portrait representation of Darius with a procession of prisoners, is carved high on the rock wall. Below are several closely written panels, one in Babylonian, one in Elamite, one in ancient Persian, giving an account of Darius's genealogy and his deeds. In the narrative is included a curse on whoever destroys the monument, which mercifully has not yet had occasion to fall. Rawlinson was the first to succeed in deciphering the ancient Persian cuneiform characters. From the results of his researches here, it has been possible to read many of the numerous clay tablets recovered from excavations in Asia Minor, part of the great King's domains. A huge panel some 500 feet long has been smoothed on another face of the mountain but left bare. In yet another place, a panel with battered figures has a wordy inscription in Arabic characters cut into the middle of it. A well-preserved caravanserai of Shah Abbas's time stands nearby, and this is no less than the grandiose monument of the fabulous Achaemenid of 2500 years before, testifies to the divine spark that has flared up in the soul of Persia through the long centuries of its history but now slumbers.

Here too a spring flows, but from the slope below the mountain and not from the cliff as on the opposite side at the Taq Bostan. Augmented from time to time as it leaves its source it becomes a pleasant stream, where numerous water birds have gathered. Kingfishers, herons, grebes, and gallinules hang on this vital thread in the waste. How different an environment from the life-crammed marshes that are their haunts with us.

Something was found wrong with the car, so our visit to the first coffeehouse was protracted till dusk when repairs arrived from Kermanshah. At Sahneh, well-watered and green, we waited an hour, all sitting in the car—even the driver had had enough sociability with the afternoon at Bisitun—till the postmaster got the mail sack ready. When at last the tiny bag appeared, it showed no signs of having anything inside it. The pass to the Kangavar Valley is called Gardan Bed Surkh (Red Willow Pass) and is over only a low ridge. Kangavar is one of the fertile spots in the western desert and here too we stopped an hour while everyone regaled himself in the desolate "coffeehouse." The Kangavar Valley is separated from Asadabad, another region of fertility, by a range of low hills like those that separate it from Sahneh. When we left Kermanshah, we were glibly assured we'd be in Hamadan by half-past four in the afternoon, a perfectly possible feat of course, but my travel experience led me to express a doubt that we should be thus catapulted through space. "It's the mailbus. It has to get there," our companion said reprovingly. At 2:00 in the morning we reached the foot of the great climb above Asadabad, and of course more refreshment was needed. I was sure we'd stay till daylight. It had grown cold and the pass ahead had probably collected ice that might make going in the dark unpleasant, but our escort had no mind to tarry. At 3:15 even his patience wearied, and when he went to prod the driver he found the company had gone to bed. It was, however, no difficult matter to get them up again and in 15 minutes, we were started once more, with no more halts till Hamadan. The pass was slippery, and at a bend near the top a truck had tipped over and lay at the very edge of the precipice. The goods had been saved in part and were collected about the wreck. At 6:30 we roused the hotel porter in Hamadan and went to bed, having achieved our trip of 100 miles on the fast mail in 18 hours flat.

January 19. The road from Hamadan to Borujird winds along on a flat expanse strewn with low hills which the road dodges except to cross the one that bars the way into the Malayer Plain. Malayer is noted for its grapes and grape produce—wine, raisins, and *shireh*—and plenty of vineyards are seen around the town. In some the vines are covered with earth, in others exposed. There are also numerous orchards, and in spring it must be a bright spot against the low bare hills. The mud-walled, flea-bitten town itself is as out of place in the landscape as a mole hill in a lawn. In the bazaar a big heavy-furred monkey had to dance, under threat of a switching, before likely spectators. We hurriedly tipped his master to be spared the pathetic exhibition. A proffered sack of raisins rejected by the monkey was seized by the master. A pair of brown *tazi* greyhounds went out on the desert to hunt and soon came back with a hare.

An hour later we were in Borujird,[1] one of the most delightful of Persia's great oases. On one side a high, harsh mountain wall bounds the narrow plain and on the other, rolling hills billow off into the horizon, each one higher than the next. Grain fields in a green lawn extend across the valley, interrupted along the eastern end by blocks of walled-in gardens and to the west, where a rivulet flows down the plain, by copses and groves of willows and poplars. Such patches of field and orchard, fresh in the mountain-rimmed desert have doubtless formed the changeless Persian landscape throughout the ages, with sometimes the stronghold-dwellings of the cultivators. Earthquakes, wars, and weather have quickly beaten down, then buried or dissolved these inanimate works of man, and in all Iran there remain mere vestiges of the architecture of bygone times. Even the great edifices of the seventeenth century have been shaken or even shattered by these forces of destruction, and those of earlier periods have disappeared almost without a trace. But here in the walled-in gardens still stand the fort-like dwellings of the landlords of the past—massive structures, their windowless walls grim and defiant. Yet they are confidence-inspiring and not repellent, like the faces of stern old warriors, survivors of a time—now all but vanished— when the Persian loved the land and dared to live in the midst of its pleasantness. Peaceful times have allowed some softening of the face of these old castles, and in the upper stories apertures for light and air have been increased, but in the lower walls the heavy iron-clad door remains the only breach. New structures have also risen in imitation of the old, but reflecting the gentler character of modern times. Roundabout on the plain are lone towers from whence sentinels gave the alarm to peasants in their likewise embattled villages.

On this page out of the romantic past, the hand of modernism has scrawled two long streets, as usual far too long and far too wide, blotted with makeshift and unsightly heaps of walls and roofs. Because wide and open fields were needed to express the renaissance, the town has been constructed at the desert's edge where its squalor intrudes the least on the unique beauty of the landscape. Two cemeteries over which the march of Progress passed have been transformed from neglected wastes of heaps and hollows into public gardens planted with trees. The few flowers like hollyhocks and petunias that flourish in this country, despise care as if conscious of the greater need of cheer and brightness and strive to make good

---

1. Borujird (33°54′N, 48°46′E, ca. 5200 feet) was a small town of 30,000 on a rich plain with many springs, certainly existing in early Islamic times but perhaps older. The population was a very mixed one of Kurdi, Luri, and Persian-speaking Moslem, Armenian Christian, and Jewish communities. The only modern industry was one of manufacturing heat-resistant bricks, but a beet-sugar factory was not far away on the road south toward Dorud and Khuzistan.

A Well-tended Garden of Assorted Trees and Flower Beds. The trees are often crowded, since exposure to sun and wind quickly dries the soil and burns the foliage of isolated trees. Thus one commonly sees a fruit garden as dense as a thicket, with various kinds planted together; the humid air they conserve for each other is of more importance than the light and heat of more open planting.

the failures and shortcomings of their feebler brethren. If these gardens lack the aspect of tended cultivation, they at least provide a bit of shady rest for the wretches who have nowhere else to seek it.

The Hotel Ferdos, named for the ancient poet, is a square of small rooms constructed around a patio with a cement pool in its center and flowerbeds in which a few rose bushes are still struggling against the growing cold to send forth to bloom. A few *Bellis* and *Muscari* deluded by the temperate weather to dream of spring have succeeded in their attempt. A half-dozen hungry hens with curved and twisted feathers of a breed called *firri* peck about the enclosure stupidly, hopefully scrutinizing again the barren pavement they have fruitlessly searched a dozen times before. A flock of house sparrows finds refuge in the rose bushes from which a swift little hawk tries from time to time to dislodge them.

The market still has grapes, large green ones, somewhat withered but with taste as fresh as ever and some melons of both kinds still good enough to eat. In one shop, the shopkeeper said he wouldn't sell the good grapes until he had first got rid of a pile of rotting ones. A black winter radish is like ours in appearance but mild and tender which ours never are. In the fields are large flocks of wood pigeons, rock pigeons, and winter sparrows from the north; on the edges of the cultivation chukors from the mountain; along the streams jacksnipes, teal, and mallards and an occasional cormorant, heron, and egret.

Our escort, like all the others we have had with us, though helpless at first has quickly learned how things are done, and let no one think that even to get a ride on a truck is such a simple matter! He has succeeded better than anyone else in getting us transportation in the daytime. Though it usually turned out that we spent the night on the road for one reason or another, we at least set forth in broad daylight.

January 23, Dorud. An enterprising, farseeing citizen has planted a grove of almonds and other trees on the slope above Dorud and has dug down for water to irrigate them. On all the thirty-odd miles of fertile and watered plain between here and Borujird, there is hardly another grove, and the owner can have no more hope of ever getting a harvest than if he planted muskmelons on a city lot. Both the muskmelons and the almonds, as it happens here, have a long period of usefulness, beginning from the time they leave the blossom. The one is always a substitute for cucumber at all stages in its growth, and the other tastes sourish in its beginnings and then is much esteemed by old and young and can be bought in the markets as *"chaqaleh."* However, the trees are thriving and their buds have swollen to pea size.

On this property has been built a wretched five-room building that nowhere else would be mistaken for a human domicile, but in Luristan, most building is rough. The Lurs generally don't trouble to make sun-dried bricks like other people but pile up their walls of stone and mud. The mixture flows and sags, and so the walls are not rigidly perpendicular. The roof is the usual one of earth piled on brush across the beams, and from the marks on wall, floor, and beam left by rills of liquid mud, it clearly is not equal to the task of keeping out the rain. We rented one room of this habitation and spent the rest of the day in trying to remove the traces of the previous occupants who apparently were pigs—real four-footed pigs. The other rooms bulged with hordes of railroad track workers who poured in and out with the sun. Fleas are so troublesome that I couldn't sleep till after midnight, and today I astonished the bazaar by looking for a Flit gun. Mice rattled and gnawed all night, though it would seem they are no better off in this environment than ours in our proverbial church. One bit Rinchen Gialtsen's toe.

The peasants are still at work sowing grain. On the slopes where the crop matures only from "drinking God's water," as the peasants often style unirrigated planting, they are sowing on land already plowed. On the plain where water can be led to the fields, the grain is scattered on unturned earth and then plowed under.

We walked up the valley a few miles and found at the foot of the mountain along a bright mountain streamlet a shrine in a grove of oaks, beautiful well-grown trees, sometimes a yard through, covering several acres of the slope and the stream bank. Among them stood a colossal plane tree. There are often in Persia such places sacred to some saint (*imamzadeh*) around which stand unharmed patriarchs, safe I suspect because of that ancient, perhaps Aryan, reverence for trees which underlies all the religions of India. The birds have collected around the mountain base: choughs, rooks, larks, snow finches, rock sparrows, linnets, and small northern sparrows, several hundred in a flock, in a variety and abundance we seldom have seen in the country. The rains collapsed the ant tunnels, and the summer convexity of the hills has changed to a concavity. A few of the tenants have ventured out and stiff-jointedly are surveying the damage.

While we were resting on the hill, a wolf came dashing past carrying a sheep, as easily as a cat a mouse, though the sheep must have been of greater weight than he. The carnivores of course have enormous strength. An Indian episode seems still so incredible that I can hardly relate it with conviction. A cattle driver spent the night with us at a mountain village, and in the morning two of his cattle, each as large as a Jersey, were lying dead 150 yards away. A leopard had attacked them while they were tethered beside the driver's bed and had dragged them off across a sandplain. The corpses were found in the morning side by side, with not a mark or blood stain on either one. That night we hid to kill the leopard. Toward midnight he came, but at a sign of life from us he vanished so swiftly that but for his tracks in the sand it might have been a dream. Rup Chand's flashlight picked up two fiery eyes in the distance, and the horrible crash of his 11 mm Mauser quickly brought a crowd around us. The eyes were those of a fox. "Really," said one of the natives, poking its carcass with his toe, "one wouldn't have thought such a little animal could have carried off those cows." He possibly would have been little less surprised if he had seen the leopard, which after all, doesn't weigh much more than a man. They told us the right front foot of a wolf is a useful remedy for treating wounds and that wolves often carry off dogs, as do our Himalayan leopards. A shepherd said there were 32 wolves in a pack one day, but we never have seen more than 9, possibly a family party.

Rinchen Gialtsen says the cotton dealer will never sell him the cotton he asks for from his stock but makes him wait till he has ginned the required quantity. Then he wants to know what he is going to do with it, and Rinchen

Gialtsen answers in Tibetan. The shopkeeper expresses his regret that he doesn't understand Arabic. If we buy seeds in a shop, they may tell us this isn't the time for seed buying, planting time is a long way off, or that we have already bought much more than for any reasonable use. A merchant will often object to selling us all his stock of a certain article, and he has little tendency to reduce the price for large scale purchases. He may freely refer us to some competitor who has better goods in case we are not suited with his. In general he asks but little more than he expects to get, while the Indian asks whatever the situation seems to warrant. To buy even a match, we will pay through the nose if we aren't sure what matches are worth.

There are some handsomely-ribbed orange pumpkins in the bazaar, a foot through, that we bought for seed. One of our neighbors pounced on the discarded shells, and later two more came hat in hand and said they'd like any we might have to discard in the future.

An ibex and her goat-sized kid came to drink at the river. When they went back up the mountain the kid looked very carefully around before he jumped to the next rock ahead. There might be a wolf behind it.

Our donkey-driver, who took us up the Tī Valley last summer, came promptly to see us on our arrival and brought with him his brother-in-law who was a brigand in the days before the present king cleaned up the country. He is not at all what one would expect a brigand to be, in fact as good natured and simple a soul as could be found if you scoured the country. Yet I have no doubt when he went marauding, it was with as clear a conscience as the short-seller; both of them were taking risks. They said one of our summer's friends at Tī had disappeared, and only his gun and cap had been found. If a bear or leopard had killed him, there would have been fragments of clothing, so they thought maybe a jinn had carried him off. Supernatural beings are fewer in this part of the world than anywhere I have ever been and even among the simple people, play little part in their life. The Tibetans, on the other hand, have great quantities of them, real flesh and blood articles not to be ignored, all named and localized in special haunts. To such folks our ghosts, confessedly unreal, seem psychopathic manifestations.

February 1. All the villages of the Tī valley that in the summer we had found empty are now inhabited, and all received us like old friends. They hadn't seen us but they had heard about us from those who had, since of course, any visitors, even Persian, are an event in this out-of-the-way place. At Baraftab where we stayed the night, the young men spent the evening with us. One finely-made youth with dirt-encased neck and hands said he'd wash in hot water, if we'd take him along. He had paid 30 tumans to have his age inscribed as 47 in the police records to be exempt from military service; he had paid 150 tumans for a wife, but he hadn't married yet because he

KURD NOMAD WOMEN MILKING THE SHEEP. Persian sheep are important animals in the native economy. In places they furnish the Persian lambskins of the luxury fur trade. Their use as carriers is not important as in Tibet, but as everywhere they are grown for their wool and meat. The nomads regularly milk them. There are many local breeds. The one in the foreground is the fat-tailed type. The best of these are to be seen in Afghanistan, where they grow largest, and the meat of these Afghan animals is of superior quality.

didn't have the 100 tumans more he needed for the wedding. One youth had lost both hands in a dynamite explosion. He had got the dynamite from the railroad workers and had intended to scare away the wild pigs from the crops, but the stuff went off in his hands. He was always wanting to bring something in his poor stubs. We had had two lame boys with us during our travels, and both had dashed down the stairs and raced down slopes as if to convince themselves that they were like other people. One of our new friends was dressed in a bellboy's coat with the word "Charlevoix" on the shoulder and always answered "Yaw" to anything you asked him. He had worked for some foreigner on the railroad tracks. They all urged us to come home and sleep with them, but we stayed on the sand by the river where there weren't any fleas.

We arrived at Tī to meet a funeral. To Lahulis, meeting a funeral or to dream of one is good luck, and I suppose we were lucky enough in our stay in the valley because nothing worse happened than that we got drenched a few times by the rain that once or twice fell night and day. The corpse was wrapped in a purple cloth on a crude stretcher lying on the ground next to the river. The men and women were seated in separate groups, and a mullah was reading something from a book. Some people coming up from below washed their hands and face and put a dab of earth on their heads before joining the party. Some men took the corpse and washed it in the river and then carried it to the grave enveloped in a clean white cloth. The women lamented, the men chanted, the mullah read for about two hours.

At four Rup Chand went with one of the villagers to look for a pig, and in a little while we heard the wild Bakhtiari yell which they said was a call to send the dogs. Then we heard several shots and toward dark, the men came back. They had killed an old boar and had left him lying half a mile up the river with one of the dogs keeping guard. He was far too heavy for them to move, so there was nothing else to be done tonight. I wanted two of the natives to sleep there so the wolves wouldn't eat the carcass, but Rinchen Gialtsen wouldn't trust such an arrangement. Instead he took a bottle of wine and some bread and went to stand guard himself.

The day which had started fair and warm turned cold and dark, and the villagers brought us one of their flimsy black goat-hair tents to protect us against the threatening rain. The tents are woven for summer use and since it doesn't rain in summer, they have not been made to shed water. This one was moreover an old one. The government, they said, had seized most of their tents because they wanted people to get out of the habit of wandering around. By dark it began to drizzle.

February 2. It rained considerably in the night, and the tent let in enough water to wet us, but there was plenty of wood about and we were soon dry. The slopes up the river from the village are well forested with oaks as yet untouched by the charcoal burners. Whenever a native passes camp he drags along one of the numerous pieces of dead wood that lie about in the forest and drops it at camp as an excuse for a visit. The oak burns with a clear bluish flame, makes beautiful glowing embers, and gives off a fragrance suggestive of vanilla. Rinchen Gialtsen dislikes seeing the wood-bringers. He is reminded of the Kuluese custom of cremating the dead: everyone brings one piece of wood to build the pyre. He asks folks to bring two pieces at a time, instead of one and pays for them.

A boy went with two donkeys and brought the boar. It was an enormous thing, in full winter dress, handsome black-brown, broadly tipped lighter, with long wooly down underneath that Rup Chand later spun and knitted into an attractive sweater. The skin came off easily, and the meat, in spite of the evident age was tender and odorless and tasted better than any quadruped I ever ate. There were no strips of lard such as our domestic pigs have, and the fat was soft, not tallow. A homemade bullet was embedded in the skin near his tail, a souvenir of an encounter with a native.

The rain we'd had in the valley was snow on the mountains, and both cliffs were white this morning to near the bottom. The snowcocks driven down a bit by the weather whistled on the slope, and one flew across the valley. Toward morning, a wood owl sang in a tree beside camp. In the dry bed of the torrent today I saw fresh marks on the sand which looked as if something had been rolling on the sand or someone sitting. I crouched to examine the ground and found a few hairs, which weren't of wild goat, sheep or pig (the animals that came at once to mind), nor were there any hoofmarks which these would inevitably have left on the soft ground. As I rose, a handsome great leopard leaped from behind me, where he had been hiding on the other side of a boulder. I could have petted him from where I stood. He had probably been sunning himself and had then slipped around the rock as I approached. He bounded off up the ravine, leaving a strong unpleasant scent behind. In another place 36 ibex were grazing in the forest. All were females and kids except one old male, much paler than the rest with black beard and saddle.

Rup Chand went up on the mountain to look for snowcock. They are digging *Muscari* and the other bulbs now greening, taking toll of the remnants the chukor missed in their harvesting in the fall. In a few weeks when the shoots grow longer, the bears will begin to grub. Sokhtazar, the guide, too appraised the sprouting landscape with the same sentiments as the birds and bears—there'd be lots to eat soon. In the grove around the big spring, the children were collecting the fresh sprouts of a carroty plant they called *gul khanami*. I bought a bunch and told them to carry it to camp. First they cleaned the greens and washed themselves pink in the ice water, then set out to deliver the goods.

Sokhtazar has a soft dry fungus from rotten oak wood that makes a perfect tinder. In the Himalayas, the Tibetans use a fungus that grows on birch, but more often they use the wooly hairs of various species of composite plants. Sokhtazar would like to divorce his wife but he can't find the money. He paid 16 tumans for her and stipulated he could send her home on the payment of 20 more, but the mullah who drew up the contract wrote 50 instead of 20 and he can't raise so much. He said she was sickly and barely equal to the simple tasks of the women here. The men tend the fields, and the women prepare the acorn bread and keep the house in fuel and water. The sheep are grazed by boys of 12 and every day they take them to a different slope. The hills now are washed a sulfur green since spring has called forth once again the tiny plants which each year for a festive moment adorn the endless barren stretches of Iran.

Most of the people are fearfully poor and some are nearly naked. Our men fitted out one lad with coat and pants and even sweater, and his companions looked on without trace of envy, but rather pleasure, in their simple faces. The men paid too for the funeral feast of some wretch who left his misery yesterday. The widow came today, with four slabs of wheatbread, one apiece and some butter!

Rinchen Gialtsen can always spare something for someone. He always has clothes to give away, though his wardrobe has no superfluities so far as I can see. But for us he has little pity. When we come home drenched and benumbed by some capricious spring cloud or meet with any of the other little accidents that befall people of our habits, he shows impatience and annoyance: "why hadn't we been more careful?" But if one of us is ill, he worries. Wangyel on the other hand is distressed at our little misfortunes and tries even to protect us from them. He thinks little of his own comfort if he can see a way to please us. Both the men share my interest in the work. Once in Afghanistan when a torrent carried off one of our horses and lost its load and its owner, they often repeated their thankfulness that it didn't happen to be another more valuable load. Rinchen Gialtsen takes a special interest in the bird collections; he inspects the day's bag and recognizes species not found before; he was annoyed that I exchanged some skins with another ornithologist. Without such friends I, a lone foreigner, should never be able to travel in remote and dangerous places, nor could I accomplish more than a fraction of what I am now able to do.

In the late afternoon our Persian companion came with a mounted police escort. He had been nearly eaten by the fleas in his last night's lodging, and I left it to him to find out that it would be worse tonight. He had brought no food, though I had warned him of the destitution in the valley, and since our supper of wild boar didn't interest him, he had to depend on what he could scare up in the village. I suppose he deduced from our eagerness to get here that the valley flowed in milk and honey. Sokhtazar, who has the best, at least the newest of the hovels, took him home with him, having first sent his wife to the neighbors, since the house has only one room. The horse worries me. They will demand grain for him, and the people have none to eat themselves.

February 9. The big fish seem to have left our river, and the largest now seen are about a pound in weight. The water is much less than when we were here in summer, except for short spells of flood. The weather continues rainy, and now and then it thunders. Clouds hang in close smoky masses around the peaks and sometimes drop down to fill the great ravines that dent the valley walls.

The dog that helped in the pig hunt spends all its time at our camp. It considers its first duty is now to us and chases away its erstwhile masters. It even makes clumsy attempts at being playful. In Moslem countries not many people play with dogs, and the poor things hardly know how to respond to friendly treatment. The handless boy from Baraftab brought us a little rooster that looks just like a jungle fowl. We expected it would at once join the village flock, but instead it spends the day at camp. The nights it rains, the rooster sits upright, neck straight, to let the water roll off its back. It crows at daybreak, at noon, around 4:30, and again last night when Wangyel got up and lit the lantern.

There is a sort of painful eye inflammation prevalent just now, and many people come to us for treatment. One woman has a husky 18-year-old son who brings her and looks after her as tenderly as any mother could want. The people here believe, as do the Indians, that the milk of a woman who has her first child is eye medicine. There is the usual smell of unwashed humanity about our friends, an impersonal, not offensively human odor, more suggestive of smoke, from which it possibly comes.

Often one sees a nice log lying in the wood with a stone or two on it, to indicate that someone is interested in it. Lahulis have the same custom designating ownership as the Eskimos in the Greenland Arctic.

Plowmen are busy sowing the spring wheat. The birds have begun to nest. A dipper is gathering moss in the stream; a rock nuthatch is cementing on the cliff another gourd of glue and pitch beside the one he made last year; woodpeckers are digging nestholes in the oaks; two thrushes sing all day in the barberry thicket. The chukors and wood pigeons that nest later are still in flocks. The bright weather stimulates them to song, and very often a golden eagle dashes into the noisy chukors and scatters them squealing across the valley. There are butterflies about and a few skinks on the warmer slopes. Clumps of a purple and blue bulbous iris, wild pansies, and patches of a large flowered waxy buttercup with anemone habit are blooming among the oaks, and along the spring are beds of purple crocus-like flowers (*Merendera*). Brighter than these are the cherry and almond bushes clothed in pink and white that cling to the hillsides. The women singing in field and forest have a song that reminds us of Mandi in the Himalayas.

March 27. One of our neighbors is sick and hasn't been able to work for weeks. His wife is nearly blind, and he has a four-year-old son. Today a creditor came and seized their rug for his debt. The child came running and told Rinchen Gialtsen of the calamity—what would they have to sleep on? Rinchen Gialtsen paid the debt and a little while afterwards the mother came with a pair of cotton pants wrapped in a cloth as a present for him. Persians give with two hands to superiors and take with one, Lahulis the opposite.

Another of our neighbors has a son who is a mason. He builds walls along the railroad track and is therefore above the other track workers. His mother always refers to him as "Master Mohammed" (*Ustad Mohammed*). She was complaining today to Wangyel that he wants to marry locally. "Think of it! A Lur, and 6 feet tall, and so homely," didn't he think so? We see no reason to share the general contempt for the poor Lurs; we find them pleasant neighbors. A man came and asked us to get a rook for a patient who has a severe cough. Another wants a raven for some other ailment. There is a peach tree in the garden, a foot high, with two flowers on each of its two branches.

I went up the river to Sangar where they say the river can be waded and so saved half an hour's walk to get onto the plain. A nice big boy with down on his lip had just crossed and stopped to visit. He was going to a neighboring village and had a round thick slab of bread, his lunch no doubt, which he

A Kurdish Dance. Persian dances are lively, and both sexes may take part. Dancing is not the popular pastime it is with the European peasant, and performances like this are rarely seen. Farther eastward, the folk dance loses all vivacity and becomes a monotonous pantomime of a few slow and simple movements. Such performances are, however, much enjoyed and may occupy performers and spectators throughout the day.

wanted to give me. He said he was twenty, but when I thought that was high, he said, "maybe fifteen." A shepherd boy whom I asked about the best place to ford wanted to give me his bread too. He wouldn't have had any lunch then. The water came to my waist but the bottom was hard ripply sand and the crossing was easy. A man and a woman crossed with me. The woman couldn't strip as we did and got her trousers soaked.

There were ten great bustards in one flock and over against the mountain a flock of more than fifty. The males are beginning to strut and make conspicuous white spots that can be discerned at the limits of vision. Rup Chand got a nice male with a wingspread of 100 inches and weight of 28 pounds—with a rifle shot at 200 yards. They are of course wary, rise easily, and fly swiftly. The stilts have come and the lapwings are anticking and wailing. There are 150 mallards in one flock. A pair of storks is busy trying to build a nest on a stub 8 feet high, but most of their sticks have fallen to the ground. There are also strange storks in small flocks on the plain (ours fly alone or in pairs) that are searching the meadow as if they had lost a needle. All I could see there was an odd cricket. The tortoises feel the elixir of spring and are roistering about in their lovemaking. The male bumps the female by way of caress, and the thud can be heard some little distance. He may also hiss. At night they look for shelter, and often one sees them at evening parked in sheds dug into the side of one of the thorny pincushions that grow commonly in places on the steppe. Most of them weigh 4 or 5 pounds and often they show scars where their shells once were broken. I don't remember seeing a small one that might be a year or two old. The scarabs are now common and are frantically rolling off their manure balls.

A native had a handkerchief full of the mushrooms that are beginning to appear now on the plain. I wanted to buy them but he said to take them, they weren't worth anything, and to come to the house for a cup of tea. "I wasn't home when you went by this forenoon or I'd have asked you then."

At Pirabad, where there is a shrine, a crowd of peasants had gathered at the edge of a little copse to commemorate Qatl, one of the numerous murders that are high points of the Shia brand of Islam. Everyone was in his gayest clothes, and the hundred donkeys on which the crowd had arrived also had bright coverings. The tenants of the dozen stork nests in the few trees beside the shrine were undisturbed by the unwonted assembly below. Their black and white plumage elegantly trimmed with red bill and legs crowned the gala scene, and their sober stamping and bill-clapping with which they hailed each other's arrival and departure were fitting rituals for the solemn occasion. Off to the side in the village, a large flock of green-headed mallards was splashing and preening. The air was soft and warm, and the sun shone fresh and clear; the landscape was clothed in tender green. Only in spring is the air so soft, the sun so clear and the green so tender, and nothing was lacking to the perfection of the scene of spring. Flowers? For the missing flowers, Nature had taken brighter things: the storks, the ducks, the festive human beings.

While we were watching, a golden eagle came flapping across the plain leisurely in pursuit of a hare. The eagle probably saw the hare had no way of escape and made no move to strike. The terrified hare zig-zagged ahead of its pursuer, and then seeing the crowd and recognizing only shelter, dashed into the midst of the people. When we got home, the Armenian pig flock was there eating up our garbage. The pigs get nothing to eat but what they can find on the desert, but they don't look as thin as the Georgian razorbacks that have richer pasture. They chew up the grass and spit out the cud, and their wake is strewn with these puzzling marks. Some musicians had arrived, too, and all our male neighbors were dancing. One of the musicians had a wooden horn that he blew for 20 minutes at a stretch till he was purple in the face. He put so much life in the tune that the dancers were intoxicated and hopped on into the night. Crowds of spectators came, too, and clapped time, and some appreciative lookers-on slipped small bills to the players.

The poor people seldom have such wholesome amusement. Oftenest the laborers after their day on the railroad tracks gather to hear someone of their more favored number, a stonemason or overseer maybe, read at the top of his voice from the Arabic Koran. It is as if our factory hands had to spend their evenings in listening to the reading of a Latin Bible. This diversion is varied some nights by the recitation of the story of the suffering of the martyrs which dissolves the audience in tears. They have no more than will keep them alive and don't know whether they'll have that tomorrow, yet have tears to shed for the sufferings of others. Sometimes too, someone comes from the home village with a donkeyload of bread and the evening passes in talk. In their conversation, our people frequently touch on finance and you often hear "*seh kran,*" "*hasht kran,*" or some such small sum float out of the conversation of a passing group of peasants or pop out of the more animated discourse of a sitting group. Chauffeurs are particularly apt to converse of money, and their fancy has wings. Hundreds and thousands of *tumans*, not *krans*, are the subjects of conversation.

The hens are now laying. They like to make nests in the seclusion of our luggage in the corner of our room, and Rinchen Gialtsen gives the gardener the eggs he buys from the market and keeps the fresh ones the hens deposit with us. Hens here don't cackle after laying, having retained the prudence of their wild ancestors. They seem also not to sit so regularly as ours.

A flock of sheep on the plain scattered in panic. We expected to see a wolf attack but instead, through the rift in their midst dashed a hare pursued by the shepherd's four dogs. For a mile went the chase, the dogs barely holding their own. Pools of water the hare struck like a shot, the waters parted, and on he flew. He shook the dogs off in a wheat field, and one by one they came back to their sheep.

Four of the villagers nearby died of eating poisonous mushrooms. Most people know better than to eat any except the parasitic mountain sort and the agarics of the plain.

PIGGIE, THE PET WILD BOAR. Piggie was 18 inches overall when he was brought to us by a neighbor in whose field his mother had come to root for wild carrots. He was as affectionate as a puppy and much more mischievous. Donkeys and cattle were terrified by him. Donkeys threw their riders in the dirt, and plowing oxen fled to the hills with their owners in frantic pursuit when Piggy willed. At night he slept with me. On account of the fleas that gather around habitations, we made our bed in the desert and more than once a wild pig came to see us, apparently mistaking me for a pig, too.

Our neighbor's mother calls Rup Chand *"Nana"* ("Mother"). Tibetan mothers also often call their children *"Ama."* She asked if he had taken the quince seed and what not she had recommended for his cough, and he told her he had tried this, showing the brandy bottle. "Oh! That is good," she said.

April 25. We got up at daylight. The rain was dripping in through the roof. Muddy trickles soaked and stained our bedding and made a soggy untouchable mess of the blotters and bundles of dried plants, and converted the mud floor of the room into mire. With some waterproofs we made a tent on an island and huddled under it with two charcoal fires that made the bedding steam. The rain came even harder than yesterday, such a rain as I had seldom seen anywhere. The river overflowed its banks and made the plain a vast lake and the village of Sangar into an island. Pieces of wood and matting rode down on the torrent, and the flood even carried off a man from the town while he was trying to salvage the flotsam. The wood woman came in spite of the rain, her thin cotton dress dripping and clinging, and brought some *kangar*, the wild greens with the artichoke flavor. The donkey couldn't cross the swollen Marbur, so they came on foot over the little bridge farther down. I have often noticed desert people don't seem to mind rain and seldom run to escape as do we who ought to be used to it.

Our neighbors were indignant at our aquatic environment and poured out on the absent landlord such abuse as the gentle Persian language allows. You can't get very abusive in Persian and ordinarily you don't hear anything worse than a suggestion that your father's ancestors were of canine origin or that he is in hell. They said to take rent for such a duckpond was *haram* (unclean) and one after the other, even our donkey driver, brought us their nice rugs, *ghilims*, and blankets to be ruined in the mud.

Before noon a man came with a little animal wrapped in a gunny sack, with only its head sticking out. The men thought it was a baby gazelle, but it was a tiny wild pig, striped and spotted a light brown. He had been captured when his mother had come to root for wild carrots in the wheat field. One of his brothers had been killed by the dogs but the rest got away. Only a few days ago Rup Chand had met a peasant bringing five piglets to town in a sack to give them to Petros, the Armenian pig raiser. Rup Chand had remarked they were nice little things and the peasant said yes, they were, "but when they grow up they're awful. They eat the wheat. Not that they eat so much but they root." He illustrated the rooting by turning his hand to the side, then corrected it to a forward pushing of the fingers. He said maybe Petros wouldn't want them, but he didn't want to kill them. Their father hadn't been with them, else he wouldn't have dared to touch them. Rup Chand said we didn't want this pig, just as he always opposes our having any pets because of the tragedy that invariably follows, but I took the piglet and paid as little as possible for fear they'd be bringing me sackfuls of little pigs. We expected he would be stubborn and hard to keep, but he promptly went to sleep in my arms and by night was drinking milk out of a saucer. He is 18 ½ inches long over all. The old lady next door petted him and told us to get a red nipple and a little box for him to sleep in. Flocks of waders lost in the rain and blinded by the electric lights of the station circled and cried all through the night.

April 26. The rain stopped before sundown yesterday, and today only some large cottony clouds were left of the gray roof of the last two days. Our piggy slept with me and at intervals came out to get a drink from his saucer of milk and then with dripping muzzle wormed his way under the blankets again. He knows Rup Chand and me from the rest, follows us about, and races from one end of the room to the other, dodging under legs and jumping over arms. He goes to the door but won't go out. He plays with a rope, chews on our buttons and fights with a finger shaken at him. We have great hopes of making something out of him.

The rain has brought out the flowers. In the orchard, glorious red poppies 2 inches across have opened, and a fragrant violet-colored iris that had stopped blooming started up afresh to make gay blotches on the plain. The red tulips of the mountain have grown unusually well, and cups nearly 4 inches long can be found, while the rare yellow one has sent up its flower stalks 2 feet high.

We found a garden of two kinds of morel mushrooms and filled our knapsacks. The frequent spring rains have given us plenty of mushrooms. The agarics of the plain have been common for a month, and the larger and tastier sort of the mountains for nearly as long. The natives say mushrooms are brought out by the thunder. Lahulis and some Americans have the same belief.

While Wangyel was looking for morels among the bushes, he disturbed a boar. The boar dashed past him, so close that it knocked his basket out of his hand and went up the slope. A little later Wangyel had another thrill: as we neared the top of the mountain, a golden eagle sailed to strike at something we couldn't see and then came to rest on a boulder. Soon two pigs came into view and one charged up the hill at the eagle and drove it off. Thirty or forty ibex were watching the performance a hundred paces above while we were twice as far below. In a rocky stretch I separated from Wangyel and a little later heard a fearful scream. Then a boar and a sow and eight very small youngsters came trotting toward me. They stopped at 10 paces. The boar eyed me a moment with a threatening look and then they trotted off. It had charged Wangyel but had stopped at five paces. On the crest, four pigs with two flocks of young were walking along a strip of snow. Climbing over the peak, I came almost face to face with a wolf coming up from the other side, perhaps on the trail of the pigs. A little farther on, some men collecting wild onions scared up an ibex flock that came within 50 yards before they saw me.

POSTSCRIPT

Some years have passed since we lived through these experiences, and we are still in Iran. Many pleasant things have befallen us since, and there have also been the cloudy days that set off the brightness of the others. We have continued to study the plants and animals of the country, but we have also tried to explore the hearts of the people. We have learned the language so to have more light in our search. The dark and stormy war years that swept over the country laid bare the souls of the people, and the lightning flashes of affliction revealed what must have always remained hidden from the candle of our talents. We saw much beauty there and no stain that the tear of compassion would not blur from the sight.